Richard P. Goldman

SPORT'S GOLDEN AGE

SPORT'S
GOLDEN AGE

A CLOSE-UP OF THE
FABULOUS TWENTIES

EDITED BY
ALLISON DANZIG
AND
PETER BRANDWEIN

———

Foreword by
JOHN KIERAN

———

HARPER & BROTHERS
PUBLISHERS: NEW YORK

CONTENTS

ILLUSTRATIONS

These illustrations will be found in a group following page 146

FOREWORD

I am not one to believe that the world is spinning rapidly downhill and that things were better in every way in the brave days of old, but there have been exceptional men, extraordinary events, and odd eras in human history. There was, to be specific, a notable array of flaming figures in sports in the wake of World War I, strong teams and brilliant individual performers in many fields of competition.

This was the era of Man o' War on the turf, of Jack Dempsey in the ring, of Bill Tilden on the tennis court, of Bobby Jones in golf, of Babe Ruth in baseball, and of Red Grange and the Four Horsemen of Notre Dame in football.

Never before had there been so many outstanding attractions in so many different fields in such a limited period of time. And never since has it happened. Perhaps the future—and may I be there to see!—will bring an even more brilliant galaxy of flashing competitors to the enthusiastic attention of the sports fans of another generation, but, until that happens, the tremendous tide of a quarter of a century ago must remain the high water mark in American sports.

What is sometimes overlooked about that glorious era of competition is that there were writers worthy of the great competitors of those dazzling days. What would we have known of Achilles, Hector, Aeneas, Ulysses, Ajax, and other heroes of ancient times if it were not for Homer and Virgil? So the champions of a great era in American sports found their personalities and their performances chronicled by a great group of writers, men who were outstanding in their own part of the field, the press section.

The old competitors, some of them now strolling the Elysian Fields, can't repeat their thunderous performances, but the same great writers can, and in this book do, describe once again the high spots, the thrills, the outstanding accomplishments, and the breathless brilliance of that great era in American sports, all of which they saw and part of which they were. Those were great deeds to see. It is a delight to read about them again.

—JOHN KIERAN

EDITORS' PREFACE

Mankind looks back beyond the veil of blood and tears to the period of Pericles as civilization's most shining hour. Sport, too, had its Golden Age. It came in the years following the First World War. Never before, nor since, have so many transcendent performers arisen contemporaneously in almost every field of competitive athletics as graced the 1920's.

Each sport has its magic name—its all-time top performer, established by the record of achievement or accepted by common consent. In baseball, boxing, golf, tennis, polo, horse racing and balk-line billiards, this champion of the ages was in his prime in the Golden Twenties.

In the case of baseball, both the greatest figure, Ruth, and the most powerful team, the New York Yankees of 1927, as well as three of the most successful managers of all time, McGraw, Mack, and Huggins, are offered.

In tennis, both the male and female of the superspecies arose, and the same can be argued for golf. Horse racing contributed the greatest thoroughbred and the leading jockey.

Boxing presented the top money attraction and the promoter who brought out the first million-dollar gate as the carriage trade paid fabulous prices to see Tiger Jack Dempsey in action, first against Gorgeous Georges Carpentier and then against Luis Angel Firpo, the Wild Bull of the Pampas.

Football, track and field, swimming, yachting, basketball, hockey, six-day bicycle racing, and rowing produced champions who, if they did not gain the very pinnacle, above all others in their sport, certainly were as famous as any to take their places in the record books.

What names are bigger in football than Grange and Rockne, than Nurmi and Paddock in distance and sprint running, than Weissmuller and Ederle in swimming, than Shore in hockey, than the Celtics in basketball? Who associated with yachting was ever the byword with the public that Sir Thomas Lipton was when he was challenging unsuccessfully for the America's Cup, even though he never skippered one of his craft? When did Madison Square Garden, the old or the new, ring to wilder cheering than was provoked by the jamming speed of Goullet, McNamara, Egg, and Belloni?

All of these and many other great figures of the Twenties challenged the most gifted writers of the nation's sporting press to rise to flights of descriptive English never before nor since attained. Some of them, upon their return from conquests overseas, received an official welcome from New York's mayor at City Hall and then paraded in triumph through a canyon streaming with ticker tape and confetti as hundreds of thousands of admirers roared their greetings.

The whole story of the period and its phenomenal performers has never before been put between covers. To present it authentically, the editors sought, and were fortunate enough to enlist, the services of men who were eyewitnesses to the deeds herein recounted, were intimately acquainted, in most cases, with the champions, and wrote spot-news reports of their exploits for the daily press. Each of them is a recognized authority in his field. Seldom, if ever, has so qualified a group collaborated on a sports volume.

—ALLISON DANZIG AND PETER BRANDWEIN

SPORT'S GOLDEN AGE

THE GOLDEN PANORAMA

by GRANTLAND RICE
Dean of American Sports Writers

Sport has been a big factor in this country since George Washington ran race horses and tossed a dollar across the Potomac; since Abraham Lincoln was a wrestler, Teddy Roosevelt a boxer, and Woodrow Wilson a football coach.

But sport's first tidal wave of popularity never struck full force until we came to the Golden Age of competition after the First World War.

Just why was this period from 1919 to 1930, in the wake of the Marne, the Meuse, Cantigny, Belleau Woods, Sedan, and the Hindenburg Line, called the Golden Age of Sport?

The answer is a simple one. It is because this postwar period gave the game the greatest collection of stars, involving both skill and color, that sport has ever known since the first cave man tackled the mammoth and the aurochs bull.

Recently one of the younger sporting set offered the idea that sport today had just as many stars and as many colorful competitors as the Golden Age ever knew.

I offered no argument in rebuttal. Age can argue with youth, but it can never win the argument. I might have mentioned just a few names—Babe Ruth, Jack Dempsey, Knute Rockne, Bobby Jones, Red Grange, Bill Tilden, Billy Johnston, Earl Sande, Tommy Hitchcock, Helen Wills, Man o' War, Exterminator, Rogers Hornsby, Frank Frisch, Charley Paddock, the Four Horsemen, Gene Sarazen, Glenna Collett—taking them helter-skelter in no set order.

I would like to ask you to look over and study this partial list at closer range. I don't believe the average sport follower quite realizes what these few I have mentioned have meant to the American sporting scene.

Most of them are as well known today and as closely remembered as they were twenty or twenty-five years ago. They had something more than mere skill or competitive ability. They also had in record quality and quantity that indescribable asset known as color, personality, crowd appeal, or whatever you may care to call it.

Suppose, for example, we start with just two names—Babe Ruth and Jack Dempsey.

Ruth started his home-run fame in 1919. That was also the year which gave Jack Dempsey his early knockout over Jess Willard.

Who would the crowds follow today in any gathering—Ruth and Dempsey, or the pick of the modern leaders?

Babe Ruth played in ball parks before more than 30,000 spectators, where the attendance before had dropped below 1,000. Jack Dempsey fought before more than $10,000,000 worth of customers in what otherwise would have been a rather drab time for the ring.

These were the two competitors the multitudes wanted to see— and still follow today.

Both were known around the world. They were known in Japan, Australia, South Africa, the Philippines, any place you might mention. They were world figures. There was nothing above Babe Ruth or Jack Dempsey, as long as you stuck to this rather minor planet.

Their main field of operation was power—Ruth's mighty slugging and Dempsey's two murderous hands, especially his left.

But they went far beyond this. They had a crowd appeal that has never been approached. For each, with all his skill and power, gave all he had to give at every start.

They had what I would like to call character in competition. When either appeared, you knew there had to be a show worth seeing.

I would rate these two men as the all-time tops in two different games. And both, a number of years away from competition, have held their grip on the masses. When Babe Ruth came down with an illness a year or so ago, he received only some 30,000 letters and telegrams. I believe that, under the same conditions, Jack Dempsey would have come close to Ruth's record.

Ruth, in addition to being the major slugger, was also a brilliant pitcher and a brilliant outfielder. But more than anything else, he was Babe Ruth.

Jack Dempsey, a tiger in the ring, has always been one of the gentlest men I've ever known outside of the ring. To me, a gentleman must first be a gentle man. Considerate and courteous, with no thought of himself, I'd rate Jack Dempsey at the top—away from the ring, where his only idea was annihilation. Which is the way it should be.

I am afraid that none of us will look upon another Babe Ruth or another Jack Dempsey. And I doubt that the next generation will have any such luck.

Ruth and Dempsey alone could have given us the Golden Age of Sport. But they were not alone. They were only a vital part of an amazing march of exceptional stars.

It was about this time that a coach by the name of Knute Rockne lifted his partially bald head against the skyline. Knute Rockne, a great coach, was also something more than a great coach—just as Ruth was something more than a great ballplayer and Dempsey was something more than a great fighter. Many, many years and yesterdays have slipped by since Knute Rockne fell from a Western sky to his death.

There have been football coaches as great as Rockne was—on the field, in the matter of systems and other factors. And Pop Warner, Hurry Up Yost, and Percy Haughton, to mention a few, ranked with him in this respect.

But, like Ruth and Dempsey, Knute Rockne had so much else to offer. Rock had a personality no other football coach has ever reached.

In New York gatherings before some big game, I noticed all coaches were asking where Rockne was. Rockne's hotel room was always headquarters for the crowd. From nearly twenty years away I can still hear the old question: "Where's Rock?"

Knute Rockne had something, something I can't explain, that no other football coach had. And beyond this, he was a brilliant and a winning coach. No amount of color can cover up failure. Above everything else, you must be a winner. Color fades out in the dark drabness of defeat.

You can move Rockne up with Ruth and Dempsey, but Rockne had the advantage of a much better-trained mind. He was a master chemist and also a Latin scholar, which few know.

Then we come to a golfer, whom I happened to know first when he was seven or eight years old. At that time he had a tremendous head on a frail body. He was watching Stewart Maiden in Atlanta giving instruction. A few years later, at the age of eleven or twelve, when I played with him, he was down in the low 70's.

His name is Bobby Jones. Here was a great artist, with only one early fault. They called it temper; what it really was happened to be the striving for perfection.

George Duncan, the British champion, once said to me: "Jones will never be a champion. He is too fine an artist. Only the perfect shot ever suits him."

Duncan was right for seven years. And then, starting in 1923, Bobby Jones came into his own. He won 13 national championships in the next seven years. Bobby quit at twenty-eight, just as he was approaching his peak. He finished with his famous Grand Slam in 1930, when he won the U.S. and British Open, plus the U.S. and British amateur titles.

"This is a crime," Tommy Armour told me. "The kid is just starting. He'd win every championship for the next ten years."

Once again Bobby Jones was something more than a great golfer. Graduating from Georgia Tech, he took two Harvard two-year courses in one year.

Looking as far back as 1916, at Merion, when he was a chubby, pink-faced kid of fourteen, he caught and held the affection and admiration of big galleries. These galleries saw something more than a fine club-swinger. They saw a personality they wanted to follow. And from 1916 to 1930, the major part of the gallery, even with Hagen and Sarazen around, always followed Jones.

Why? Because he was Bobby Jones. Just as Ruth was Babe Ruth. Just as Dempsey was Jack Dempsey. Skill? Certainly. But beyond that, character, class, and crowd appeal.

Bobby Jones, like Ruth and Dempsey, was known around the world. "I found that out in the Fiji Islands," Gene Sarazen told me. "When I was there they were asking me about Bobby Jones. If I had played with the pygmies of Africa, it would have been the same."

Ruth, Dempsey, and Bobby Jones have been our three leading world-wide names in sport.

And then there were Red Grange—the "Wheaton Iceman"—and the Four Horsemen for football, who wrote chapters that still belong to the classics of competition.

The Galloping Ghost from Illinois, under Bob Zuppke's able direction, startled the football world when he scored four touchdowns against Michigan in 12 minutes. Later on, Red lured over 73,000 into the Polo Grounds against the New York Giants after he had turned pro.

Red Grange was by all odds the greatest crowd collector and pleaser football has even known. Red, with Rockne, was football's leading contributor to Sport's Golden Age. Who could ask for two better leading men in any play? The Four Horsemen of Notre Dame who followed—Stuhldreher, Crowley, Miller, and Layden, with an average backfield weight around 165—are still remembered for their speed, skill, and craft against the greater brawn they had to face.

For this Golden Age, I'll stand on Red Grange, Knute Rockne, and the Four Horsemen as far as football goes.

The amazing part of this period is that every sport had more than its share to offer.

Who can forget the "hell-for-leather" riding and the big hitting of Tommy Hitchcock, barely more than a kid, who was to give the ancient game of polo a new angle?

It was Tommy Hitchcock who brought power to this great sport, power above finesse. Hitchcock rode hard, with reckless daring, and he hit even harder when his mallet had a crack at the ball.

Tommy Hitchcock came from the skies to resume his polo play after the First World War, and it was from the skies again that he left on the long, long trail in making a diving test he refused to let others face.

Here again we have the character of a brilliant competitor that stands out even above his playing skill. Tommy Hitchcock holds a high place in the ranking of these incredible years.

From baseball, football, and other games we can turn to racing. Who is the jockey best remembered over a long period of time? His name is Earl Sande, who made a habit of winning Kentucky Derbies. You may recall Damon Runyon's famous verse:

> Gimme a handy
> Guy like Sande
> Bootin' them horses in.

And when they talk of great race horses today, such as Armed, Assault, and Stymie you will hear the old-timers say: "Yes, but you should have seen Man o' War and Exterminator—Big Red and Old

Bones. They were the best. There never was a three-year-old in Man o' War's class. There never was a handicap horse like Exterminator, who could win from six furlongs up to two miles and who could carry 138 or 140 pounds."

Exterminator won 50 races in 100 starts. Man o' War was beaten only once—by Upset, at Saratoga. His famous duel with John P. Grier remains a racing classic.

Sande, Man o' War, and Exterminator—the triple threat of all time.

Man o' War raced at odds of one to 100 more than once. Exterminator ignored both weight and distance. The two were racing nonpareils.

Tennis has known its share of stars year after year. But I can't recall another competitive period to match the years from 1919 to 1925, when Big Bill and Little Bill fought out their famous duels. Johnston, weighing less than 125 pounds, was badly outmatched physically by the tall, bounding Tilden. But he beat Big Bill in the championship of 1919 at Forest Hills, and the slight Californian gave Tilden all he could handle later on. The control and power of Little Bill's forehand, plus his unequaled competitive heart, made up the physical difference.

And there were Helen Wills and Molla Mallory to take high places on the tennis side. Both were a vital part of this Golden Age.

Charlie Paddock, the "fastest human," was another member of this brilliant cast. So was Rogers Hornsby, one of the greatest hitters of all time, who averaged above .400 for four successive years and led the National League many times against strong challengers.

Just what odd turn of evolution brought forward so many outstanding stars in this postwar period? No such individual fame has followed World War II, although attendance figures show that sport has reached a new peak in the way of public interest.

There is no answer to this mystery. When a Ruth, a Dempsey, and a Tunney come along together in a cavalcade that also includes a Jones, a Sarazen, a Hagen, a Red Grange, a Hitchcock, and so many others, it must be listed as something that just happened beyond rhyme, reason, or the Milky Way.

All that we know is that this Golden Age offered a flame that lit up the sporting skies and covered the world.

The war drums were silent, the bugles were still—and suddenly there they were.

It might be easy enough to explain why so much skill and ability should suddenly emerge around the same period. But skill and ability were not the major factors in this Golden Age. They were, of course, important factors, but they were, after all, only a minor part of the story.

It was their color and their crowd appeal, their vivid splash against the skyline, their remembered deeds, that write their story.

For those were the unforgettable days—Ruth, Dempsey, Bobby Jones, Man o' War, Hitchcock—the ones they still talk about long after they have passed from the active scene. The answer is that most of those from the Golden Age would draw larger crowds at any gathering than most of those who lead the pack today.

They had the glamor and the crowd lure of John L. Sullivan from 1882 to 1892. They had that indefinable quality that comes from championship ability plus the love and admiration of the masses on the personal side, which sport has never even approached since—and probably never will again in the life span of this generation.

BASEBALL

by J. ROY STOCKTON
Sports Editor, St. Louis Post-Dispatch

HOW IT GOT THAT WAY

Something big happened to baseball as the Twentieth Century edged into its third decade, and historians probably will agree that there were many factors—some human, some spun by fate—that combined to make the ten-year span one of the most glamorous in the history of the sport.

There was Babe Ruth, who moved from Boston to the New York Yankees and made the country home-run conscious by knocking 54 prodigious four-baggers over the ramparts of American League parks. If you insist on one outstanding figure to personify that Golden Era of our national game, the Bambino will do.

Then there was a new dignity that the game acquired as the picturesque and confidence-inspiring Kenesaw Mountain Landis moved from his Federal court bench to baseball's high throne as Commissioner. The Old Judge played a big part in making Beowulf Q. Phan certain that the game was all right.

Radio was a factor, too, as it began to carry baseball into homes from coast to coast, entertaining, puzzling, educating, and each October, at World Series time, making a nation do a country-wide sit-down for listening.

No doubt, too, the returned service men of World War I, coming home with a post-war adoration of American institutions all out of proportion to the apple-selling jobs some of them were destined to do years later, did much to gild the pedestal on which baseball was finding its place. These doughboys, in the slime of French battlefields, in cootie-infested trenches, had dreamed of things back home; bleachers and grandstand were a big part of those dreams.

Fate lent a hand, too, as the Cleveland Indians, the Washington

Senators and the St. Louis Cardinals won maiden victories for pennant-hungry cities and set the nation's baseball fans, otherwise nonpartisan, to rooting for underdog heroes of the game's October struggles.

We'll never forget the amazing spectacle of Washington as Bucky Harris, the boy manager, and his Washington Senators, battled the Giants of John McGraw for the 1924 world championship. Washington, the national capital, the home of diplomats, stuffed shirts and yokels with great problems. Whoever thought that in that staid city there would be frenzy over a mere game, played with bat and ball? But Washington forgot all its other problems for that October World Series week. Traffic, after a Senator victory, ceased to be a moving thing. Automobiles and streetcars were stalled, block after block, packed from curb to curb with milling throngs. All you had to do was shout "Hurrah for Walter Johnson," and pretty girls would embrace you. If you had given a cheer for John McGraw, you soon could have been the corpse in a first-class mass murder. Being country boys from the Middle West, we were startled that baseball could do this.

No doubt the same thing had happened in Cleveland when Tris Speaker's Indians in 1920 broke that city's long pennant drought. And we saw the same thing happen in St. Louis, when the Cardinals of 1926 won the city's first pennant in thirty-eight years. St. Louis went stark mad, too. Ticker tape from office windows filled the air, crowds jammed streets from curb to curb. Returning warriors from battle fields of victory never got a bigger welcome than St. Louis gave Rogers Hornsby and his Cardinals of 1926.

That fabulous decade of baseball was one of star-studded rosters, too, which didn't hurt the over-all picture. You can pick an all-star team that will do for a long all-time in the national game from the teams that battled for glory and ever-increasing purses during the Golden Era. Perhaps you'd prefer to go back a decade for your shortstop, so Honus Wagner would be in your all-star, all-time lineup. But you'd have a pretty good country infielder if you put Travis Jackson at short.

For the rest of the infield you could have George Sisler, one of the greatest stars the game has known, at first base, or Lou Gehrig, if you were a Yankee partisan. There'd be a wide selection for second base, with Eddie Collins, Rogers Hornsby and Frankie Frisch standing out. And unless you are a real-dyed-in-the-past old-timer, you'd accept Pie Traynor as about as brilliant a star as you could find to take care of third base.

Rarely does a baseball notable name an all-star team without picking the nonpareil fly-chasing trio of the Golden Twenties as the top combination—Ty Cobb, Tris Speaker and Babe Ruth.

Old-timers, of course, will go back frequently to the Mathewsons and the Youngs and the Waddells for all-star pitching talent, but most of us grandstand managers—and those who are paid for it, too—would be satisfied if we had a Grover Cleveland Alexander, a Walter Johnson, a Herb Pennock, and a Burleigh Grimes on the staff. And the catching would be taken care of satisfactorily by a Mickey Cochrane, a Gabby Hartnett, a Jimmy Wilson, or a Bob O'Farrell.

Nor was the brilliance of that Golden Era confined to the diamonds. There were baseball writers, gifted magicians of the typewriter, who put glowing words together to keep the country informed about the courage, skill and foibles of the heroes who battled on the baseball fields.

For a long time the sports departments of most newspapers had been treated much like the segregated districts, and many managing editors wondered if the baseball writers really were necessary. But after a world conflict, whether in the second or fourth decade of a century, newspaper customers become a bit weary of reading of wars and threats of war. A ball game, or the story of a ball game, is a welcome respite from the ominous foreign news. Circulation-conscious publishers began to notice, as the Golden Era dawned, that good baseball stories made for reader interest.

And so there was a lot of talent in press boxes as major-league teams fought down the stretch for pennants and when battle was joined in what each year is called baseball's great October classic. Ring Lardner was there in the Twenties, owl-eyed and inimitable. The great Damon Runyon was dramatizing the derring-do of erstwhile plough-jockeys, who could throw hard, or hit a baseball a long way. Grantland Rice was making immortals of the Ruths, the Cobbs and the Speakers, as he had done with the great Mathewson. Westbrook Pegler—Bud to us—was doing baseball, as was the erudite John Kieran. Heywood Broun was crowding his bulk into a skimpy World Series seat, next to Tommy Rice, of Brooklyn, Joe Williams, of Cleveland and later New York, and Bill Corum, the eminent Missourian. Quent Reynolds was on the sport beat, too, along with Bill McGeehan, Dan Daniel, Jim Crusinberry, Ed Wray, Boze Bulger, Bill Phelan, Jack Ryder, Fred Lieb, Harry Neily, Sid Mercer and Bill Hanna, just to mention a few.

Even if you didn't know a fielder's choice from a naked reverse, you had to keep on reading if you ever started a Lardner, Rice, Broun or Kieran opus. Unquestionably these masters of the written word did much to spread the gospel of baseball, make the country sports-conscious and help build the Golden Era into a glamorous period. No statisticians these, but spinners of thrilling, gripping yarns.

They were a merry group, too, for all their brilliance, never too busy or tired for a laugh.

Bill Hanna was writing for a New York paper and he knew his stuff. He ought to, they'd tell you, probably having given Abner Doubleday several tips about new hit-and-run signs. But Bill had an idiosyncrasy or two, one of them a stubborn, life-long conviction that he wasn't feeling as well today as he had felt yesterday and most certainly would feel worse tomorrow. He'd scowl if you so much as suggested that he was looking well.

On one of his frequent visits to doctors, he was told that perhaps he wasn't getting enough exercise and advised to take a walk each day. He was taking this prescribed walk one afternoon, on the way to the ball park, when Jim Gould, of St. Louis and several other press box cronies, on their way to a subway station, passed Bill and exchanged the usual pleasantries. At the next subway stop, Gould and his companions left the train, returned to the street and walked back, again greeting Hanna, but as though it was their first meeting of the day. When they left the slightly confused Hanna, they repeated the routine. After the same foursome had greeted Hanna the fourth time, Bill was a wreck. Instead of continuing to the ball park, he hailed a cab and rushed hell-bent for a psychiatrist.

HERE A STAR, THERE A STAR

Baseball served notice early that the first year of the Golden Era was to be a spectacular, record-setting one. The season of 1920 was only half a month old when the Boston Braves and Brooklyn Dodgers met in a game at Boston that still stands in the record book as the longest ever played.

Brooklyn scored a run in the fifth when Krueger walked, Leon Cadore grounded out, and Olson singled to left-center. The Braves came back in the sixth. Walton Cruise tripled after one was out. Walter Holke flied to Wheat in short left, and Cruise, thinking the ball would fall safe, raced half-way to the plate but was able to return to third because nobody covered that bag. Cruise then scored on Tony Boeckel's single, Tony taking second on the throw home.

As Eddie Murphy of the New York *Sun* wrote after that historic game, "It was one that neither side was meant to win. You could sense it from the start."

Walter Maranville followed Boeckel's hit with a drive that was scored as a double, although Boeckel was thrown out at the plate.

And so it went. In the 17th inning, the Dodgers filled the bases with one out, but Joe Oeschger took a tap to the mound and started a double play.

At the end of 26 innings, Cadore and Oeschger were still going strong. Cadore had allowed Boston 15 hits, while Oeschger had held the Dodgers to nine. Players were weary, but Ivan Olson of the Dodgers pleaded with Umpire Barry McCormick to "Give us one more inning."

"Why the one more inning?" the weary umps wanted to know.

"So we can make it three full games in one afternoon," the record-book conscious Olson explained.

"Not without miners' lamps on your caps," McCormick cracked, walking off the field. You see, in those days nobody thought of floodlights on the diamond.

That 26-inning stint did something to Cadore and Oeschger. Neither was quite the same thereafter. Cadore went to bed that Saturday evening and stayed there until Monday morning. And Olson, who wanted to make it 27 innings, got some extra baseball. The following day, Sunday, Brooklyn, back home, lost a 13-inning game to Philadelphia, 4 to 3, and then returned to Boston on Monday and lost in 19 innings, 2 to 1. Thus the Dodgers played 58 innings on three consecutive days.

That year marked, too, Babe Ruth's first full season with the

Yankees and his first as a full-time outfielder. The Babe stepped up his home-run pace from 29 to 54, and the home run became the thing. Thus began a great change in baseball technique. More and more the game veered from the bunt, the sacrifice, the hit-and-run. Never mind that single run. Don't choke that bat. Grab it by the nob and swing from Borough Hall. Players quickly began to strive for distance, and the club owners were willing to help the trend along. Nobody has ever admitted it, but Babe Ruth's home runs constituted such excellent box-office attractions that new jack-rabbit qualities suddenly found themselves in the major league baseball.

Many historians insist that the Babe's 54 home runs were more remarkable than his 59 the following year or his 60 in 1927, for there was more jack rabbit in the ball in later years. And despite the added bounce to the ball, only three other hitters have ever knocked more than 54 homers in a year. Hack Wilson finished a season with 56 and Jimmy Foxx and Hank Greenberg each reached 58.

George Sisler put a record into the book that year. For the first time the brilliant first baseman of the St. Louis Browns led the American League in batting. George batted .407 and, in compiling that average, he made 257 hits, an all-time record for total safeties in one season. It was a St. Louis year as Rogers Hornsby of the Cardinals found his way to the top of the National League for the first time, batting .370.

The question of who was the greatest ball player of all time is largely a matter of opinion and important largely to two persons— the one expressing the opinion and the one who quickly challenges and disagrees.

We saw Sisler at his peak, and it is not difficult to pick him as the greatest in our book. He didn't hit home runs at the Ruth pace. Detroit will laugh at the suggestion that Sisler be ranked above Ty Cobb. But we'll stick to Sisler, nevertheless.

George was a great athlete, and don't think he wasn't as aggressive as Cobb. There were stories around St. Louis in his early days that he had to whip several stalwart veterans in the Brownie clubhouse before the polite college boy from the University of Michigan was accepted as one of the crowd. Of course George had no fights with fans in the stand and he stole his bases without any reputation as a flasher of spikes.

Spiking was a Cobb copyright. Gabby Street, the old catcher, who handled Walter Johnson's shots, caught a ball thrown from Washington Monument, and later managed the Browns and the Cardinals, told us a story about Cobb. Ty was Gabby's dinner guest one evening and enjoyed the family atmosphere. The next day there was a ball game, and in a late inning, with Cobb on third base, a grounder was hit to a strong-armed infielder. Gabby had the ball in plenty of time, waiting for Cobb. But Ty almost undressed the Old Sergeant, as he slid in, spikes flashing, conceding nothing.

After the game, Gabby saw Cobb again and chided him, his friend, for almost cutting his throat with his spikes.

"Friend, hell," said Tyrus. "I'll cut my grandmother's throat to steal a base or score a run."

Sisler didn't have that same philosophy, but he put everything he had into his baseball. He'd walk to the plate, size up the outfield and infield, and then go to work on the pitcher. If they pitched him inside, he'd cut the ball to right. If they pitched him outside, he'd line a base hit to left. If the third baseman was back, George would beat out a bunt.

Defensively, George ranked with Hal Chase. Hal, in his late and unhappy years, was asked about first-base rankings. He paid Sisler a compliment:

"I think I could do things around first base that Sisler couldn't do," Chase said, "but I was no match for George with a bat in my hand."

We saw more of Sisler than we did of Chase, and then George was in a St. Louis uniform. Perhaps, therefore, we were partisan. But Sisler did amazing things. He would rush in for a squeeze bunt, tag the batter as he tried to get started for first, and then dive for the runner trying to score from third and tag him. Sisler made that play the other way, too, tagging the runner trying to score from third on a squeeze bunt, and then wheeling and firing the ball to first base in time to double the bunter.

Sisler also had a great competitive spirit, an instinctive urge that made no distinction between a title game or a college campus exhibition. When the Browns were training at Mobile one Spring, the squad journeyed to near-by Spring Hill College for a courtesy exhibition with the institution's team. In a late inning, with the Browns a dozen runs ahead, George was on third when he noticed that the pitcher was taking a wind-up. And so on that cow-pasture college diamond, with nothing at stake, George stole home.

Cleveland's Indians, led by the old Gray Eagle, the brilliant Tris Speaker, and the Brooklyn Dodgers, piloted by that delightful, doughty old Baltimore Oriole, Wilbert Robinson, battled in the 1920 World Series. Baseball fans still talk about the many remarkable individual achievements of that series.

Cleveland had been handicapped by the tragic loss of its star short-stop, Ray Chapman, in mid-August. Ray was hit on the head and fatally injured by a ball pitched by Carl Mays. The Indians were in a three-way race at the time with the White Sox of Chicago and the Yankees of New York. But Speaker found a shortstop replacement in Joe Sewell, up from the University of Alabama by way of New Orleans; the White Sox blew up in September after the Black Sox Scandal delayed bombshell exploded, and the Indians won the flag.

Brooklyn took the lead in the title struggle by winning two out of three games at Ebbets Field, but the Indians hit their stride on their home grounds at Cleveland and bowled over the Dodgers for four straight to take the winners' share, which amounted to $4,204 a man that year. The Dodgers' consolation prize was $2,387 a player.

Stanley Coveleskie, husky Pole from the Pennsylvania mining country, was the outstanding pitcher of the series. He used his spitball judiciously to win three games, the first, fourth, and seventh, and no pitcher gained three triumphs in a series again until Harry (The Cat) Brecheen turned the trick for the Cardinals in 1946.

The prize record-book game of the series was the fifth. In that contest, Elmer Smith, Cleveland right fielder, hit the first grand slam homer in a World Series. It was in the first inning, and Burleigh Grimes was the pitcher who watched the ball sail over the rampart and four enemy runners tag home plate.

In the fourth inning, Sergeant Jim Bagby became the first pitcher to hit a homer in a World Series. Two men were on base, and again Grimes was on the receiving end.

In the fifth inning, Pete Kilduff was on second base, Otto Miller was on first, and Clarence Mitchell, pitching replacement for Grimes, was the batter. Mitchell hit a sharp line drive toward second base, and Bill Wambsganss, playing second for the Indians, was moving over to cover the bag. He found himself in line with the flight of the ball, leaped high, and made the catch. The runners were in full flight, and Wamby quickly touched second, doubling Kilduff, and then tagged Miller, who was charging, head down, from first, to complete that rare gem, a triple play unassisted.

It so happened that Mitchell later grounded into a double play and so in two times at bat he hit into a total of five outs.

One of the colorful figures in the series was Walter (Duster) Mails, a left-handed Dizzy Dean of that era. Mails, the only ball player we can remember who would be a conversational match for Dean, came up from the Pacific Coast League, and his pitching was as good as his words, which were many. The Duster won seven and lost none as the American League season waned, and in the sixth series game he scored a key victory, a three-hit, 1-to-0 shutout against Sherry Smith, to put the Indians within one triumph of the championship. Coveleskie's third victory ended the series the following day.

STRUMMING, CROONING, AND SLUMPING

The Pittsburgh Pirates of 1921 were a merry band. As they breezed into the Polo Grounds on August 19, they were 7½ games ahead of the field, Charley Grimm was strumming a ukelele, batting for his more-beloved left-handed banjo, and Rabbit Maranville and Cotton Tierney were singing happily. The Pirates were glad to pose for the photographers, who wanted pictures for World Series time. The Yankees, over in the American League, were winning their first pennant.

John McGraw, widely accepted as a model for managers, an old master in the business of directing baseball campaigns, looked at the crooning Pirates and sneered.

"Look at those damned comedians," John said. "They're ready to be taken."

McGraw hadn't decided that it was a Pittsburgh year. As Pittsburgh built that early lead, the Little Napoleon of the diamond was doing things too. He made a late-season deal with the Phillies and obtained a second baseman, Johnny Rawlings, and an outfielder, Irish Meusel, to bolster his Giants for the stretch run.

In one of the historic upset series of baseball, the Giants took the crooning Pirates for five straight games, and the Buccaneers never recovered. They moved over to Brooklyn and continued their stumbling, and the Giants, forging to the front, stayed there.

There had been checkbook operations in the American League, too, with brisk traffic between New York and Boston. Ruth, obtained in 1920, hit 59 home runs for the 1921 Yankees. Carl Mays, another former Red Sox star, won 27 games, and young Waite Hoyt, also from the Boston store, scored 19 victories. And by that time even Ed Barrow, former Red Sox manager, was business manager of the Yankees. The investments all paid off—in the first Yankee pennant for the Colonels Ruppert and Huston.

That World Series of 1921 will always stand out in our memory. It was our first as a baseball writer and we were properly bug-eyed.

Mays and Hoyt shut out the Giants in the first two games, each by 3 to 0, and the Giants were thus at a disadvantage that no club previously had been able to overcome in a World Series. But there was no quitting on the part of the Giants. It was after these two Giant defeats that we first met John McGraw, off the ball field. The Giants were holding open house at their hotel, and we tagged along with a fellow-writer. Scotch, bourbon, rye, and champagne were flowing like water. Huge tables were laden with roast turkeys and plates of lobster. In a bathroom off the suite, John McGraw and his coach, Hans Lobert, were standing in a tub, opening a keg of beer.

Eddie Brannick, the friendly secretary, was there too. And when somebody offered sympathy for the state of the series, Brannick grinned and bristled.

"We're going to win," he informed us gravely. "I just bet my overcoat."

Eddie didn't lose his overcoat, either. The bats of Frankie Frisch, George Kelly, Dave Bancroft, Irish Meusel, Ross Youngs and Frank Snyder couldn't be silenced that way forever. The Giants won the third game, 13 to 5, and the fourth, 4 to 2. Behind the brilliant Hoyt the Yankees won the fifth, 3 to 1, but the Giants struck back to take the next two games, 8 to 5 and 2 to 1, and then finished off the Yankees with Art Nehf's 1-to-0 triumph over Hoyt, a game that ended most spectacularly.

The Giants scored their lone run in the first inning on passes to Bancroft and Youngs and Peckinpaugh's error, with two out, on Kelly's grounder.

Ruth, who had missed three series games because of an ailing elbow and knee, batted for Wallie Pipp to open the ninth inning and grounded out. Aaron Ward walked, and the veteran Frank Baker shot a sharp grounder toward right field. It looked like a sure hit, but Johnny Rawlings lunged for it and made an amazing stop. Rawlings fell making the play, but from a sitting position he threw to George Kelly in time to retire Baker. Ward, with a long start on the play, rounded second and headed for third. Kelly, who had a remarkable throwing arm, probably was the only man in baseball at the time who could have made the play that followed. He rifled a throw to Frisch, and when Frankie tagged the sliding Ward, the series was over and the Giants were world champions. The checks were getting bigger now. Each Giant pocketed $5,265, each Yankee $3,510.

That year was the first of Judge Landis' tenure as Commissioner. As his first big official act, he expelled from baseball eight White Sox players, although they had been acquitted by a Chicago jury. Commenting on that phase of the Black Sox scandal, Commissioner Landis told the world in a statement:

"Regardless of the verdict of juries, no player that throws a ball game, no player that entertains proposals or promises to throw a ball game, no player that sits in a conference with a bunch of crooked players and gamblers where the ways and means of throwing games are discussed and does not promptly tell his club about it, will ever play professional baseball. . . . Just keep it in mind that regardless of the verdict of juries, baseball is entirely competent to protect itself against the crooks both inside and outside the game."

STRANGE STORY OF A BOTTLE

The Ruppert-Huston Yankee dynasty was firmly established now, and the club made 1922 another pennant year. It was a close squeak, however, as George Sisler batted a gorgeous .420, Urban Shocker pitched brilliantly, and the Browns made a serious challenge, ultimately to be eliminated on the final day, one game behind New York.

There were other factors to make it a close race. Babe Ruth and Bob Meusel had ignored Judge Landis' edict against barnstorming after the World Series of 1921 and were suspended until May 1. Then, after being back in uniform only five days, the Babe jumped into the stands at Washington and took a punch at a fan. Ban Johnson slapped a fine of $200 on the Babe and ordered the great slugger relieved of his rank of team captain. Ruth hit only .315 that year and knocked only 35 home runs as Ken Williams of the Browns won the four-bagger title with 39 over the fence.

That baseball had become an important part of national and civic affairs was indicated when the St. Louis Chamber of Commerce indignantly adopted a resolution denouncing the Yankees for lack of sportsmanship. The trouble was that on July 23, the Yankees traded three utility players to their favorite talent store, the good old Boston Red Sox, for Joe Dugan, a great third baseman, to replace the aging Baker. It was checkbook baseball, the good and seething people of St. Louis insisted.

Rollicking merrily on their way, with fist fights among the players and discipline merely a word in the dictionary, the Yankees were brought up short in mid-September. Leading the Browns by a mere half-game, the New York Americans, arriving in St. Louis for a three-game series, found the city a hotbed of hope and expectation. On street corners, in front of theaters and public gathering places, were small brown barrels. The cab drivers, taking the Yankees to their hotel, explained that a committee of fans was taking up a city-wide collection to buy presents for the Browns when they clinched the pennant.

However, the presents, if they were ever bought, didn't go to pennant winners. The Yankees won two of the three games to stave off the St. Louis challenge.

The pennant was lost for the Browns in the first game. Whitey Witt of the Yankees, chasing a fly ball, was hit on the head and knocked unconscious by a pop bottle. The assumption, of course, was that an overzealous fanatic in the bleachers or pavilion threw the bottle that hit Witt. At any rate, the incident did something to the Browns and to the fans. Buck O'Neill ran out of adjectives telling of the dastardly deed, as he termed it, and the "thin veneer of sportsmanship masking a hoodlum," who would do a thing like that to a fine, clean gentleman like Witt.

The Yankees won the game from a newly listless Brownie team, Bob Shawkey shading Shocker, 2 to 1, and the St. Louis team seemed to surrender.

Ban Johnson, properly enraged over such an untoward incident in one of his ball parks, made a thorough investigation and offered a reward for the identification and apprehension of the bottle-throwing culprit. The response was quick. As a result of Johnson's offer, a spectator informed Ban that the bottle was lying harmlessly on the grass when Witt, as he sped over the turf after the fly, stepped on the neck, causing the bottle to leap into the air and strike Witt, inflicting a two-inch cut.

It was a good story. It was much better to have a bottle do that than to have one of Ban Johnson's American League customers hurl a hunk of glass at a visiting outfielder. So Johnson accepted the explanation as an official report of what had happened, and the observant spectator received $500 as a reward for being so observant. Never before, or since, has a bottle done the same trick in any league.

Over in the National League, the other St. Louis club, the Cardinals, ran into New York checkbook trouble too. With Rickey's Redbirds pressing the Giants for the lead in July, McGraw, who during the Winter had obtained Heine Groh, got out the checkbook again and paid the handy Boston Braves $100,000 for Hugh McQuillan. The Giants won the flag by seven games, with Cincinnati second and St. Louis third, and it was during that race against the checkbooks that Branch Rickey conceived the idea of a farm system, to enable the poor club owners in small cities to compete with the rich.

That was the season, too, in which Shuffling Phil Douglas broke training rules after an amazingly long period of reform and, following a hot session on the carpet, with McGraw doing the burning, allegedly wrote a letter to outfielder Les Mann of the Cardinals, suggesting that he would go fishing if the Redbirds would make it worth while. Judge Landis put Douglas on the suspended list.

The loss of Douglas was a blow to McGraw's shaky pitching staff, and John was in the mood to take a chance when Jack Scott showed up at the Polo Grounds and insisted that if he were given a chance, he might help the Giants. Scott had been released in May by the Reds. He had a sore arm and seemed to be all washed up. Fire destroyed his tobacco crop at Ridgeway, N. C., and the veteran right-hander used what little cash he had left to make the trip to New York. McGraw, always a soft touch for an old ball player in trouble, staked Scott and told him to try to get in shape. Scott ran and ran, pitched to the bat boy, and worked out for a time with the Yankees.

"Look at that poor old sore-armed boob working himself to death for nothing," the New York Americans told each other. But Scott got into shape. He won eight games and lost only two as the Giants went down the stretch, and then, as a surprise starter in the World Series, the "poor old sore-armed boob" shut out the Yankees with four hits, 3 to 0, in the third game.

The October competition was another victory for McGraw, the Giants winning four games. The only break in their triumphant march came in the second game, a 3-3 tie, called on account of darkness in broad daylight. George Hildebrand was the umpire who decided that it was too dark for any more baseball, despite the sunshine, after 10 innings, but the cash customers chose to vent their spleen on Commissioner Landis, there handily in his box seat.

The Judge backed up Hildebrand at the moment, but after he was booed as never before or afterward, he ordered that receipts of the game be turned over to charity and directed that henceforth the Commissioner would decide about darkness and daylight.

Aside from the tie game and Scott's dramatic appearance, the series was noteworthy chiefly because Babe Ruth was such a flop. Climaxing a sad season, in which his average and home-run total had fallen off badly and during which he missed 44 games and fanned 10 straight times when facing the butterfly curves of collegian Hubert Pruett of the Browns, the Bambino made only two hits in 17 times at bat in the series, with nary a home run.

You have to go back to 1922 to find a perfect no-hit game in the record book. On April 30, Charley Robertson, right-hander of the Chicago White Sox, pitched the gem. The heavy-hitting lineup of the Detroit Tigers included Ty Cobb, Harry Heilmann, and Bobby Veach, but not a Tiger reached first base. That was the first no-man-reach-first game since 1908, and the last time we looked nobody had turned the trick since Robertson did it.

YANKEES SPEND AND WIN

Stung by the World Series defeat at the hands of their hated National League rivals, the Yankees made two important deals in the

Winter before the 1923 pennant race. They acquired—yes, from Boston again—pitchers George Pipgras and Herb Pennock. Pipgras needed a bit of time before becoming a big winner, but Pennock, who had done only so-so at Philadelphia and Boston, quickly became a star of the first magnitude for the New York Americans. With Pennock, Joe Bush, Waite Hoyt, Bob Shawkey, and Carl Mays, the Yankees had a truly great pitching staff and ran away with the pennant, finishing 17 games ahead of the Tigers.

Even so, it was not yet perfection to Colonel Jake Ruppert. He called Hoyt aside one day and said: "Hoyt, what's the matter with you? You win all your games by 1 to 0, 2 to 1, or 3 to 2. Why can't you do like the other fellows? Pennock, Shawkey, and Bush win their games by 9 to 1 and 15 to 1. I wish you would try to do better, already."

It must have been a happy year for the Colonel, however. The Yankee Stadium was opened April 18, and the Bronx Bombers had a home of their own. A crowd of 60,000, the largest baseball gathering to that time, witnessed the opener, and through the year the customers attended in large numbers and cheered the man who built the stadium, the great Babe Ruth. The Babe had a big season. He batted .393, only 10 points below Harry Heilmann, the league leader, and hit 41 home runs. For the only time in his career he was named the most valuable player.

The Yankee machine was good enough to thwart McGraw in his bid for an unprecedented three straight world championships, as the American Leaguers won the series, four games to two. Ruth continued brilliantly through the title competition. He batted .368 and his hits were three homers, a triple, a double, and two singles. He also drew eight bases on balls. There was only one Babe. Oldsters like to believe there never will be another. Who could hit as he has done in World Series, and who else could hit that way and also be able to point to the record book and show 29 consecutive scoreless innings as a World Series pitcher? The Babe did that stint back in his Boston days with the Red Sox.

All financial and attendance records were smashed in that third straight all-New York series. Cash customers totaled 301,430, and they paid $1,063,815 for the show. Each Yankee got $6,143.49, tops until 1935, and each Giant was consoled with a check for $4,112.88.

A young athlete from Columbia University, destined soon to share the plaudits of Yankee fans with Ruth and the other Bombers, made his first business call at Yankee Stadium early that season. His name was Lou Gehrig, a young pitcher-first baseman. The Yankees signed him and shipped him to Hartford. Two years later, he began his record string of 2,130 consecutive games. On May 2, of 1923, a month before the young athlete showed that he could hit a baseball into Ruth's bleachers, a veteran shortstop, Everett Scott, had received a gold medal for having played in 1,000 consecutive games.

GHOST IN THE DUGOUT

There was drama and pathos in the 1924 pennant races and World Series. An underdog qualified for the October classic. A boy manager won his spurs. A foolish young man was banished from baseball with his career barely in the bud stage because he was naïve and fell for what oldsters, who should have known better, said was just a prank. And the World Series, between the Washington Senators and the New York Giants, was played with the ghost of that sad affair in the dugout.

Both races were close. In the American League, where fans had been hoping through the years that some day the great Fireball King, Walter Johnson, would get into a World Series, Washington finally made the grade. Under the scrappy leadership of Stanley (Bucky) Harris, a young man from the coal fields, for whom baseball was a smooth avenue to economic security and social graces, the Senators squeezed in ahead of the Yankees by two games, breaking half of the New York major league monopoly. Johnson, gentlemanly, and virtually an institutional figure, was a 23-game winner in his 18th season with the Washington club. And Firpo Marberry, a great relief pitcher, lent an important hand.

The Yankees got off to an early lead, but Harris held a stern whip hand over a team inclined to the playboy side, and his Senators moved from an early seventh and took first place in June. It was a red-hot race, with Detroit, and later New York again, leading, but the Senators were a team of destiny. With a nation pulling that way, Washington took two out of three at the Yankee Stadium in late August and, with Johnson's fireball accounting for 11 straight victories, the Senators went on at a dizzy pace to win, though the Yankees were victorious in 18 of 22 September games.

The great McGraw made it the coveted fourth straight in the National League, his last pennant, by the way. The Giants were strong, perhaps stronger than usual, except in pitching. Bill Terry was up from Toledo, dividing first-base assignment with George Kelly, who occasionally went to center field. Frisch was Frisch. Jackson, who had played 100 games in his 1923 freshman year after Bancroft suffered a pneumonia attack, was gaining brilliance. And when Heine Groh's trick knee faltered, an eighteen-year-old, Freddie Lindstrom, did an adequate third-base job.

Dazzy Vance won 28 and Burleigh Grimes 22 for the Dodgers, threatening as usual in an election year—they won in 1916 and 1920 —but the Giants pulled through by a game and a half, though not without a struggle—and the Jimmy O'Connell case.

Jimmy was a rookie outfielder with the Giants, a likable, green kid, purchased from the Pacific Coast League a year before for $75,000. As the season approached the nip-and-tuck finish, with the leading Giants playing the hapless Phillies, Heine Sand, the Phillies' shortstop, reported to his manager, Art Fletcher, that O'Connell had offered him $500 not to bear down too hard in the series at the Polo Grounds. Sand brushed off the offer. Then he got to thinking that at least one member of the Chicago Black Sox had been banished forever, not for being a party to the conspiracy but because he knew about it and did not report to headquarters. So Heine went to Fletcher. Fletcher called John Heydler, president of the league, and John called Judge Landis.

O'Connell readily admitted to the Judge that he had made the offer to Sand. He mentioned Cozy Dolan and players Ross Youngs, George Kelly, and Frank Frisch as the ones who seemed to know about the plan.

Youngs, Kelly, and Frisch convinced Landis that they had no part in the plot. They were cleared by the Commissioner. O'Connell was placed permanently on the ineligible list. Dolan, who asininely tried to hide behind a "don't remember anything" defense, also was banished.

Nobody in the picture ever wanted to talk about it, but many a baseball writer believes still that it was a sad case of the miscarriage of justice, if unavoidable, for O'Connell to bear the brunt of the penalty. If it was a joke, somebody should have been big enough to tell the Judge that a foolish young rookie (to be pardoned if he believed anything a great diamond star, in Giant uniform and in the Polo Grounds, told him), had been tricked into ruining his career. Nobody was big enough to do that.

But the ghost of the Jimmy O'Connell case haunted the Giant dugout as McGraw's men played the Senators for the world championship. And if the Senators were a team of destiny, victory-bound, there was a curse, too, over the Giants.

The ghost did its stuff in the sixth game. The Senators were ahead, three victories to two, though the popular idol, Johnson, had been hammered savagely and defeated twice. The Giants led in that sixth game, 3 to 1, until the last half of the eighth. Then Nemo Liebold, a pinch hitter, led off with a double. Muddy Ruel followed with his first hit of the series, a single that scored Liebold. The next two men went out, and, with Ruel on second base, the Giants were within one out of safety.

That out seemed to be at hand when Harris sent a grounder toward Lindstrom. But the ghost in the dugout deftly flipped a pebble out there in the way of the grounder. The ball struck the pebble and took a ghostly bounce over Lindstrom's head, and Ruel raced home with the tying run.

The idol, Walter Johnson, went out to pitch as the Giants batted in the ninth and the press box prepared to tap out another sad story about the great Walter, when Frisch tripled with one out. But the ghost in the dugout put fresh strength in Johnson's arm. The Big Train walked the dangerous Youngs, then struck out High-Pockets Kelly and retired Irish Meusel on a grounder that found no ghostly pebble.

Johnson was in trouble again in the 12th inning, which opened with a Giant hit. But Walter borrowed an extra bit of fire from the ghost. He struck out Lindstrom and Frisch, again walked the troublesome Youngs, and then gloriously fanned Kelly.

The ghost was through with teasing, now. Ruel, with one out in the Senator 12th, sent up a puny pop fly, a soft touch for a catcher, with no ghost dogging his heels. But the ghost was there, and Gowdy, stepping clumsily on his discarded mask, dropped the ball. Ruel then doubled for his second hit of the series. Johnson hit a grounder to the usually reliable Jackson, but Travis fumbled the ball and Ruel held second.

Without the ghost, the Giants long since would have closed out the inning. There was one more chance for the Giants. Earl McNeely hit a double-play grounder toward Lindstrom. But again there was a ghost-strewn pebble, and the ball bounced over Freddie's head. Ruel scored, and the Senators had the world championship and Walter Johnson his first World Series victory.

"It may have looked like a double-play grounder to some people," Billy Southworth, then a member of the Giants, told us years later. "We all knew what was coming. We were grabbing our gloves and sun glasses. We knew this was a series we couldn't win."

You see, Southworth and the Giants on the bench knew about that ghost.

SOME FALTER, OTHERS ACHIEVE

Washington, having broken the Yankee reign in 1924, went on for a second pennant, in 1925, and the fleet-footed Pirates, without ukulele or crooning now, smashed the McGraw dynasty and broke the string of four Giant pennants by finishing 8½ games ahead of the field. It was a popular victory, the Pirates' first flag in 16 years. Barney Dreyfus, the league's oldest magnate, and his manager, the gentlemanly Bill McKechnie, had fielded a team that boasted spectacular base running with Kiki Cuyler and the agile Max Carey, who batted .357 and .343, respectively, and stole 87 bases between them.

The Yankees folded completely in the American League, dropping to a dismal seventh as Ruth, a tempestuous figure all season, hit only .290 and contributed only 25 home runs in 98 games. It was the year of the "world's most important stomach ache," to quote Bill McGeehan, the New York author. Ruth was stricken en route home from training camp and at New York was rushed to a hospital, while grown men, with and without typewriters, and small boys, the nation over, grieved and worried. The Babe whipped the illness, supposedly brought on by too many scads of hot dogs and soda pop, but he was weak and wan when he returned to the wars and became increasingly unhappy. There was a showdown in St. Louis when

Miller Huggins, the Mite Manager, fined his top-salaried star $5,000 and suspended him indefinitely.

The Babe thought he was a bigger man than Huggins and went swearing to New York to have Miller "told off" by Ruth's pals, Ed Barrow and Jake Ruppert. But the front office gave Huggins its full backing. Ruth, whipped, took it like a man. He contritely apologized to Huggins, returned to the lineup, and spurted, but the Yankees were beyond spurting.

Important new figures appeared on the diamond. For Spring delivery, the Yankees bought Tony Lazzeri from Salt Lake City, and a fresh rookie, named Leo Durocher, from Hartford. That same season a sixteen-year-old boy walked into McGraw's Polo Grounds office, with a letter of introduction from Harry Williams, New Orleans lumber man. The boy was Melvin Ott.

Ott reported as a catcher, but McGraw quickly saw that he could hit too well and belonged in the outfield.

"Did you ever play the outfield?" John asked the sixteen-year-old Melvin.

"Yes, Mr. McGraw," the boy said bashfully, "I played a little outfield when I was a kid."

On May 6, 1925, an old gaffer named Everett Scott, who had played 1,307 consecutive games, was benched, ending the string. A few feet from Scott on the Yankee bench was a young rookie named Lou Gehrig. On June 1, Gehrig was sent in as a pinch hitter. The next day, Wallie Pipp, the regular first baseman, told Huggins his head ached and he was in a slump; better be benched. Pipp was benched and he never got to first base again. From that day until May 2, 1939, Gehrig was in the lineup of every game the Yankees played.

There were happenings in the National League, too. Just before Memorial Day, Rogers Hornsby, on his way to a .403 batting average and his sixth successive batting championship, replaced Branch Rickey as manager of the Cardinals.

Walter Johnson, smiled on by a ghost-nudged fate in that final game of 1924, wasn't so fortunate in the 1925 series. He yielded only one run while winning the first and fourth games, but his defense, chiefly in the person of Roger Peckinpaugh, fell apart, especially in the seventh and deciding game.

There were other extenuating circumstances. The final game was played in rain that was much more than a drizzle and Johnson found it difficult to grip the ball. He and the Senators had a 7-to-6 lead after their eighth inning in the final contest, played at Pittsburgh, but in the Pirate half the rain fell with increasing force and the field was in terrible condition. If it hadn't been that the weatherman was predicting worse weather, with possibly snow and a blizzard, they probably never would have started that game. Once started, everybody wanted it finished.

Johnson, making frequent use of towels to dry hands and baseballs, retired two batters in the Pittsburgh eighth, but doubles by Earl Smith and pinch hitter Carson Bigbee tied the score. Moore walked, and Carey hit a grounder to Peck, who fumbled for his eighth error. Then Cuyler sliced a drive down the right-field line and the ball kicked up water in that corner, two runs scored and Johnson was beaten, 9 to 7.

Press-box wags remarked that Johnson had missed a great chance to be a three-time World Series winner and that Peckinpaugh had missed about everything else. Twenty years later, Peck still was being reminded of his 1925 fielding. Early in 1945 there were rumors that Buck Newsom was likely to be traded to the Indians for a couple of current doghouse inmates, Jeff Heath and Jim Bagby. General Manager Peckinpaugh of Cleveland snapped, "I wouldn't have that screwball Newsom on my team." To which Bobo cracked, "And I wouldn't play for Papa Goat Peck, either. I may be a screwball, but I never made eight errors in a World Series."

Walter Johnson, one of the all-time greats of baseball, has passed on, but the legendary speed of the fireball king will live as long as men talk of baseball. On an overseas USO trip, entertaining soldiers in the ETO, Emil (Dutch) Leonard, at that time a Washington pitcher, regaled the GI's with a Johnson yarn.

Johnson was pitching against the Athletics at Philadelphia. It was getting late, the Senators had a one-run lead, and two were out in a late inning, Leonard would tell the boys. Everybody knew the game would be called after that frame, and after the second out, with Jimmy Dykes at bat and the count two strikes and nothing, Muddy Ruel, catching Johnson, walked out to the mound.

"I'm pretending to give you the ball, Walter," Ruel said. "But I'll keep it. Now you just go through the motions of pitching and I'll do the rest."

So Walter took his position on the mound, went through his smooth windup and pitching motion. Ruel, behind the plate, slapped the ball hard into his glove. Bill McGowan, umpiring behind the plate, blinked a bit and then yelled, "Strike three, you're out!"

Dykes protested, but Umpire McGowan insisted, "Jimmy, that ball was right through the middle." And Dykes cracked, "Bill, I know damned well now that you're blind. That ball was a foot outside."

HORNSBY FOR MAYOR

Young men figured prominently in the battling on the diamonds as the Cardinals broke a long St. Louis pennant drought and the Yankees bounced back in 1926 to win the major league pennants.

In New York, Miller Huggins won with an infield that was all-rookie except for Joe Dugan at third base. Mark Koenig was the shortstop, Tony Lazzeri at second, and Lou Gehrig, a regular now, at first. Ruth bounced back, too, for the Mite Manager, hitting .372 and contributing 47 home runs. Herb Pennock, at his brilliant peak, gained 23 victories. But the steadying influence, the big human factor, it seemed, that enabled the club to rebound from a bad seventh to the top was young Lazzeri. Quiet, reserved, with the baseball instinct of a veteran, he also was blessed with strong arms that could hit a long ball.

The Yankees finally clinched the flag, in a close race, by taking a double-header at St. Louis on September 25. The night before, at the old Buckingham Hotel, they had been kept awake by the hilarious celebration of St. Louis fans, maudlin happy over the Cardinals' first pennant, clinched September 24.

Rogers Hornsby personified the triumph for St. Louis. His batting average dropped from a robust .403 to .313, but he gave the club a driving leadership. Two mid-June deals were important, too. Just before the June 15 trading deadline, Heine Mueller went to the Giants for Billy Southworth, who hit .320 and played a steadfast right field. Eight days later, with Manager Joe McCarthy of the Cubs sweeping with a new broom, an old gaffer named Grover Cleveland Alexander was offered for the waiver price. Four clubs lower than the Cardinals passed, and St. Louis claimed the thirty-nine-year-old right-hander.

Lester Bell, booed in the Spring, listened to the cold-blooded Hornsby, who said, "Let those damnfools boo, Kid, they're paying your salary." Bell led the Redbirds with .325, Jim Bottomley slumping along with the Rajah. Freshman Taylor Douthit, a gentle young man from college, much out of place in tough baseball, helped with a .307 average and a great year in center field. Flint Rhem had a 20-7 record; Bill Sherdel, 16-12; Jess Haines, 13-4; Alexander, 12-10; and Art Reinhart, 10-5.

Whenever anyone is looking for thrilling ball games to dramatize, in print or on the air, he quickly picks the final game of the 1926 World Series, a thrill-packed natural if there ever was one.

The Yankees were favorites with the wagering gentry. They deserved to be. They were a better team. But the Cardinals, very much the underdog, were the popular favorites. Hornsby's mother had died on the eve of the big series, but Rogers agreed that she would have wanted him to go on with his duty. He was manager of the Cardinals. And so grimly he went on, while his mother's remains rested in a Texas mortuary. The boy who had just lost his mother, leading a team in a city that had just broken a thirty-eight-year-long pennant famine—it was natural for the country to be rooting for the Cardinals.

The series was tied at 3-3 when the two teams met in the finale on a raw, drizzly Sunday, October 10, at Yankee Stadium. Jess Haines started against Hoyt and in the third inning yielded a homer by Ruth, the Babe's fourth of the series. But in the fourth, with Hornsby out, Bottomley singled to left and Bell was safe on a fumble by Koenig. Chick Hafey's short fly fell between Meusel and Koenig, filling the bases.

Bob O'Farrell followed with a drive to left-center, a ball that Earl Combs or Bob Meusel could catch. At the last moment, Combs stepped aside. It was good baseball thinking, for Meusel had a rifle arm and would have a fairly sure play at the plate. But the Cards were a team of destiny that year. Meusel dropped the ball, Bottomley scored, and the bases remained filled. Then Tommy Thevenow, a .255 regular-season hitter, rising to .417 heights in the series, shot a two-run single over second.

The Yankees scored a second run in the sixth on Dugan's single and Hank Severeid's long double, and then came the dramatic seventh. Combs walked and Koenig sacrificed. Ruth was passed intentionally. Meusel forced Ruth, but Haines couldn't get the ball over the plate and walked Gehrig, filling the bases.

Hornsby called a halt and talked to Haines. Jess showed him his finger, raw and bloody from pitching knuckler after knuckler. It was no wonder Haines couldn't control the ball.

Only the day before, Alexander had pitched nine innings. But after that game, before going off into the night, Old Pete had told Hornsby, "If you need me tomorrow, I'll have a little left. This was fairly easy today." And Hornsby had grinned and thanked Old Pete, and told him not to have too rough a night.

With the bases filled, two out, and the Cardinals one small run ahead, Hornsby called on Alexander. Old Pete was down in the bullpen, dozing as he caught up with some of the sleep he had missed the night before. They say that when word was received that Rog wanted Old Pete, the grizzled veteran handed to Bill Sherdel something that looked like a bottle.

Hornsby walked halfway to the bullpen to meet Alexander and was glad to see that Old Pete's eyes were open.

"How are things, Rog?" Alexander asked.

"Two out, we're a run ahead, and the bases are filled and Lazzeri's up," Hornsby replied.

"Nothin' much left to do except give Tony a lot of hell, eh Rog?"

Lazzeri, a tough .275 hitter, with 114 runs batted in that season, second only to Ruth among the Yankees, took Alexander's first pitch, low, for ball one. A curve nicked the inside corner to even the count. On the next one, inside, Lazzeri whipped a vicious line drive to left, and the Stadium stands roared. But the drive was pulled a bit too much. A foul. Strike two. On the next pitch, a curve that looked good but wasn't, Lazzeri struck out.

On the train that night, as the Cardinals journeyed back home triumphantly, Old Pete was being steadied by large quantities of black coffee. Somebody cracked about heroes.

"Ain't baseball funny?" the old gaffer asked rhetorically. "You know, you never want to take this hullaballoo and hero stuff too seriously. Yes, I struck out Lazzeri; but suppose that line drive he hit on that second strike had gone fair? Boys, Lazzeri would be the hero tonight and I—well, I'd just be a bum."

Scarcely had St. Louis settled back from its frenzied celebration of its first pennant in thirty-eight years and its first world title in forty, when rumors began to circulate that all was not well between Hornsby and his employer, Sam Breadon, president of the Cardinals. It was true, and in December it was announced that Hornsby had been traded to the Giants for Frank Frisch and Jimmy Ring.

St. Louis was properly indignant. Breadon was hung many times in effigy, the Chamber of Commerce censured him, fans swore never to attend a Cardinal game again. But you know the story. Frisch had a great year in 1927, the turnstiles continued to click, and the wounds all healed.

It was a case, of course, of two too-rugged individualists being one too many. Hornsby was one of the greatest hitters the game produced and had one of the keenest baseball minds. But he was a man of solid opinions, to which he subscribed without stint. He felt that if he earned a few thousand dollars and wanted to bet some of them on a horse race, that was his right and his business.

"I can't see the difference," he would say, "between me betting a few bucks on a horse and getting a big kick out of it, and Mr. Rickey betting on Air Reduction or American Can, and getting a big kick out of hoping he'll win."

Hornsby also believed that if you had an honest opinion and expressed it honestly, it was all right, even if you were a bit vulgar about it. One day in the Pittsburgh clubhouse, after a Cardinal defeat, Breadon appeared, to announce that he had been unable to get a couple of exhibition games canceled. Hornsby had asked for the cancelations, so that his team, in the thick of the pennant fight, could have a bit of badly needed rest. When he told Breadon, too vulgarly, what he could do with all exhibition games, Breadon made up his mind he wouldn't have such a rude man as an employee any longer. Before the club's train had arrived in St. Louis for a triumphant home-coming, he had asked Bill Killefer, then a Hornsby coach, if he would accept the management of the club.

Hornsby continued a stormy petrel through his playing career. For a time, John McGraw considered him his heir apparent as manager of the Giants, and when the Little Napoleon missed a trip, the Rajah acted as a leader of the Giants. But friction developed there, too, and Hornsby was traded to the Braves. The Cubs then offered a big roll of dough, and the Rajah went to Chicago, where subsequently he became manager, succeeding Joe McCarthy. But Hornsby kept on saying what he honestly thought and ran into trouble with the Cub front office. The club had bought Frank De-maree, for a substantial sum, for a look-see. In a pinch, the Rajah used Frank as a pinch hitter. The front office thought he should have picked a pinch batter of more experience.

"Why the hell did they pay all that dough for him, and why the hell is he in a Cub uniform?" Hornsby retorted angrily. "Baseball is a game of pinches. I want guys with guts who can hit when it counts and I wanted to find out about this guy."

Hornsby later managed the Browns, but there was trouble with Don Barnes because the Rajah still had more than academic interest in the ability of one horse to run faster than another. Barnes paid him off.

Through it all, Hornsby always was a prime favorite with the press, whose most important yardstick is forthright reliability. And when Hornsby said something, you could believe him and you could quote him. Rogers is doing all right now, as year-around director of baseball school activities for the Chicago *Daily News*, which broad-mindedly believes there is something academic about the financial aspects of horses when they run.

THE GREATEST YANKEE TEAM?

There have been so many great Yankee teams, so many New York American pennants and world championships, that a popular fanning-bee topic through the years has been the question of which was the greatest.

We'll take the Yankees of 1927 and 1928, a team with a devastating punch and airtight pitching that made observers overlook the fact that here was a stalwart defensive club, too. In 1927 the Yankees won by 17 games, and in 1928 they built up a similar lead at one stage of the race.

Combs, Ruth, and Meusel were the outfield, and the infield included Gehrig, Lazzeri, Koenig, and Dugan. The catchers were

Pat Collins and Benny Bengough, and Hoyt, Pipgras, and Pennock were a pitching staff unto themselves, especially with the incomparable Wilcy Moore as the one-man bullpen.

Ruth, hitting 17 home runs in September of 1927, set the season record of 60 and batted .356. Gehrig, fast moving to the front, hit 47 home runs and batted a stout .373. The club hit 157 homers, nearly three times as many as the total of the second-place Athletics. The Yankees broke up so many games with explosive big innings, usually in the late frames, after they had dallied with the enemy, that Combs coined the expression "five o'clock lightning," the approximate time of the eighth inning and booming Yankee bats.

In those two years, the National League was a poor match for the Bronx Bombers, who knocked over the Pirates in four straight in 1927 and made equally short work of the Cardinals in 1928.

New York, the historians will tell you, won the 1927 series in batting practice, hitting so many balls into the stands at Forbes Field before the first series pitch that the Pirates became terrified.

The 1927 series will be remembered for its most spectacularly unspectacular finish. With the fourth-game score tied in the ninth at 3-3, relief pitcher Johnny Miljus walked Combs, and then Koenig, up to sacrifice, beat out a bunt. With Ruth at bat, a wild pitch advanced the runners, and Manager Donie Bush of the Pirates ordered the Babe passed intentionally, to fill the bases.

Pirate hopes rose when Miljus struck out Gehrig and Meusel, but as Lazzeri stepped to the plate, Miller Huggins, the dugout sage, called the turn. "He's bearing down too hard," the Miller murmured. "He'll throw that ball away."

Huggins was right in a hurry. On the first pitch to Lazzeri, Miljus threw one too high and too hard. Johnny Gooch leaped desperately, but the ball was out of reach and the winning run thus scored, undramatically.

The Cardinals were about as poor a match in the 1928 series. Strangely enough, it opened amid reports that the Yankees were all crippled up, several of the stars would have to appear in wheel chairs, and that the Redbirds ought to win handily.

But despite Pennock's sore arm, Combs's broken finger, Lazzeri's bad right shoulder, Dugan's old knee injury, and Ruth's charley horse, Huggins found enough bailing wire to put everybody back together, and the Yankees breezed through in four straight.

St. Louis will remember it as the "Series of the Quick Pitch." Bill Sherdel, a good World Series pitcher but never a winning one, had a 2-1 lead until the seventh inning of the fourth game. With one out in the seventh and a two-strike count on the Babe, Sherdel kept his foot on the rubber and, after taking Jimmy Wilson's return throw, fired across a quick-return third strike.

A terrific argument followed. Umpire Cy Pfirman said Ruth wasn't out, that Sherdel would have to pitch to the Babe again. Cardinal Manager Bill McKechnie, Frisch, and Rabbit Maranville screamed that the quick-return was legal in the National League and that this was a National League game. However, the other umpires, Cy Rigler, Brick Owens, and Bill McGowan, upheld Pfirman, explaining that at a conference meeting with Judge Landis the umpires had agreed to bar the quick-return in the series. But nobody had told the managers or the pitchers about it.

When quiet was restored, Ruth stepped to the plate and belted the next Sherdel pitch into the right-field stand, tying the score. Gehrig followed with an even longer four-bagger, and the Yankees were ahead. Sherdel and Alexander were routed. The final score was 7 to 3.

MORE FAMINES END

Baseball's most glamorous decade went out as it had come in, with two long pennant famines broken, with two fresh flag winners. The races weren't very hot, as the Athletics, who hadn't won in fourteen years, triumphed for the venerable Connie Mack by the wide margin of 19 games, and the Cubs of Joe McCarthy took the National League honors by 10½. It was Chicago's first flag since the ill-fated Black Sox of 1919, and the first for the Cubs since 1918.

McCarthy's team had great right-handed batting power. Hornsby, obtained from Boston, hit .380 and 40 home runs. Riggs (Old Hoss) Stephenson batted .362, Cuyler, .360, and Hack Wilson, with 39 homers, had a .345 average. Charley Grimm, at first base, was the only left-handed hitter in the lineup, and the punch would have been even more potent if Gabby Hartnett hadn't missed the season with a sore arm. Charley Root, Pat Malone, Guy Bush, and Fred (Sheriff) Blake headed the pitching staff.

Connie Mack's team had a fine punch, too. Al Simmons batted .365 and hit 34 homers. Jimmy Foxx, a youngster of twenty-one, finally found his place at first base and hit 33 four-baggers as he batted .354. You were a bum on that club if you weren't comfortably in the 300's. Mickey Cochrane had .331, Bing Miller, .335, and Mule Haas, in center, hit .313. A couple of youngsters, Joe Boley and Max Bishop, made a smooth middle-of-the-infield combination, permitting the ageless Jimmy Dykes to move over to third. The still sullen Lefty Grove and large George Earnshaw were the big winners, with 20 and 24 victories. Left-handed Rube Walberg helped with 18, Ed Rommel was the relief ace, and the veterans John Quinn and Howard Ehmke worked in spots.

As was the case with other title struggles of the Golden Decade, the 1929 series produced incidents and thrills and furnished fuel for the Hot Stove League down through the years. Ehmke was the surprise hero, and the stocky Hack Wilson the outstanding goat.

Ehmke, widely regarded as all washed up, had won only seven games and lost two and had worked only 55 innings as the Mackmen breezed to the pennant. As a matter of fact, Mack was about to release the veteran but played a hunch when Howard wistfully told him that he always had longed to pitch in just one World Series game, if only for a few innings.

"I think I've got one more good game left in there," Ehmke told Mack, as he flexed his right arm. So Mack told the pitcher to pass up the final Western trip of the season and scout the Cub hitters.

Mack then pulled the biggest "sleeper play," the biggest surprise in World Series history. Even the Athletics were amazed when Ehmke began to warm up for the opening game of the series at Wrigley Field.

"Are you going to let that guy pitch?" snapped an unbelieving Simmons.

"Yes, I am, Al," Mack answered quietly, and Mackmen on the bench tapped their temples suggestively. The Old Man had gone nuts at last.

But Connie Mack wasn't "nuts." Ehmke's side-arm curves, sweeping past the Cub sluggers from a white-shirted bleacher background, mowed down batter after batter. The veteran, who had told Mack so pleadingly that he had just one more good game left in that arm, was right. He scattered eight hits and set a World Series record for strikeouts by fanning 13 Cubs, as the Athletics won the game, 3 to 1, to take command.

Hack Wilson's goat horns bloomed in the fourth game. The Macks had won the second game, and the Cubs the third, and the National Leaguers seemed to be safely on their way to a 2-2 tie in the title struggle as they battered Quinn, Walberg, and Rommel and led, 8 to 0, after their seventh inning. Charley Root, who had lost to Ehmke in the opener, was sailing along.

Then suddenly things happened. Simmons hit a home run, and Dykes wisecracked, "Well, we're not shut out, anyhow."

Foxx, Miller, Dykes, and Boley singled in succession, scoring two more runs. George Burns, batting for Rommel, popped to Woody English. But Bishop singled, scoring Dykes. The score was a more respectable 8 to 4 now, two men were on base and only one was out.

McCarthy, playing it safe, called on Art Nehf to replace Root. Haas hit a line drive to center. It looked like an easy second out. But Wilson misjudged the ball, started in, became blinded by the sun, lost the ball completely, and it sailed over his head for a home run, inside the park. Nehf walked Cochrane, and right-handed Blake replaced Nehf, only to have singles by Simmons and Foxx tie the score. Pat Malone relieved Blake and hit Miller with a pitched ball, filling the bases. Dykes doubled, just out of Stephenson's reach, and Simmons and Foxx scored. It didn't make any difference, then, that Malone struck out Boley and Burns, the latter a pinch batter who accounted for two of the outs in the ten-run inning.

Lefty Grove struck out four of the six Cubs he faced in the last two frames, and the final score was Macks 10, Cubs 8. The Athletics went on to take the fifth game, and so the beloved Connie Mack, coming back to the title wars after a long famine, was leader of world champions once more.

Yes, it was the Golden Era of baseball, with stars studding every roster, and jammed stands feasting on thrill-packed baseball. The greatest years of baseball? Well, they're still doing all right at the gate. It must be a great game in any era.

BOXING

by JAMES P. DAWSON
Boxing Editor, The New York Times

Any reference to the 1920-1930 era in boxing must be made in terms of golden splendor. It was truly the Golden Age. The ring sport never before touched such stratospheric heights. In popular appeal it knew no parallel period; nor has it attained a similar level since. It is to be doubted that it will again in our time.

The Twenties saw the world's greatest fighter and the promoter of the ages operating in close harmony and giving the sport a tone and affluence hitherto unknown. The biggest "gate" on record for a boxing bout became history. The ring attracted its largest "paid" crowd. The top purse ever received by a fighter for a single contest was presented. The period furnished boxing's outstanding bouts on an over-all basis. It also provided the most controversial fight in all ring history, past or present, a controversy that has been handed down by chroniclers whose prejudices reflect the slant of their arguments, and doubtless will be argued for a long time to come.

All this was so because all classes, from flyweight to heavyweight, were crowded with performers of conspicuous merit. From the diminutive Jimmy Wilde, who was the "mighty atom," antedating the smashing of the more volatile neutron, to Jack Dempsey, the Manassa Mauler, who was the ring's front-page "killer," boxing boasted a list of champions and near-champions, recognized challengers for titles, such as has not since been equaled. Nor, from the current outlook, will this array be equaled for years to come, if ever.

This may be dismissed as the biased conclusion of an old-timer in a nostalgic mood. Each generation favors its own in any retrospective appraisal; that is human nature. But a look at the record, an inspection of the library files which have grown yellow and musty from the passing of time, will supply confirmation.

Dempsey, Tunney, Leonard, Firpo, Carpentier, Tendler, Gibbons, Greb, Walker, Loughran, Delaney, Canzoneri, Flowers, Wilde, Sharkey, McTigue, Berlenbach, Risko, Siki, Stribling, Slattery, Dundee, Mandell, Kilbane, Villa, Schmeling, Criqui—these were the names in boxing that became bywords the country over in the Golden Twenties. When shall we see such a group again in any one period?

Equipped as it was with fighters who fought, with boxers who gave superlative demonstrations of the sport's finer points, with punchers of paralyzing force, durable practitioners who were human shock absorbers in resistance to punishment—exponents whose appeal at the box office was like some irresistible, overpowering magnet—and unsullied by the cloud of suspicion subsequently to discredit the sport, boxing emerged from the shadows in which it had been cloaked and sparkled in the sunshine of popularity.

Where it had been a sport merely tolerated before World War I, it became "big business," an enterprise with a tremendous following. Not so many years away from the era of clandestine exhibitions on river barges, in well-hidden barns, or in isolated suburban rendezvous, boxing came boldly forth into the open. Legal barriers were gradually removed. Laws sanctioning the sport were adopted by first one state and then another in a sweeping national movement, stemming in part from recognition of the fact that fisticuffs were a vital part of the conditioning of the doughboys who shattered Kaiser Wilhelm's armies in the first world conflict.

The sport that had been an outcast went through a transition to become a major fixture on the entertainment calendar of the nation. Where once it had been the plaything of a select coterie, just outside or within the law, depending on the point of view, it achieved recognition for its true value as one of the manliest and most appealing of athletic endeavors.

The "best" people, who once shunned the ring and shuddered even at the mention of the "vulgar" sport, became its most confirmed supporters, not in a patronizing way but because there was no resisting the allure of a clash between two perfectly trained, evenly matched, highly developed boxers.

The idea of the exclusive club in American boxing was born. The International Sporting Club came into being. Patterned along the lines of the ancient National Sporting Club of London, steeped in tradition and boxing history, it attracted some of the country's most influential names. It matters not that the venture blew up in the face of those who conceived it, that the breath of scandal chilled a bond-selling project which was to provide a huge boxing arena but resulted only in "the famous hole in the ground" at Forty-ninth Street and Lexington Avenue in New York City.

In its conception it was all right. Complaint came only from the execution. Yet, notwithstanding the jarring collapse of the I.S.C., the plan served a purpose. The project was launched during the days of the old Madison Square Garden and, before the organization crashed in ruins, it had played a part in influencing the adoption in New York State of the Walker Law, legalizing boxing, had conducted several important bouts, and shared in the herculean task of establishing the respectability of the sport. It served as the model for the mythical "600 millionaires," exclusive club associated with the new Madison Square Garden, which opened its doors in 1925 on the site of an abandoned car barn at Fiftieth Street and Eighth Avenue, New York, as the greatest indoor arena in the world.

The affluence of boxing in its gaudiest era is attributable to the influence of just two men—William Harrison (Jack) Dempsey, and George Lewis (Tex) Rickard. The record is there for all to see, and it will remain as a lasting memorial to these two figures, whose fame has become legendary. Individually, each was a leader. As a team, they were the greatest boxing ever knew, probably ever will know.

There may have been a greater heavyweight champion than Dempsey. Corbett, Jeffries, Sullivan, Fitzsimmons, Johnson, and Louis all have their proponents, and it is idle speculation to say that Jack would have beaten any one or all of them, or vice versa. It's simply one of those things that can't be proved. But in this corner the greatest fighting man of them all was William Harrison Dempsey, and that's the way the world felt when he was in his prime. That's the way many whose opinions count feel today.

The blazing hot Fourth of July in 1919 that the 187-pound Dempsey hammered six-foot-seven-inch, 245-pound Jess Willard into a shapeless mass of beef was the start of the greatest gold rush since the days of the Forty-Niners. The word and photo picture of the butchery committed by the lean, scowling, black-browed challenger upon the enormous hulk of the champion electrified the sports world.

Then and there was born the greatest star the ring had known, a magnet of such irresistible appeal, with his murderous fists, as to bring millions of dollars into Rickard's till and make Jack and Tex rich beyond the dreams of any fighter or promoter before them.

In five Dempsey appearances under the Rickard banner, the gate passed a million dollars, for a total of $8,500,000. Two of them were with Gene Tunney, and one each with Georges Carpentier, Luis Angel Firpo, and Jack Sharkey. In every instance it was Dempsey who brought on the stampede toward the box office. His name carried a magic that made people forget their business, time, distance, and the cost in their rush to get down their money to see the deadliest killer operating outside the jungle.

Nothing like this Tiger Man had been known in the ring since the days of Stanley Ketchel, the Michigan Assassin. This bobbing, weaving engine of destruction had the same "color" as the handsome, tawny-haired Ketchel. He had the same heart of an oak, the same aggressiveness to the point of recklessness, the same savage instinct to tear into action and rip and slash his opponent into instant helplessness, hooking wickedly with both hands. For combined speed, hitting punch, fighting spirit, ability to take a punch, and contempt for consequences, the ring has never seen Dempsey's equal among the heavyweights.

On his way up to the championship bout with Willard, he left a wake of destruction. His terrible fists wrecked men like Bill Brennan, Gunboat Smith, and Carl Morris. In 17 seconds he finished Fred Fulton. And then, getting into the ring with the Pottawatomie Giant, who towered above him like a mastiff over a bulldog and little suspected the frightful beating he was in for, Dempsey went berserk. The punishment he inflicted upon Willard in the first round has probably never been equaled. The bell saved the champion, and only his gameness enabled him to carry on after Jack, who had left the ring in the belief that he had won, returned to finish his man. At the end of the third round, Willard's seconds threw in the towel as the giant sat helpless on his stool, beaten to a pulp and his face almost shapeless.

The world never could forget the memory of that awful carnage wreaked upon the giant. Dempsey's fists became associated in the public mind as double charges of dynamite, too powerful for human flesh and blood to resist, and the association continued throughout his career, even after he lost his crown to Tunney in their first meeting in Philadelphia in 1926. Every time Jack went into the ring, Rickard was fearful that he would kill his opponent, just as he had been afraid of Willard killing Dempsey. Tex was so sold on the lethal content of the Tiger Man's punches—like everyone else—that, even after Tunney had given him a thorough beating, the promoter was convinced that Jack would whip him in their return fight in Chicago.

The legend of Dempsey's stark ferocity in making the kill was responsible for making him the greatest ring attraction in history. In his early years Jack was far from being a popular figure. He was accused of being a draft dodger in the First World War, although he was exonerated of the charge later. From the time he left grammar school in Salt Lake City, Utah, he had known only the hardest kind of work, in mines, lumber camps, on railroads, and in shipyards, as he moved restlessly on from one job to another.

But whether people liked Dempsey or not, in those early years, before he became one of the most idolized heroes of sport, they wanted to see him in action and paid their money. They had to see the most spectacular showman, the most savage fighter, and the hardest hitter the ring had known. And so Rickard had the greatest attraction in boxing history to launch fistiania's Golden Age.

Rickard came off the frontier area to dazzle the effete East with his promotional daring and business acumen. He gave the world its first million-dollar gate; also the biggest gate a bout ever has drawn—the $2,658,660 taken in at the second heavyweight championship battle between champion Tunney and challenger Dempsey in 1927. He gave Tunney the largest purse ever paid a boxer—the staggering sum of $990,445, a far cry from the $67 Gene collected for a bout against K.O. Jaffe in the New Polo A.A. in New York before joining the Marines in the First World War. He accommodated the largest paid crowd ever to witness a boxing bout—the 120,757 fans who witnessed Dempsey's dethronement by Tunney in Philadelphia's Sesqui-Centennial Stadium in 1926. His boxing promotions in nine years brought in the staggering total of $15,000,000.

It was Rickard who introduced the elite to boxing, or vice versa, through the medium of the fight carnival held in old Madison Square

Garden for the Fund for Devastated France, under the sponsorship of Miss Anne Morgan, in the wake of World War I. And having brought the elite to his door, he kept them coming back, because, unlike other promoters of the day and before, he guaranteed them the seat their ticket called for. His name became the trade-mark of integrity and of the best in prize-fight entertainment. With the confidence he inspired, he popularized every one of the eight standard ring divisions, set a new vogue in boxing, and marshaled the funds with which the new Madison Square Garden was erected after the relic that stood in Madison Square had outlived its usefulness. They could have named the new plant "Rickard Stadium" when he died in 1929, and the tribute would have been deserved and approved.

To say that Rickard accomplished all of this by himself would be stretching the truth. He had a monopoly on the world heavyweight title, introducing a departure from established custom which proved highly profitable and set a definite pattern and, of course, he had Jack Dempsey. The tremendous box-office appeal of Tiger Jack, in conjunction with the daring, foresight, and brilliance of Rickard as a promoter, made for the greatest combination boxing or any other sport has known.

Gambler, rancher, lumberjack, gold prospector, Rickard came out of the Western frontier towns to command attention as the greatest sports impresario of the twentieth century. Tex had imagination, an amazing conception of the popular appeal of any specific event, an unerring appraisal of the public desire in boxing. He established a reputation for providing only the best in a field of almost unlimited selection. His personality overrode the objections of boxing's enemies (and they were counted in large numbers in the early days of the sport's restoration to legal status under the law sponsored by the late James J. Walker) and crushed the jealousies of rivals who resented the signal success of this outlander after their own failures. He had the Midas touch.

The perfect illustration was the immediate success which followed his acquisition of the old Madison Square Garden. The famous arena, a plaything of political intrigue before the advent of Rickard, was more or less of a white elephant, largely because of mismanagement. Charles J. Harvey had failed as its promoter. So had Billy Wellman, who cut a spectacular figure at the time as a dashing, youthful impresario, particularly in the automobile racing field. So had Harry Pollok, who is remembered as the manager of Freddy Welsh, predecessor of Benny Leonard as world lightweight champion. Billy Gibson, who piloted Leonard and Tunney into world titles, had a crack at boxing promotion in the old Garden—and failed. So did Jimmy Johnston. Not necessarily in this order were these established, experienced boxing men tossed for a loss by promotional difficulties of the old Garden, but they are names which come readily to mind as casualties of a system which Rickard, with his daring and magic touch, overcame.

Representing boxing's leading figures of the time, they were typical. They mixed politics and promotion in overbalance; not to the advantage of the sport. Rickard, too, had to meet the political influence of a hungry, corrupt Tammany Hall machine, but he handled the situation astutely, until the weight of his reputation ended early apprehension.

Tex was unheard of until 1906—as a sports promoter, that is. Then he created something of a furore by signing Joe Gans and Battling Nelson for a lightweight championship bout in Goldfield, Nevada. A mystery man came into focus, and a rough, rambling frontier town became the world's sport center with the announcement of the match. Increasing the attention his bout attracted, Rickard offered a purse of $30,000 for this fight and startled the world by placing the entire amount, in gold coin, on display in the window of the gambling saloon which was his headquarters, "The Northern." No one had ever heard of such a procedure. Indeed, the accepted order at the time was a reduction of pledged purses, on one pretext or another. The bout went 42 rounds, with Gans the winner on a foul.

Next on the Rickard calendar came the Jim Jeffries—Jack Johnson world heavyweight title bout. Johnson's escapades as titleholder had aroused resentment. Jeffries, in retirement since 1905, was induced to return to the ring in 1910 in an effort to dethrone Johnson and restore the crown to the white race. For a match which attracted world-wide attention and excitement, Rickard, with Jack Gleason as his partner, provided a purse of $101,000 and pitched the battle in Reno, Nevada, far off the beaten track, but not altogether inaccessible, as was proved when the fight drew a gate of $220,000, an unheard of sum in those days.

The yellowing newspaper files record the wild disorder throughout the country which followed Johnson's knockout of Jeffries in 15 rounds of a bout which Rickard not only promoted but refereed because he could not get the boxers to agree upon a satisfactory arbiter. Racial feeling ran high in advance of the match and exploded into riots in various sections of the nation in its wake.

It was on this very feeling that Rickard capitalized. But the battle aftermath had a salutary effect. Rickard thereafter shunned "mixed" matches for the heavyweight title, although he promoted them frequently in the lighter divisions. Indeed, the promoter repeatedly confided to me that his fear of the repercussions influenced in no small measure his failure later to arrange a match between Dempsey and Harry Wills, for which a clamor had been created during Dempsey's reign as champion and which unquestionably was the most lucrative bout available when the demand was hottest.

Rickard's success with the Nelson-Gans and the Jeffries-Johnson fights made him not altogether insensible to the possibilities of sports promotion as a permanent thing. These triumphs dimmed somewhat the luster of the reputation of James W. Coffroth, a Californian affectionately called "Sunny Jim," who was the country's leading boxing entrepreneur at the time. For five years Rickard weighed the matter, meanwhile pursuing the more or less nomadic role of gambling-house proprietor, prospector, and rancher, traveling far and wide over the world as opportunity beckoned.

In 1916, Rickard again was in the sports headlines. He came into New York in the old Frawley Law days with a heavyweight championship bout between the towering Jess Willard, who had acquired the title on a 26-round knockout of Jack Johnson on April 5, 1915, at Havana, and Frank Moran, a rugged flame-haired Pittsburgh heavyweight, who had made a triumphal tour of England and France.

Old-timers will recall Moran as the owner of the famous "Mary Ann" punch, a looping right-hand drive to the jaw which started almost from his shoe tops and was paralyzing if it struck the target after arching through the air. Twice Moran had knocked out Jim Coffey, an imposing Irish giant, with this punch. Bombardier Wells, perhaps the cleverest heavyweight England ever sent to America, had fallen victim to the blow in London. Coffey and Wells were known as "glass-jawed" heavyweights. Their chins responded like china to such a punch as Moran's "Mary Ann," which generally exploded after Moran had been subjected to withering fire chasing his foe. This punch and Moran's rugged durability were his only claims to ring fame.

The two knockouts of Coffey, one in the third round, in 1915, and the other in the ninth round, early in 1916, created a demand for Moran as a challenger, despite the fact that Willard towered above him and outweighed Moran proportionately. Under the Frawley Law no decisions were allowed. Contests were limited to 10 rounds, a regulation of the State Athletic Commission.

Rickard, having established relations with Willard through his manager, Tom Jones, moved quietly in getting the champion's approval for his only title appearance in New York away from the circus tent, and speedily signed Moran. As quietly, Tex proceeded to engage Madison Square Garden, satisfying the political demands he encountered, meeting the requirements of the State Athletic Commission in partnership with John Ringling, and overcoming the petty jealousies of rival promoters who lacked the imagination or daring to envision such a match.

The bout was held March 25, 1916. It attracted a crowd which made the old arena figuratively bulge at the sides and resulted in a "popular" decision for Willard in the newspapers, which gave the only decisions of the day. Indirectly, too, the fight hastened the death of the Frawley Law, outlawing a sport which had been disfranchised earlier through the abolition of the old Horton Law.

The writer recalls "covering" a boxing-law hearing held in the Bar Association Building in New York, at which charges of bribery were under investigation as a prelude to killing the Frawley measure. It would be untrue to say that the agitation for the repeal of the Frawley Law stemmed from the Willard-Moran fight. This battle was a box-office attraction to the tune of $152,000. It enriched Willard to the extent of $47,500 for 10 rounds of what amounted to little more work than Big Jess would have expended in a gymnasium workout. It brought Moran $23,750 for 10 rounds of diligent but futile effort, in which his only chance to win the title was by scoring a knockout. This sum, incidentally, was $3,750 in excess of the amount Rickard had guaranteed Moran. The extra compensation was exemplary of Rickard's generous disposition.

But the fight provoked jealousies which developed into enmities. To begin with, Rickard was compelled to pay a rental of $15,000 for the use of the Garden. This compares with the $1,500 for which he rented the old Garden when he assumed control, and the $3,500 which was the minimum rental fee when he opened the new plant. It provides an insight into the obstacles Tex had to overcome in establishing himself. These obstacles were nothing new to him. He had encountered them wholesale in connection with the Jeffries-Johnson bout.

Rickard had to do some adroit manipulation to get the 1910 battle. He laid the foundation when he secretly met Johnson and advanced the Negro champion, always a loose man with a dollar, the sum of $2,500, at a time when the Galveston ex-stevedore was short of money. This endeared him to Johnson to such an extent that the champion advised Rickard that rivals, represented by Gleason, were going to bid $100,000 for the fight. The information spurred Rickard to increase his offer to $101,000. When the seals were opened and twenty crisp $1,000 bills were revealed as Rickard's binding deposit, Johnson rejected other propositions, which had been accompanied by checks, and swung the fight to Rickard.

A condition of his successful bid was that Rickard take Gleason in as co-promoter, a stipulation he always resented but to which he felt himself obliged to yield. In the many discussions we had, Rickard always insisted Gleason had been "wished" on him, and that he conducted the fight alone.

It had been planned, with the sanction of Governor Gillett, to hold the bout in San Francisco. Rickard proceeded with arrangements accordingly, among them the construction of an arena costing $35,000. Almost on the eve of the battle, Governor Gillett withdrew his approval without explanation, and Rickard was faced with the problem of a quick transfer. He had gone to the expense of paying out $6,000 for a license. Since the California law barred non-residents as promoters, he had to purchase another's permit. The Governor's decision came as a shock to Rickard. He had known a reform element was against the fight. But there was no explanation for the sudden about face on the part of Gillett, and no expectation of it whatsoever.

The situation was serious. Rickard told me that he had originally intended the bout as a Salt Lake City attraction and had been induced to shift to San Francisco only by the concentrated pressure of a variety of business representatives. He couldn't go back to Salt Lake City even had he wanted to, he often said in recalling the circumstances surrounding the bout. In desperation he contacted interests in Reno, was assured of wholehearted co-operation, and forthwith transferred his base of operations. He then proceeded with a venture that drew $270,775 and enriched Johnson by $120,600 for his hollow knockout triumph. Jeffries' pain for the cruel beating he withstood until the 15th round was assuaged with $117,066.

Fortified with all this experience, Rickard was looking to the East, to New York in particular, as the boxing hub of the world, when the sport was outlawed in the Empire State through the repeal of the Frawley Law on November 15, 1917. Animosities, engendered when Rickard staged the Willard-Moran fight, gradually led to an aggravated situation which exploded suddenly and had its repercussions in the hearing conducted in the Bar Association Building.

The vicissitudes that confronted him were disillusioning to Rickard without being altogether discouraging. More were to be encountered before he launched boxing's Golden Era. There was, for instance, the tragic end to the Australian light-heavyweight, Les Darcy, whom Rickard imported as a heavyweight title possibility in an elaborate plan for international competition. Arriving here while his country was fighting in World War I, Darcy was stigmatized as a "slacker." He never appeared in an American ring. He died in May 1917, while visiting Memphis, Tennessee, a victim, many said, of a broken heart.

All the time, however, Rickard was quietly bending his efforts toward big things for boxing. His association with Willard in the Moran fight of 1916 gave him a tacit priority on the Pottawatomie giant's services, to the exclusion of rival promoters. Willard did no fighting. He confined his activities to circus appearances and exhibitions, and few of these were boxing exhibitions at that.

Meanwhile, a young unknown was booming along, barnstorming through the country wherever a match offered, knocking over rivals with unerring marksmanship and amazing regularity. His name was Jack Dempsey. He was likewise embroiled in managerial complications. In his hungry days Dempsey had acquired managers with prolific disregard of legal responsibilities and without attracting particular attention—until he threw in his lot with Jack Kearns. Then, Dempsey rocketed through a succession of engagements that swept him past all opposition on the challengers' path to Willard, his most notable achievement being his 17-second knockout of the gigantic Fred Fulton at Harrison, New Jersey, in 1918. Battling Levinsky, Porky Flynn, Carl Morris, Gunboat Smith all bowed to the devastating Dempsey punch in an uninterrupted string of victories which focused attention on the battering newcomer.

Rickard had moved into New York. With the repeal of the Frawley Law he joined forces with William A. Gavin in the promotion of the proposed International Sporting Club. Differences arose between them and Rickard started working independently, with headquarters in the old Waldorf-Astoria on Thirty-fourth Street, New York City. Here he met with boxing writers every day, outlining plans for the future. They encompassed an immediate heavyweight title match between Willard and Dempsey. Rival interests also wanted the match.

Kearns, naturally striving for the best bargain obtainable, played one set of promoters against the other. One day he was loudly proclaiming he would ignore Rickard and sign Dempsey with a rival promoter. Again, he would profess to be considering putting on the bout himself. All this went on interminably, most of it while promoter and manager were separated by the breadth of the continent. Through it all, however, the fact was overlooked that Rickard had Willard committed to an agreement.

Finally, Rickard coaxed Kearns and Dempsey to come to New York City. Kearns was not disposed to rush into Rickard's embrace and meekly sign a contract. He felt he had the man who would conquer Willard under his management. He wanted Dempsey to have the chance to prove it. But he wanted, also, to get as big a price for his challenger as the traffic would bear. It developed into a test of endurance until, ultimately, Rickard got Kearns seated at a round table in the old Waldorf bar one evening, surrounded by newspapermen. The monetary difference between promoter and manager amounted to $5,000. Kearns had boosted his price to $30,000 for Dempsey. Rickard could not see his way clear to paying this figure and held out for a $25,000 maximum.

They were deadlocked until, his eyes twinkling, his gambler's instinct asserting itself, Rickard proposed they submit the issue to the assembled newspapermen. Hype Igoe was there. Fred Keats was another writer, among a group of about six of us. As I recollect, Slim Farnsworth and Ed Curley also were there. All of the group were on intimate terms with Rickard through long association. Few of us knew Kearns.

I know I resented strongly the impudence of this Johnny-come-lately trying to impose his will against the better judgment of a man who was even then an outstanding promoter. I was later to become an intimate of both Kearns and Dempsey. But, at the time, I was convinced Kearns was unreasonable. Here he was offered a chance at the world heavyweight title, sure he could win the crown with his fighter, yet delaying actual signing for the match with his demands for what amounted, in my appraisal, such as it was, to a king's ransom.

Kearns agreed to the vote plan. He was confident that the ballots would be in his favor. We all wrote on slips of paper whether we thought Dempsey should receive $30,000, $25,000, or a compromise figure. The compromise carried. Dempsey was committed to the fight for a guaranteed $27,500.

There remained the actual signing. This presented difficulties. Boxing was banned in New York State. This meant it would be illegal even to sign a boxing contract in the state. Aside from whatever penalty might result, legal advisers told Rickard such a contract would not stand up in court action.

The solution was simple. There was no law against boxing in New Jersey. Rickard therefore arranged for a safari across the Hudson and, at the appointed hour, we all went by ferryboat to Weehawken, New Jersey, just across the river from the Forty-second Street dock. With the group assembled around an improvised desk in the ferry-house there, a fountain pen was produced and the documents were signed.

This important detail was the cheapest item paid for by Rickard in connection with the fight. The ferry fare was three cents each, and a maximum of thirty cents is all that was expended for a group numbering eight or ten. Not having gone beyond the gate on the Weehawken side, we all boarded a returning boat without having to pay a return charge. Tex often chuckled about this business in later years.

He didn't realize it at the time, but the ferryhouse incident sealed for delivery a contract that was to start Rickard on a fabulous career. For, when he signed this fight, Rickard secured what amounted to exclusive control of the world heavyweight title, with but two experimental exceptions. One of these was Dempsey's three-round knockout of Billy Miske, disintegrating St. Paul heavyweight, at Benton Harbor, Michigan. This occurred in 1920, after Jack had been champion for more than a year. Dempsey made the finish as painless as possible in a bout that brought the titleholder $55,000 and Miske $25,000. The other departure came in 1923, when Dempsey fought Tommy Gibbons 15 rounds at Shelby, Montana. But that is another story.

Rickard had a heavyweight championship match in his inside coat pocket. He was operating out of New York and he had skirted the law in signing the bout. Also, he had no place in which to pitch his battle. This, however, was of minor consequence to the promoter. He was soon flooded with offers from business and civic officials.

Canada wanted the bout. So did Mexico and Havana. European battlegrounds were submitted for consideration. Rickard listened to the counsel of friends, consulted railroad maps intently, and finally hit upon Toledo, Ohio, as the battle site, because of its transportation convenience. The date for the struggle was set for July 4, 1919.

In no time at all the interest of the sport universe centered around Toledo. Writers from all over the world assembled there.

Willard, at six feet seven inches, towered five inches over Dempsey and, at 245 pounds, outweighed the challenger by 58 pounds. The disparities made the deepest impression on the writers about the camp, some of whom became fearful for Dempsey's well-being. Reformers voiced protest against a match declared to hold possibilities of a fatality.

Rickard constructed an arena with a capacity of 80,000. He expected, at the least, the plant would be half filled for the battle. He pictured a gate of close to $800,000. He was disappointed when only about 19,000 spectators turned up and the receipts were $452,000.

But Rickard's disappointment was short lived. Dempsey, as previously related, knocked out Willard in three rounds of savage ripping that made for one of the most spectacular heavyweight title fights in history. The battle was waged in 120-degree heat. The excitement of the crowd was accentuated when Dempsey left the ring after a first round in which he floored the giant Willard seven times, in the mistaken belief he had knocked Big Jess out. Dempsey had to be recalled hurriedly when the gong clanged a resumption of hostilities.

Rickard thrilled to this spectacle, a throwback to the Dark Ages, which ended with Willard a pitiful, battered hulk, unable to respond to the bell for the fourth round.

The thrill for Tex was in the future he envisioned. He had been working to arrange a lease of the old Madison Square Garden. He had marshaled the financial backing with the aid of John Ringling. He had confidential information that the Walker Law would be enacted. He had the world's heavyweight champion, Jack Dempsey, under a contract which forbade him to defend the title except under Rickard's express approval. He had the greatest gate magnet boxing ever knew.

The Walker Law passed the State Legislature on May 24, 1920. Tex leased the old Garden two months later.

Through Gans and Nelson, Jeffries and Johnson, Dempsey and Willard, Rickard had received a liberal education as a promoter. He was on the threshold of a period that was to see him soar to fantastic heights and pull boxing with him until his death in 1929, when his empire crashed into the dust to which he had returned. The master's touch was removed with the passing of Rickard. It has never been applied in the Rickard degree since.

Oh, I've sat in groups where I've listened to oracles of a later day expatiating on "how lucky Rickard was," and how "he was fortunate because the money was around, then," and "he had the field to himself." But these deprecations generally came from those who weren't around to know firsthand the magic Rickard touch, or the overpowering, magnetizing influence that was the name of Dempsey. And I've heard it said more than once that Mike Jacobs was the power behind the throne of Rickard, that it was Mike's business acumen and sagacious manipulation that accounted for the tremendous success of the man who came off the Chilcoot Pass, away from the gaming table where he once threw dice at $35,000 a roll, to become a legendary figure in boxing. And I know that Mike knows how lightly these exaggerated claims are to be dismissed.

To set down even sketchily a review of everything with which Rickard was connected, everything he did in advancing boxing to a plane the sport never before attained in popularity and patronage, would require volumes. But some of the more important, most vivid recollections of a great promoter are set forth here as part and parcel of a romantic era which likely will never be surpassed and as the simplest way of presenting the great fighters of the time. They come from memory, refreshened by an old, dog-eared, blood-spattered notebook, musty with more than twenty-five years of age, which has held an obscure corner of a desk drawer, unnoticed until recently.

We fellows who wrote about the prize ring in those long-ago days led an adventurous life. Going to a fight, gaining admittance to clubs under the old Frawley Law and club-membership days, acquiring your seat in the working-press row to which your ticket was supposed to entitle you, getting away from the club in a safe retreat from managers who wanted to know your decision in a period when there were no official decisions—all this could at times be exciting.

We did not have the modern facilities we enjoy today on every hand. You went to a fight club by subway or trolley, set down your notes as the fight progressed, flew out of the club with the last bell, and started your story on the return journey to the office. You wrote longhand, of course, in a school-boy's ordinary notebook. On the other hand, we did not have the mechanical hurdles in newspaper offices that obtain today; the terrific pressure for material to meet an early deadline. In the old days the early-edition deadline for sports copy for *The New York Times* was 1:10 A.M. Today, the same edition is put "to bed" at 10:40 P.M., sometimes earlier.

I recall clearly one night in John (The Barber) Reisler's Harlem Sporting Club on 135th Street in New York, when an usher tapped me on the shoulder while I was concentrating on some of the preliminaries and said: "You'll have to get out of there. That's Rube Goldberg's seat." Rube then was a cartoonist on the New York *Evening Mail* and occasionally covered fights. He was a quiet-spoken, dignified youth with a modest, retiring disposition. I am afraid I was rather outspoken and extended a belligerent invitation to be forcibly removed. Rube told the usher not to make an issue of it. I held the seat which my ticket called for. Rube and I have often laughed over the occurrence since.

Another time, Jimmy Johnston—"the Boy Bandit" they called him affectionately—had the St. Nicholas Arena in no-decision days and was also the manager of Joe Welling, top-flight Chicago lightweight. He had Welling in with Johnnie Dundee and, at the end of the bout, made it his business to get to me at the ringside to ask my decision as I was leaving for the office. When I told him, quite frankly, my decision would be for Dundee, he let forth with a line of criticism. Astigmatism and mental disorder were just a few of the afflictions of which, he informed me, I was a victim.

There was another time, at the old Clermont Rink in Brooklyn, when Mike O'Dowd, of St. Paul, and Al McCoy, the original "Cheese Champion," were fighting for the middleweight title and the bout ended in a six-round knockout victory for O'Dowd—and a riot. The fans didn't like the way McCoy succumbed. By an eyelash, one of the bottles thrown at McCoy's corner missed crashing against my skull. That was back in 1917.

Again, there was the night at the old Star Casino, at 107th Street and Park Avenue, New York City, when the club was run by Moe Smith, later to gain fame as a prohibition agent under the Volstead Act. Benny Leonard was going against Frankie Conifrey, who was known as "the Fighting Fireman."

Leonard was fighting his way to the lightweight title at the time. It was 1916. A superlative boxer, a paralyzing hitter, Leonard was going to content himself with outboxing Conifrey through 10 rounds in a no-decision bout. However, when Conifrey became abusive in the clinches, Leonard forgot all about his restraint and battered Conifrey so badly the fight was stopped in the sixth round.

In the ensuing riot, Promoter Smith came up with a gaudy-colored "shanty" on his eye, and Johnny (Kewpie) Ertle, then a claimant of the world bantamweight title, his manager, Mike Collins, and I scooted under the ring for protection until the trouble subsided with the arrival of the police. I shall never forget Ertle, a diminutive fellow, walking erect beneath the ring. Collins and I had to bend almost double to get under. All this was adventure, more attractive in retrospect. Rickard changed that, with the aid of a boxing commission that commanded deep respect.

With Dempsey under agreement, Rickard launched boxing's Golden Age with the inaugural of the old Madison Square Garden regime in September 1920, featuring a fight between Welling and Johnnie Dundee. Welling won this 15-round bout. Tex closed the arena in May 1925, with a 12-round battle between Dundee and Sid Terris, which the latter won.

He used Dempsey first as champion in the old Garden against K.O. Bill Brennan, a Chicagoan, who was a recognized challenger at the time. They fought in December 1920, three months after Dempsey knocked out Billy Miske at Benton Harbor in a bout with which Rickard was not associated. The Manassa Mauler did little or no serious training for Brennan and proved something of a disappointment to a crowd which packed the arena. Finally, Dempsey tagged Brennan with a right to the jaw in the 12th round and Brennan went down and out.

In January 1921, when he had Dempsey and Georges Carpentier signed for the first large-scale international heavyweight title bout, which proved also the first million-dollar gate attraction in boxing, Rickard drew the carriage trade to the ring through the instrumentality of Miss Anne Morgan, philanthropic sister of the senior J. P. Morgan.

Miss Morgan was interested in raising funds for war-stricken France as head of the American Committee for Devastated France. Co-operating with her, Rickard arranged a lightweight title match between Benny Leonard and Richie Mitchell, which not only filled the old Garden with the most distinguished crowd a boxing bout had attracted up to that time but provided a battle which will always be referred to as one of the most exciting in lightweight title history.

Leonard floored Mitchell three times in the opening round, the first time for a count of eight, the next two times for counts of nine each. Leonard looked supreme. He was butchering one of the deadliest hitters among the lightweights of the period, and the class was replete with dangerous challengers.

It appeared so easy, in fact, that as I look over the fading notes in my ancient book I can see Leonard nodding to friends at the ringside, winking confidently, as Mitchell struggles to get up inside the 10-second count from that third knockdown. Mitchell finally made it, with a great effort.

To the astonishment of the onlookers, and the complete surprise of the cocky Leonard, he came up fighting. My notebook says, with laconic brevity, "M [Mitchell, that is] l hook j, L 9." This means Leonard was down before the first round ended for a count of nine, bowled over by a terrific left hook to the jaw.

Staggered early in the second round under Mitchell's fire, Leonard came back to send the challenger wobbling to his corner at the bell. Again in the third round Mitchell staggered Leonard. In the fourth, Benny came back to shake Mitchell with a right to the jaw and they proceeded cautiously through the remainder of the round, and the fifth, Leonard out-boxing his foe. In the sixth, the champion's deadly right dropped Mitchell for a nine count. A right and left to the jaw and Mitchell went down for nine again. Another right and left to the jaw and down went Mitchell for the third time in the round, helpless but game. This time the referee, Johnny Haukop, stopped the bout. The round had gone 1 minute 55 seconds.

I can look back now and picture the excitement of the crowd, the hysteria in the corners of the champion and his challenger, as this fistic drama went into history. Many more terrific Garden battles occupied Rickard as he led up to his first grand-scale undertaking. This was the fight between Dempsey and Georges Carpentier on the afternoon of July 2, 1921, in which the champion stowed away Gorgeous Georges in four rounds.

I can still see the Frenchman curled up on his right ear, his left leg spasmodically kicking the air in convulsive movement as he gently subsided to be counted out by the referee, Harry Ertle. I can still see, too, the mammoth pine stadium Rickard erected in Jersey City on the property of a man named Boyle, remembered to this day as "Boyle's Thirty Acres."

I recall the vicissitudes through which this bout went. In my possession is one of the copies of the contract Rickard distributed among the writers when the match was signed. On the back of the legal-looking cover, written down in ink, are listed some of the developments in connection with the fight.

To begin with, Rickard undertook the bout with two partners. They were William A. Brady, who had managed Jim Corbett and Jim Jeffries as world heavyweight champions and then became a leader in theatrical productions, and his London associate, Charles

B. Cochran. The trio tried to sign the fight on a percentage basis. But wily Francois Descamps, manager of Carpentier, would have nothing of this. Nor would Jack Kearns, Dempsey's manager.

Rickard, secure in the conviction he had a million-dollar gate attraction, finally consented to guarantee a $500,000 purse for the battle, $300,000 to Dempsey and $200,000 to Carpentier, an arrangement that astounded the sport world. Many expressed the opinion that Rickard was insane. Brady and Cochran may not have subscribed to this conclusion, but they did not share Rickard's confidence in the success of the bout on such a financial scale.

They withdrew, leaving Rickard alone with his project. Indeed, Kearns was none too sure of the bout's success. He demonstrated this when he insisted on a $300,000 guarantee. His percentage of the $1,789,238 the fight drew would have amounted to more than $600,000.

Rickard survived a plethora of difficulties and anxieties to promote the venture, which attracted world-wide attention. Not the least of these was his own fear of a fatality. Carpentier was a legitimate light-heavyweight, matched with the most killing fighter of modern times. Tex later recalled how he visited Dempsey's dressing room and requested the champion to "go easy with this young fellow out there today and give all those nice people a show."

Dempsey did start to "go easy" with Carpentier, or as easy as a fellow who did not know the meaning of restraint could go. I say this advisedly and from experience because I know Dempsey's good-natured embraces when he was being playful with friends were bone-crushing experiences. When Carpentier tagged Dempsey with a solid right to the jaw that made Jack blink, in the second round, all "go easy" impulses left the champion. He was a tiger after that, and his killer instinct was not satisfied until he had battered Carpentier helpless with vicious short-arm body blows at close quarters and set up the knockout punch that sent Carpentier on his ear.

This was one of the few fights in the career of the Orchid Man about which there could be no complaint from his handlers. Most of his bouts ended with a claim of a foul or a disagreement over application or interpretation of the boxing rules.

I have never rated Carpentier as a great fighter, or even a good one. To me he was the most artificially built-up boxer I have encountered.

There was nothing to impress in his record before he came here to knock out Battling Levinsky in four rounds of a bout in Jersey City as a steppingstone to the Dempsey engagement.

Weighing 170½ pounds, Carpentier won recognition as world light-heavyweight champion in this Levinsky fight, the record of which follows a match between Ted (Kid) Lewis and Marcel Thomas in my old notebook.

Away from the jurisdiction of Rickard, and against the promoter's advice, Dempsey undertook his next title defense against Tommy Gibbons, St. Paul challenger, at Shelby, on July 4, 1923. Kearns prevailed upon Rickard to let this match proceed unhampered when a syndicate of influential Montana citizens, taking a leaf from the Rickard book, decided they would attract attention to Great Falls and Shelby with a heavyweight title bout.

Rickard could have prevented the fight had he exercised his claim on Dempsey's services but, because he did not regard Gibbons as a suitable challenger for an extravagant production and had no thought of promoting the bout himself, withheld any objection, although he cautioned Dempsey and Kearns against the venture.

Banks crashed in the wake of the battle, and lives were blighted. On the eve of the fight, Kearns had to take over the box-office receipts in an effort to salvage what he could of a $200,000 guarantee for Dempsey. The night before, one of the associates in the promotion visited Kearns' suite in the Park Hotel, Great Falls, with the depressing news that Dempsey's $200,000 guarantee was not in sight. Kearns threatened to withdraw Dempsey from the match, despite the fact that for six weeks the champion had been in training and writers from all over had been attracted to a battle locale which defies description.

Great Falls was a booming town, but Shelby was little more than a whistle stop on a railroad trunk line. A frame hotel was improvised (that is the correct word) to take care of correspondents who attended Gibbons' workouts. Accommodations there were primitive, particularly by comparison with the modern quarters at Great Falls. It was nothing unusual to request your room key at the hotel desk, only to be informed that somebody else was occupying the room. Handling of preliminary details for the bout was equally chaotic.

Little surprise was occasioned, therefore, when one of the promoters informed Kearns the fight was a financial flop. Kearns exploded. Writers eagerly awaited the outcome of a conference which dragged through the night. Bulletins were issued in which Kearns insisted the fight was off.

Newspapers on the East Coast went to press with the fight off. Benefiting by the difference in time, editions in Chicago and way stations underwent rapid postscripts to meet changing bulletins. Finally, Damon Runyon, Warren Brown, and Scoop Gleason, writers who were closeted with Kearns during the vital interview, prevailed upon the hotheaded manager to assume direction of the promotion, take what money was realized on the sale of tickets, and let Dempsey fight. Dempsey won a 15-round decision and once and for all was through with itinerant campaigning.

I have been to countless training camps in my time. Montana was the camp to end all camps for bizarre experiences. Not the least of these was the arrival of a coyote as a gift for Dempsey. No stranger collection of characters was ever attracted to a midway than the crowd which converged on Shelby. "Certified" checks, placed as bets in advance of the fight, were bouncing all over the place long after these characters had transferred their operations to the next stop.

I opened my hotel-room one night to find a party going full blast. Men and women filled the place, which was littered with liquor bottles. My remonstrances were unavailing. The hotel manager's son was the host and he "knew" me. Leaning against my dresser and using diplomacy to "break it up," I felt a pickpocket trying to lift the wallet out of my rear trousers pocket. There was the world's champion optimist.

There I was leaning against the "poke" he was after, yet he made his play without organizing the traditional "bump." That was the end of diplomacy. The party dissolved in a few minutes. At the ringside, and scattered through the pine arena the day of the fight, bulging hips were as conspicuous as hedges in a suburban development, and the owners weren't carrying oversized handkerchiefs.

Newspapers went the limit in covering this bout. Feature writers, literary lights who scarcely knew a fight from a ball game—and cared less—specialists in anatomy, and experts on boxing form, along with photographers, were added to the lists of regular boxing correspondents, who were more or less dwarfed by the "names" engaged for the occasion. Countless columns of space were devoted to an undertaking that was singularly unique. Unhappily, Shelby couldn't capitalize on the publicity the small, isolated town received.

Dempsey and Kearns came out of the Montana crash with little or no money. (Eddie Kane, who was Gibbons' manager, once told me the St. Paul challenger received only the money he made on a short vaudeville tour in advance of the fight.) The Dempsey-Kearns living standard required plenty of cash.

To Rickard, the Shelby flop was a bonanza. Any ideas Dempsey and Kearns entertained of dealing independently with promoters were dissipated. Thenceforward, the champion cast his lot with Rickard, inseparably and with mutual advantage to both.

At the time, Rickard had an enormous foreigner, an ungainly, shaggy, beetle-browed giant who had come up from the Argentine in process of development. His name was Luis Angel Firpo. Damon Runyon was to nickname him "the Wild Bull of the Pampas" because he reminded you of nothing so much as the bull in a china shop in action and had all the strength of the bovine of the Argentine plains.

Cumbersome, awkward, crude, he was. But he had mastodonic strength and a wild conception of himself as heavyweight champion of the world. Some enthusiastic friends convinced him that his six feet four inches and 216 pounds equipped him as the man of destiny who was to destroy Dempsey. And, strangely enough, he almost did, to the astonishment of his friends, not to mention the brief spasm of consternation he caused Dempsey, Kearns, and the champion's legion of admirers, who accepted Firpo merely as another human hulk, below the Willard order.

Firpo's "development" had progressed satisfactorily from his arrival here, with Guillermo Widmer, early in 1922. The giant had launched an American campaign by putting away Sailor Tom Maxted at Newark, New Jersey, on March 20, and followed this with a succession of knockout conquests—over Bill Brennan, in 12 rounds, Jess Willard, in eight, and the clever, shifty Charlie Weinert, in two. There were other knockouts as he gradually accumulated American ring experience, gained popularity, and created a demand for a chance at the title.

Dempsey was eager for the fight. Rickard signed it with customarily elaborate formality, after the traditional period of haggling over terms, and on September 14, 1923, at the Polo Grounds, New York, Dempsey and Firpo provided the greatest battle this observer has ever seen. In less than four minutes of actual fighting, through two rounds, Firpo was knocked down 10 times, Dempsey twice.

For blazing fury, cyclonic action, there has been nothing to approach Dempsey and Firpo since. Rickard often told me the greatest thrill of his lifetime came in that battle.

Dempsey, as was customary with him, came tigerishly out of his corner at the opening bell, only to be clipped with a ponderous right that bounced off his jaw and sent him to his knee in the first five seconds of action. Arising before a count could be started, the champion ripped and slashed at Firpo, flooring the giant seven times under an avalanche of wicked, savage rights and lefts to the body and head.

I still have a clear mental picture of one of those knockdowns on which it seemed inconceivable that Firpo could possibly come erect. But he got up with a gameness that was unexpected and, with a courage that was magnificent, lit into Dempsey after the seventh knockdown, bowling the champion out of the ring with a right that glanced off Dempsey's jaw as he was backed to the ropes.

The spectacle of Dempsey down on his knee with the first rush and punch of the fight stunned the crowd. The savage fury of Dempsey upon arising is a vivid memory even now, after the lapse of a quarter of a century. For those who viewed it, the picture will never dim.

When he came erect, the champion went into a blazing offensive. Fighting out of his famous crouch, flailing rights and lefts in a thundering fusillade against a sluggish target, Jack dropped Firpo with practically every barrage. And, when he sent his gargantuan foe down, Dempsey, the urge to kill upon him, the utter destruction of the giant his all-besetting thought, stood within a stride of Firpo and at times directly above him, waiting for him to arise.

Each time Firpo started scrambling to his feet, it was only to be knocked down again, until it seemed human endurance could stand no more.

But Firpo stood it and fought back in a blind rage of his own. Like an infuriated bull, he came charging up from the seventh knockdown to rush Dempsey to the ropes near the challenger's corner.

There, with a terrific right that glanced off Tiger Jack's jaw, Firpo toppled the champion through the ropes. Men and women who had been yelling themselves hoarse gasped at the spectacle of the champion falling through the ropes, his feet in the air, his shoulder blades hitting the ring apron as he tried to break the fall, reaching futilely for the ropes.

It has always been a disputed point, but it is my recollection that Dempsey landed above the seats occupied by Sheriff McGeehan, Jack Lawrence, and, I believe, Jane Dixon, who were covering the bout for the New York *Herald Tribune*. Indeed, in his descent, Dempsey narrowly missed crushing Lawrence's typewriter. There is no questioning the fact that Lawrence gave a helping heave to the floundering, topsy-turvy Dempsey, while a startled referee, Johnny Gallagher, confusedly delayed starting a count until the champion, partly on his own, partly through Lawrence's assist, got back inside the ropes.

Lawrence often told me afterward that when Dempsey's body landed on the ring apron, he could be heard muttering "You big ――――, get me back in there; get me back in there, I'll fix him."

Dempsey gave it the old Leon Errol coming erect and avoided further damage only because, in his wild eagerness to press his advantage, Firpo was ludicrously futile. The champion was on unsteady legs when the bell ended the round.

There was nothing to it in the second round. Like a panther, Dempsey leaped at his foe with the gong, swinging both hands to the body. I can still see Firpo crumbling slowly under the fire, like a deflated gas bag. Arising, he was crushed to the floor again. When he came up from the second knockdown in the round, his ninth trip to the canvas, Firpo was helpless. With a savage fire of both fists to the body and jaw, Dempsey stretched his giant opponent inert on the floor.

Out of the battle came boxing's second million-dollar gate. The receipts were $1,188,603. Out of it, too, came a lot of criticism for Dempsey's unbridled fighting style. It brought the rule that compels a boxer, when knocked out of the ring, to get back under his own momentum, inside the 10-second count, or suffer a knockout. And, more important than all else, it brought the rule that was to cost Dempsey the distinction of becoming the only heavyweight champion in history to regain his title, the night he "knocked out" Gene Tunney four years later in Chicago.

For, in response to the hue and cry raised over what practically everybody condemned as Dempsey's unfair tactics—standing almost directly above a prostrate foe—there came the ironclad regulation that a boxer scoring a knockdown must proceed to the farthest neutral corner as soon as the count is started over the fallen fighter. Failure to observe this rule delays the count or interrupts it if it has started, with the result that the boxer scoring the knockdown is penalized accordingly.

As a matter of fact, there was nothing technically wrong with Dempsey's action, although, ethically, it left much to be desired. He was perfectly within his rights standing within striking distance of his fallen foe, in the absence of any restraining rule. His plan was to hit the second his man was up, which, technically, was when his knees and hands were off the floor. This was the school he had been educated in. It was the only method he knew. His adherence to this style was to cost him dearly later.

Rickard didn't have a suitable opponent for Dempsey in the succeeding three years. The champion and his manager, Kearns, became involved in differences which ended with a dissolution of their partnership. Harry Wills, the Brown Panther of New Orleans, was pushed forward in a campaign for a match with Dempsey. This caused Rickard some uneasy moments and not a few embarrassing situations. But he was developing champions in other classes, filling the old Garden with bouts between lightweights, featherweights, bantamweights and, sometimes, with flyweights, and converting the Garden into a summer indoor pool to lighten the financial drag.

There was, too, the construction of the new Madison Square Garden to occupy the attention of the promoter. The ancient building, located on the entire square block from Twenty-Sixth to Twenty-Seventh Street and from Madision to Fourth Avenue, was falling into decay. Its activities had outgrown the plant, and the increasing popularity of his attractions among New York City's growing population, permanent and transient, dictated a bigger and better building.

Rickard marshaled the capital for a new arena. He acquired an abandoned car barn, and construction work started as soon as the transfer of the property was completed.

In May 1925, Rickard closed the old Garden. While the new Garden was under construction, Tex was like a child with a new toy. He could be found every day stumbling around the mass of planks, pipes, steel, brick, and mortar, stargazing there in the vast, gaunt, naked structure, impeding the progress of the skilled laborers. He would converse with the workers and point out to guests, for whom he was always conducting inspection tours, the advantages of the new building.

Tex would take you to a corner where a section of the flooring, finished, had been covered with a paper protection. With the cane he always carried, he would slap some of the covering away, jab the stick at the floor, and expound on the improvement. "This is something new; it's terrazzo," he would say. Its advantages had been explained to him.

But, I daresay, Tex didn't know terrazzo from chenille. He was enthusiastic, and you were infected with his enthusiasm, the excitement that lit up his gaze as, day by day, his magnificent dream approached completion.

He opened the new arena with a six-day bicycle race in November 1925. The structure was incomplete; some laborer's planking was still in place. And, forthwith, through the magic that was Rickard's, the plant flourished and, with its varied attractions, became a place of world-wide renown.

Meanwhile, Gene Tunney was clamoring for a crack at Dempsey, and in this campaign Rickard saw a refuge from the Wills embarrassment. He had often told me, off the record, he could not promote a Dempsey-Wills bout. Dempsey was eager for it, confident that Wills' style was made to order for him, and convinced that the most money would come from such a "natural." Rickard's private explanation was that he had been advised by governmental sources not to undertake such a match. The riotous aftermath of the Jeffries-Johnson battle in 1910 was recalled.

Stinging criticism rained upon Rickard and Dempsey, chiefly the former. He had Dempsey under contract and no other promoter could use him, although any number of them leaped into the publicity fanfare with fabulous offers. The State Athletic Commission in

New York, under which Rickard operated, insisted Tex would not be permitted to stage a Dempsey bout in New York unless the opponent was Wills. Civic groups entered the controversy, which developed into a racial issue.

But Rickard proceeded quietly on what was for him a routine scale. And all the time Tunney was fighting his way to a position where he commanded attention. Negotiations with Tunney's manager, Billy Gibson, had been progressing without attracting notice, but when Tunney knocked out Bartley Madden in three rounds at Minneapolis and followed this with a Cleveland victory in 12 rounds over Johnny Risko in 1925, the Dempsey match for him was assured.

Gene Tunney was not only one of the great figures of boxing's Golden Age; he was one of the most unique personalities the ring, or any sport, has known. In a profession that was a little beyond the pale for genteel folk, that was infested with characters of questionable, if not shady, reputation and in which a man of learning and refinement was largely out of his element among those who made their living with their fists, Tunney was the rare exception and an enigma. He was a self-made man, just as he was a "made" fighter, and what he made of himself was baffling, incomprehensible, and irritating to many ring followers as well as to the public. The result was that he became one of the least popular champions boxing has known, even though at the same time he had qualities far superior to most of his competitors and contemporaries.

Although he never went far in his schooling, Gene was a man of appreciable learning, the associate of Professor Billy Phelps, of Yale University, and Thornton Wilder, the novelist. He could quote Shakespeare and contemporary literature. That was enough in itself to get him in wrong with a lot of people and make him misunderstood. That did not bother Tunney. He had a lofty indifference to what people might think of him, and he was not the most tactful person in the world.

Regardless of what ring followers and fans thought and said about him, he was a person who commanded attention for more than what he accomplished with his fists. He was a fine figure of a man, handsome, clean cut, and intelligent, a man whose character, courage, and determination were written in his bearing and features.

It was that character and determination and intelligence that made Tunney the world champion in the face of disparaging, almost contemptuous, estimates of his chances. No one except Gene himself and possibly a close friend or two thought there was the remotest possibility of his defeating Dempsey in their first fight or even of escaping an early-round knockout. His answer to the overwhelming mass of expert opinion that picked Dempsey to put him away was that if the champion would slug it out with him, Jack would be the first to back up; he (Gene) would beat him to the punch every time.

Everyone thought Tunney was merely talking to keep up his courage or just being smart. But Gene wasn't speaking for the effect. He believed what he said, and his confidence in himself was born of years of study he had made of Dempsey's style and methods.

No one knew—Dempsey least of all—that from as far back as 1921 Tunney had been preparing himself for a meeting with the champion. In all the history of the ring there probably never was a boxer who made a more thorough, scientific study of his prospective rivals than did Gene, or who was more successful in ferreting out their weaknesses and plotting ways and means of taking advantage of them by adjustments or changes in his methods.

When Tunney fought Tommy Gibbons in June of 1925, Gibbons had no way of knowing that Gene had had him in a test tube for three years. Tunney had a tremendous respect for him, so much so that he had ignored the challenges Gibbons hurled at him all through 1924 and 1925. From the time he saw Tommy in a fight at the Pioneer A. C. in New York, in 1921, he decided he wanted no part of him until he was satisfied that he was ready. Gibbons at that time showed him what Gene called "the finest exhibition of effective boxing I have ever seen in the ring."

To the time that they met, he ranked Tommy as the best fighter in the country next to Dempsey. From early 1923 on, he prepared himself for the time they should get in the ring together. At that time he was getting ready for a bout with Harry Greb, and he called in Jock Malone from St. Paul as a sparring partner. He wanted Jock because he had boxed a great deal with Gibbons. In 1924, when he was training to fight Carpentier, Gene called in Jack Delaney, who had helped Gibbons get ready for Carpentier. The result was that when Tunney fought Gibbons he knew all he wanted to know about

Tommy's style, mannerisms, leads, and punches. He had the answer to his feints and leads, beat him to the punch, baffled him, and the experts at the ringside, too, and knocked him out in the 12th round.

The victory over the man Dempsey had failed to knock out did more than anything else to advance Gene's candidacy for a fight with the champion, who cabled his congratulations from Germany. Little did Jack know that, long before, this Tunney had been making the same, thorough scientific analysis of Dempsey's style that he had made of Gibbons'.

For every hour he had given to Tommy's style of ring peculiarities, Gene said, he had given five to Dempsey's. In 1921, after the Dempsey-Carpentier fight, he had engaged Larry Williams, Jack's chief sparring partner, to come to his camp in Red Bank, New Jersey. After that, he worked with any other heavyweights he could get who had sparred with the champion. He saw the Dempsey fights with Brennan, Carpentier, and Firpo and he studied the moving pictures of these bouts.

From the Brennan fight he came to the conclusion that Dempsey lacked boxing skill; from the Carpentier fight, that he was not invincible. The Firpo fight, he said, revealed to him that Dempsey was an open target, that there was no improvement in his technique and that he depended on his deadly punch and did not interest himself in skill. When he was ready to start his training for Dempsey, he worked out a program to add to his hitting power, increase his endurance, and add to his weight. He was confident before he went into the ring that he had the speed, skill, punch, and endurance to win, regardless of the expert opinion.

It took a lot of courage for Tunney to get into the ring with a killer such as was Dempsey, particularly in view of the fact that they were picking the champion almost to a man to finish him in a round or two. We know how that courage was found wanting in so many who faced Joe Louis in later years.

But there never was any question of Tunney's heart. They said of this former steamship clerk from Greenwich Village and ex-Marine, who won the light-heavyweight championship of the A.E.F., that he did not have his heart in prizefighting and that he had a distaste, if not an actual revulsion, for the vulgar business. But no one could ever say that he was afraid of being hit. The fact is that he

was one of the gamest men ever to put on the gloves. His fights with
Harry Greb were enough to prove that.

Tunney met Greb for the first time in 1921, at the old Madison
Square Garden. He was defending the American light-heavyweight
title, which he had won by defeating Battling Levinsky in January
of that year. His victory over Levinsky, a cunning, tricky fighter, who
was as game as they came and took on all the big men of his time,
marked only his third appearance in the Garden. His first had been
with Jack Burke, of Pittsburgh, and his second with Eddie O'Hare.

In getting ready for Greb, Tunney suffered a number of mishaps.
His left eyebrow was opened and both hands were injured. Also, he
had a recurrence of an old trouble with his left elbow. In the first
exchange of the fight, he suffered a double fracture of the nose, which
bled to the end. It was one of the messiest fights ever seen, and
Tunney took a sickening beating from the Pittsburgh Windmill. Six
bottles of adrenalin chloride were used in the effort to stop the bleed-
ing of his nose and the cut over his left eyebrow. Also, at the end
of the 12th round, he took some brandy. This, with the blood and
chloride he had swallowed and the physical drubbing he had absorbed,
brought him to such a state that he collapsed as he was climbing the
stairs to his dressing room.

One would have thought that Gene Tunney had had enough of
Greb to last him a lifetime. The next day he went to the office of
the boxing commission and placed on file a challenge for a return
fight, backed by a check for $2,500! Gene said that he discovered in
the early part of the fight in which he took the worst licking of his
life that he could lick Greb!

Abe Attell came into his dressing room after the bout and said:
"Kid, you're the gamest fighter I ever saw. I lost $2,500 on you,
but to hell with it." He kissed Tunney's battered face and told him,
"You certainly will be the next heavyweight champion of the world."

Tunney met Greb again and again and again. They fought five
times. Concentrating on a right-hand punch to the heart almost exclusively, Gene battered the spectacular Greb into defeat in 15 rounds
in the second fight. After their fifth bout, which followed Tunney's
knockout victories over Emilio Spalla, champion of Europe, and then
over Carpentier, at the Polo Grounds, in July 1924, Greb came into
Gene's dressing room in St. Paul and said: "Gene, you and I have

fought five times. I am through! I will never fight you again. Let the other guys have a dose of you from now on."

This from one of the greatest, gamest fighters the ring has known, a whirlwind, cyclonic attacker, who swarmed all over Tommy Gibbons and Brennan, who had amazing speed and endurance, despite the fact that he did part of his road work on the dance floor, and who took on all comers regardless of size and was most contemptuous of the big fellows.

This, then, was the Tunney with whom Dempsey was matched to defend the world heavyweight championship in 1926. Rickard signed the bout, only to find that New York was barred to him. He had several sites available but selected Philadelphia when promised the co-operation of local and state authorities as well as businessmen of the city.

The insistence of the New York State Athletic Commission on a Wills bout and then the refusal of the License Committee to issue a permit to Dempsey forced Rickard in the Philadelphia move, embittered Tunney, at least temporarily, and deprived the Empire State of the income from the largest gate in all boxing history up to that time, $1,895,733, paid by a gathering of 120,757, the record paid crowd for a prizefight. The business turnover in the vast assemblage, which flocked from all over the country and overseas to see this match, an item of income also lost to New York, can well be imagined.

Dempsey trained for the battle at Atlantic City, harassed on all sides because of litigation started or threatened from every conceivable angle by his discarded manager, Kearns. Gene Normile was handling Dempsey's business, doing a good job, too, in so far as was possible. But, he wasn't exactly a Kearns.

Covering the doings at Dempsey's camp was akin to police reporting. Mysterious individuals, suspected of being process servers, hovered all over the place, trying to serve body attachments on Dempsey. They were frustrated because Dempsey was surrounded by an impregnable police cordon. Indeed, one day Dempsey made his departure from the training site through a hole in the board fence surrounding the unused race track which had been selected for him. That is fairly illustrative of the tension under which Dempsey prepared himself for what proved the toughest fight of his career.

Little wonder he became upset. Small wonder this nervous condition manifested itself in a skin rash that spread over his body, particularly about the armpits. He was a scowling, vicious animal, in his abbreviated workouts—on the surface; underneath, he was a highly distraught individual.

Tommy Loughran came down to spar with Dempsey and gave him a boxing lesson, as might have been expected. The very fact that it was expected led many of us to overlook the significance of the workout. There before our eyes was the spectacle of Dempsey, against a clever boxer, being made to appear crude, awkward, altogether ineffective. But, we reasoned, this was only a camp workout. Dempsey must surely catch up with Tunney once in 10 rounds, and when he catches up with him it will be all over.

The only thing wrong with this reasoning was that Dempsey didn't catch up with Tunney until a year later. And then the success of his pursuit didn't pay dividends.

Tunney hied himself to Stroudsburg, Pennsylvania, for training, and there busied himself with daily concentration on the fighting method that would overcome Dempsey's undeniable strength and punching power. Regularly, Tunney proclaimed to all who would listen his confidence in dethroning Dempsey. Few paid him heed. The majority attributed these declamations of confidence to excessive enthusiasm. Some even said it was all a pose.

Expert opinion was preponderantly against Tunney as the training of champion and challenger progressed, and forecasts on the outcome of the bout began to decorate the pages of newspapers. When Tunney flew from Stroudsburg to Philadelphia for the weighing ceremony on the day of the bout, this departure from traditional caution was regarded as just another evidence of misplaced bravado by those who expected Dempsey to annihilate the challenger. The recklessness gave Rickard a distinct shock. His nervous reaction was not adjusted until Tunney finally stepped on the scales. Tex dubbed this incident one of the craziest he had ever known of, and the furore it caused in newspaper accounts proved this conclusion was widely shared.

Here was a challenger risking his neck in a plane flight to the rendezvous for what was to prove boxing's greatest gate up to that time, a spectacle that dwarfed anything that had gone before. The situation wasn't eased any by the knowledge that only a short time before Bernard Gimbel, dry-goods merchant-sportsman and Gene's close personal friend, had cracked up taking off from a visit to Tunney's camp.

It fell to my lot, incidentally, to inform Tunney of Gimbel's narrow escape from injury as he was being rubbed down after a workout. I had hardly finished telling Tunney in the presence of his trainer, Lou Fink, when Gimbel strode into the dressing quarters, smiling broadly, unhurt, unshaken, bemoaning the damage to a new suit. The right knee of the suit had been ripped in the take-off mishap.

Tunney's relief at this evidence of his friend's well-being was matched only by the relief that overcame Rickard after the Philadelphia flight. And, a few hours later, we were to discover that Tunney's air journey, far from being the superficial gesture of an exaggerated ego, was instead the manifestation of the spirit of a man who was supremely confident in his own ability to handle the biggest assignment of his life and was taken for the reason of the psychological effect it might have upon Dempsey.

It rained the night of September 23, 1926, in Philadelphia. It rained as it had never rained before, but not early enough to bring a postponement of the battle. Trying to beat the downpour which threatened, Rickard ordered the title bout started ahead of time. But the move was wasted. Rain fell in torrents while Dempsey and Tunney struggled for the championship. Everyone in the record crowd was soaked to the skin. No protection was offered at all. You were just out there in the wide-open spaces, sitting and taking the watery drenching that was comparable only to the punching drenching to which Dempsey was subjected as, for the first time in history, a world heavyweight title changed hands on a 10-round decision.

Telegraph instruments at the ringside short-circuited. Radio broadcasting was done under difficulties. I recall a particularly vitriolic outburst against Graham McNamee, who was sitting in front of me in the working press row, trying to broadcast while I was dictating a round-by-round description. Near the end of the battle, in the eighth or ninth round, my wire went dead.

Edition time was approaching, the fight was nearing its end. It was imperative my line be clear of all disturbance, and there I was, pulled to my feet unconsciously under the nervous tension of the battle and the approaching rendering of a decision. Throaty shouts of the fans made it difficult for me to be heard by the operator above the din. I know now I was shouting, although it never occurred to me at the moment. I must have been interfering with McNamee's broadcast. He signaled me to be quiet. I dislike to recall now what I told him. But it all provided laughs later in some of the fanning sessions we enjoyed.

Tunney did everything to Dempsey that night but knock him out. The killer of the ring was helpless before the superb boxer that was Tunney. Dempsey chased and chased, slipping and sloshing over the rain-soaked canvas covering, pursuing Tunney to all corners and all sides of the ring, flailing out of his crouch with that deadly left hook of his, trying to nail Tunney with a right to the jaw. And all Dempsey did was run into a bewildering, blistering, blinding barrage of stiff left jabs, accurate left hooks, to the face and head, and an occasional right cross to the face or head, in an exhibition of skill no heavyweight had flashed since the days of Jim Corbett.

Had Tunney the punching strength, he would have knocked Dempsey out as he boxed his way to the decision and the title in his most impressive exhibition and the most methodical demonstration of an unalterable battle plan a fighter ever followed. Nothing Dempsey did disturbed Tunney. The fighting ex-Marine knew he was Dempsey's master and proceeded accordingly, to become the world's heavyweight champion and collect $200,000 in the process. Dempsey received $711,868, since his 37½ per cent of the receipts exceeded a $450,000 guarantee for which he had signed. He had the privilege of working on the higher percentage and held to it—after the experience of the Carpentier fight in 1921.

The defeat of Dempsey stunned those who expected to see him knock out Tunney. In the wake of the battle came reports that Dempsey was "doped," that he was overtaken by illness. Nowhere, however, was there any protest over the decision. Tunney had seen to that by outboxing Dempsey by a margin that left no room for doubt.

In the traditional acclaim for a new heavyweight champion, Tunney was hailed on all sides following his victory. Modest in the extreme, Gene accepted this acclaim graciously. He held to seclusion while postbattle details were being straightened out in Philadelphia, and when he returned triumphant to his native New York a few days later, it was to a reception such as few public figures have received.

Not for weeks did the hubbub over the Tunney conquest abate in the newspapers. Through it all, Gene maintained a dignified calm which amounted almost to aloofness. It was as if he couldn't understand all the noise and excitement about a fellow accomplishing exactly what he knew he could accomplish. He had a distaste for what he regarded as notoriety. He had a wide acquaintance among wealthy businessmen and figures prominent in the affairs of the nation, state and city. This circle grew with the passage of time.

In time, also, demand grew for a return bout between the new champion and the old. Tunney was agreeable to this for a variety of reasons, not the least among them being his confidence that he could whip Dempsey every time they met and the knowledge that another Dempsey fight, no matter where held, would bring him a huge purse. The $200,000 he collected for the Philadelphia bout represented a sum that had been only in Tunney's imagination up to that time. The $711,868 Dempsey received opened his eyes to the immediacy of the independent wealth he envisioned when, an ex-marine of the First World War, he adopted boxing as a profession with a seriousness that saw him overcome the handicap of fragile hands and other discouraging obstacles in his path.

If the wide road to affluence had at last opened to Tunney, it had not exactly been closed to Rickard. He was yet to achieve the pinnacle of his career as a promoter—the greatest gate that has even been drawn to a boxing bout, the staggering sum of $2,658,660, paid by 104,943 persons to see the second meeting of Tunney and Dempsey, in Chicago. He was yet to pay the record individual purse to a boxer, the amazing sum of $990,445 which he handed over to Tunney for the famous battle of "the long count."

The disappointment over Dempsey's collapse as heavyweight champion, the fact that the title changed hands for the first time on a 10-round decision, the conviction that Dempsey had not boxed up to his best because of the difficulties that beset him on all sides as he tried to prepare himself for the bout, the undercurrent of feeling that, Tunney's masterful exhibition of superlative boxing notwithstanding, Gene still had to prove himself a better man than Dempsey

—all this sustained interest in heavyweight activity at fever pitch and created a demand for another Dempsey-Tunney battle.

Dissatisfied with his Philadelphia showing, disillusioned as well, and enriched with the $711,868 he collected in defeat, Dempsey, in his immediate reaction, was for quitting the ring. He took his setback graciously.

Ugly stories were circulated in the battle's wake. One of them was to the effect that Dempsey had been mysteriously drugged. Someone was supposed to have tampered with his food in the training camp, although how this was accomplished, despite the guard of trusted associates with which Dempsey surrounded himself, was not explained.

Max (Boo Boo) Hoff, a character of wide notoriety during the prohibition era, actually started court action against Billy Gibson, Tunney's manager, on the basis of an arrangement he claimed was effected before the bout, by which Hoff allegedly was to provide "protection" for Tunney. This claim overlooked entirely the fact that Tunney carried all the "protection" he required in his glove-encased fists that night.

Dempsey's pride was hurt. He confided to Rickard his own conviction that he could beat Tunney if given another chance. With visions of a still greater box-office match in the offing, Rickard was not unreceptive to the idea.

Biding his time until the celebration of Tunney's triumphal return to New York began to wane, Rickard moved toward the re-match. He organized a publicity safari to St. Louis on January 6, 1927, formally to sign Tunney to a bout contract. Tunney had business in St. Louis at the time, and Rickard, alive to the news value of such a trip, underwrote the journey. The investment paid handsomely. World-wide publicity resulted from Tunney's signing.

With Dempsey, however, it was different. The ex-champion wanted one tune-up fight to equip himself for a second meeting with Tunney. Actual combat would sharpen his fighting edge, Dempsey felt. There was also the consideration that at the time it was questioned whether Dempsey was the outstanding contender. Jack Sharkey, fighting ex-sailor from Boston, was booming along the challengers' trail at the time and won support in his insistence upon recognition. The "hysterical horticulturist" had come up in the picture by stopping Harry Wills in 13 rounds.

Rickard decided a Dempsey-Sharkey elimination match would solve the problem. The victor would fight Tunney in 1927. Dempsey welcomed this arrangement. So did Sharkey. They were signed to fight it out at the Yankee Stadium on July 21. Dempsey engaged Leo P. Flynn, then a leader among fight managers, to direct his training. The ex-champion took himself off to Saratoga Lake, New York, for the conditioning campaign. The question was whether Dempsey could attain a physical soundness with which to withstand the rough, gruff "garrulous gob." While Sharkey proclaimed to all who would listen that he was going to hammer Dempsey out of a second Tunney match and detailed exactly how this was to be accomplished, Dempsey proceeded quietly with his training.

But the ex-champion's road was not as smooth as had been anticipated. A younger brother went berserk in Schenectady, within a week or so of the battle, and murdered his wife before committing suicide. This jarred Dempsey badly. The ordeal of identification to which he was subjected didn't help much. It was a red-hot story, and we were all on it, uninterruptedly. We tried to be as considerate of Dempsey as we could be. A group of us accompanied him to Schenectady for the police hearing, which found Jack highly nervous, as can be imagined. But he came back admirably from this shock, aided no little by the paternal care of the gray-haired Flynn.

The night before the fight, when the writers were preparing to leave camp, Dempsey celebrated with a modest party in his secluded cabin. Jackie Farrell, then on the News in New York, was the only writer present. One of the clown acts of the affair was a dance in which the diminutive Farrell was Dempsey's partner.

In grasping the left arm of the ex-titleholder, Farrell detected a bandage. He kept his own counsel until he returned to the boarding house of old Tom Luther, where we were quartered. He had a story that was a sensation, but was timid about using it. He was sure he had felt the bandage, yet there was that uncertainty. He interrupted my packing for consultation. I was leaving with the late Harry Cross of the New York Herald Tribune, for New York. Our stories had been filed. Our work was finished.

My decision was to go whole hog on the story, qualifying it, of course, in the absence of any announcement from Flynn or Dempsey about an injured arm. Farrell explained he had mentioned the bandage to Dempsey and had been advised that the champion was suffering from what he thought was a minor muscular complaint.

Any "complaint" in connection with Dempsey's left arm could not be relegated to the "minor" category. Cross and I filed stories about the sensational discovery of Dempsey's condition.

Not the least of those alarmed when the papers appeared was Rickard, who immediately communicated with Dempsey and was reassured. However, the gamblers, who had made Dempsey a prohibitive favorite, scurried for cover in their pre-fight "action," and the odds tumbled.

That, it developed later, was the object of the "injury," which had been carefully planted by Flynn. It was aimed, too, at making Sharkey overconfident. It failed of this purpose.

Dempsey knocked out Sharkey in the seventh round at the Yankee Stadium. That is what the record shows. I have always maintained Dempsey fouled Sharkey no less than four times with right-hand drives delivered at close range. The action took place directly above me, with the boxers in a position where I had perhaps the best ringside view of what happened.

Of course, there was a noisy aftermath to the battle. Sharkey and his manager, Johnny Buckley, announced they would attempt to have the decision reversed. Failing that, they set up a clamor for a return bout on the ground that Dempsey's victory was inconclusive. Fans took sides on the issue. But the State Athletic Commission, of which James A. Farley was then chairman, ruled against setting a precedent by reversing an official, and the decision of Referee Jack O'Sullivan stood.

Dempsey, naturally, moved into the return match with Tunney. Rickard pitched the battle in Chicago, on September 22, 1927, with the assistance of George F. Getz, millionaire coal merchant, and a coterie of similarly wealthy Chicagoans. Because he was a non-resident, Rickard was ineligible for a promoter's license in Illinois. This obstacle was hurdled when the permit was issued to Getz.

Dempsey selected the race track at Crete, Illinois, as his conditioning camp. Tunney picked the country club at Lake Villa, Illinois. While the training proceeded, the demand for tickets swamped Rickard and his box-office staff. They poured in from all over the world. Everybody, it seemed, wanted to be at this fight. The top price was $40.

The fight itself was a resumption of Philadelphia for six rounds. Dempsey chased Tunney, and Tunney boxed circles around the ex-champion, thrusting aside Dempsey's savage lunges for the most part with no more effort than would have been necessary in a gymnasium workout. The champion was the epitome of boxing skill, courage, grace, and resourcefulness. Dempsey couldn't hit him with a solid punch to a vital spot—until the seventh round.

Then it happened. Dempsey banged Tunney against the ropes with a long left hook to the head out of his crouch. The champion fell backward into the ropes almost above me, shaken and hurt. Like a tiger, Dempsey was upon his foe, vicious, savage, a man berserk. A volley of wicked lefts and rights to the head and jaw, and Tunney crumpled, his brain numbed, his consciousness gone, oblivious of the earsplitting din which grew into a crescendo of wild cries echoing over Soldier Field's excited populace.

Referee Dave Barry stepped to the side of the prostrate Tunney to begin his count. The knockdown timekeeper, Paul Beeler, rose across the ring to tick off the seconds on the watch in his hand. Dempsey, his arms spread over the ropes in the corner above me, stood tense, waiting for Tunney to be counted out or come up for further punishment.

Barry's arm swung down in "one," and he motioned Dempsey to leave the corner above Tunney and cross to the opposite neutral corner. Dempsey ignored the motion. I was shouting myself hoarse trying to tell him to heed the referee. Tunney was heaving convulsively there on the floor. The count went to "five" before Dempsey moved. Tunney now was an inert mass struggling to grasp the rope, with the instinctive effort of pulling himself erect. Dempsey finally raced to the corner diagonally across from the fallen Tunney.

Barry resumed his counting—at "one." That was "six" in elapsed time. Tunney was still feebly pawing the air, as thoroughly "out" as any boxer I have ever seen. At "seven" he managed to grasp a rope. That was "twelve" in elapsed time. By superhuman effort he was up at "nine," which should have been "fourteen." Dempsey leaped after him in a furious bid for a knockout that was frustrated only because Tunney had recovered enough of his senses to dodge out of the way of Dempsey's annihilating fists as the ex-champion rushed in. They resumed near the knockdown spot, and then Tunney danced away from harm through the remainder of the round.

In the eighth round Tunney was himself. He came boldly forth with a right to the jaw, under which Dempsey went down to one knee. But, even before Dempsey hit the canvas, Referee Barry was above him, photographic records show, with his arm raised aloft in the count of "one."

Tunney was on the floor for anywhere from 14 to 21 seconds in the seventh, independent watches held on the event showed. I have always maintained Dempsey was the victim of an injustice that night. It has been and always will be my contention that Dempsey knocked out Tunney in Chicago. His popularity since seems to reflect a pretty general support for this view.

Yet, whatever injustice occurred was brought on by Dempsey. Had he obeyed Barry and raced to the farthest neutral corner without delay, Tunney must have been counted out. Or, even surviving a "slow" count, must have been in such helpless condition as to have been finished with the next onslaught. Instead, Dempsey stood there above Tunney, wasting precious seconds in futile insistence to Barry that "you start counting."

There has been no more controversial ring issue in history. Tunney always insisted he knew what was going on at "seven." That was "twelve." If he had heard "five," it was "ten."

Dempsey's camp protested furiously. His handlers insisted Jack was robbed of a merited victory. They carried their protest to the Illinois State Athletic Commission the next day, in the following letter to John Righeimer, Paul Prehn, and Samuel Luzzo:

Gentlemen:

Please take notice that the undersigned, in behalf of Jack Dempsey, files a formal protest against the decision rendered by your honorable body, individually and collectively, on Sept. 22, 1927, in the boxing contest held at Soldier Field Stadium, and further, the undersigned hereby formally files notice of appeal from the decision as rendered in behalf of James J. Tunney and against Jack Dempsey, on the grounds that:

First, the said James J. Tunney was actually knocked out in the seventh round of the said contest.

Second, that the said James J. Tunney was down longer than the prescribed ten seconds, as provided by the rules and regulations governing a boxing contest.

Third, that through a lack of proper co-ordination by the referee and the counting timekeeper the said James J. Tunney was on the floor from three to six seconds more than the time prescribed by the rules and regulations governing boxing contests.

The undersigned, therefore, on behalf of Jack Dempsey, pursuant to the rules and regulations made and provided, respectfully demands that an immediate hearing be granted so that all persons who are within the jurisdiction at the present time of the honorable body in the State of Illinois may be given an opportunity to give testimony and be heard before they depart for their respective homes.

The petition was signed by Leo P. Flynn, manager of Dempsey.

Chairman Righeimer and Commissioner Prehn rejected the petition on the ground that Flynn had no standing with the Commission as Dempsey's manager, and insisted that the Commission would consider only a petition signed by Dempsey. The ex-champion never submitted such a petition.

In the aftermath, much was made of the claim by the Commission that Dempsey was aware of the knockdown requirement, that it had been very thoroughly discussed in a prebattle meeting among the principals and the Commission. It was insisted that the minutes of the meeting would reveal the discussion. I can recall Hype Igoe and myself asking Prehn, whom we knew well, for a copy of this section of the meeting minutes. It could not be found.

Timekeeper Beeler explained it as follows:

"When Tunney was floored I began to count. With my eyes on the watch, I tolled off the seconds. I looked up and saw Barry pushing and waving Dempsey to a neutral corner. Dave Barry then picked up the count. I called 'five' and he called 'one,' showing that the count started from that second. Instead of calling 'six' on the second, I called 'two' and then counted up to nine, when Tunney got up. Thus, the total time Tunney was on the floor was 13 seconds."

Tunney said:

"I was in possession of my faculties all the time. I felt myself hitting the floor and, whether it was the jar of that fall or not, I was counting with the referee all the time. I was getting up at four, but the men in my corner waved me down, and I took advantage of the extra seconds to get a rest."

Dempsey picked up a check for $884,500—a record sum for a loser —paid Flynn off with $75,000, and his championship career was over. The greatest drawing card the ring ever knew was in eclipse, and with his retirement Rickard lost the prize meal ticket of all time.

Rickard's specialty, of course, was the heavyweight championship. For him there was an irresistible appeal about the "big fellow." But an abundance of good fighters in the seven other ring divisions provided him with plenty of business activity, the thrills that go with exciting combat, and the profits accruing therefrom.

Looking back on the field, I can recall the sweeping popularity he created in the flyweight class with such fighters as Jimmy Wilde, Pancho Villa, Joe Lynch, Frankie Genaro, Fidel La Barba, Frankie Mason, Abe Attel Goldstein, and Young Zulu Kid.

In the bantamweight class there were Pete Herman, Lynch, Jack Sharkey (not to be confused with the Boston heavyweight of the same name), Frankie Burns, Pal Moore, Johnny Buff, Eddie (Cannonball) Martin, Abe Attel Goldstein, Joe Burman, Joey Sangor, and Midget Smith.

The featherweight class was excessively equipped with talent, which included Johnnie Dundee, Eugene Criqui, Vincent (Pepper) Martin, Young Erne, Dutch Brandt, Charley Beecher, Louis (Kid) Kaplan, Sammy Nable, Benny Bass, Sammy Sieger, Gene Delmont, Steve (Kid) Sullivan, Jack Bernstein, Mike Ballerino, Tony Canzoneri, Bat Battalino and Andre Routis.

Leonard topped the lightweights, never lacking for contention from Lew Tendler, Johnnie Dundee, Willie Jackson, Richie Mitchell, Charley White, Joe Welling, Pal Moran, Rocky Kansas, Patsy Kline, Al Singer, Jimmy Goodrich, and Sammy Mandell.

The welterweight class boasted Jack Britton, Jock Malone, Pete Latzo, Lou Bogash, Pinky Mitchell, Johnny Tillman, Dave Shade, Nate Siegal, Mickey Walker, Oakland Jimmy Duffy, Morrie Schlaifer, Joe Dundee, and Jackie Fields.

In the middleweight division, Johnny Wilson, an unexciting southpaw, was the champion when Rickard assumed the Garden helm, but the class interest was stimulated in the reigns of Harry Greb, Tiger Flowers, and Mickey Walker.

Gene Tunney was among the topnotchers in the light-heavyweight ranks, which also commanded interest through the influence of Harry Greb, Battling Levinsky, Battling Siki, Mike McTigue, Paul Berlenbach, Tommy Loughran, Jack Delaney, and Jimmy Slattery.

Benny Leonard and Joe Gans are usually ranked together as the two best lightweights of all time. Benny had everything, this lad who came up from New York's teeming underprivileged to win world renown and gave all the credit to his mother with the words, "She always made me live right."

Benny was smart to the nth degree. He was one of the cleverest operators ever seen inside the ropes, a master boxer with lightning speed of hand and foot who often left the ring with his patent-leather hair unruffled. He could punch with both hands and he was a great finisher.

It was in 1916 that Leonard first came into prominence. In February of that year he got the referee's decision over Joe Mandot and in March popular verdicts over Johnnie Dundee and Freddy Welsh. On May 28, 1917, at the age of twenty-one, he won the world lightweight crown by knocking out Welsh at the Manhattan A. C. in the ninth round. That year, too, he knocked out Johnny Kilbane, the featherweight champion, in the third round at Philadelphia and received the popular verdict under the Frawley Law over Jack Britton, who had ruled the welterweight division.

Until 1924, Leonard was supreme among the lightweights and then retired unbeaten. He fought anybody anywhere. His title bouts with the left-handed Tendler, a great fighter, were among his most famous. In their first meeting, at Boyle's Thirty Acres, in Jersey City, July 27, 1922, Lew landed a terrific left to the jaw in the eighth round that knocked Leonard groggy. Benny fell into a clinch and talked his way out of the crisis. "Is that as hard as you can hit?" he asked with feigned amusement. Tendler was taken back and hesitated in following up his advantage, giving his opponent the chance to recover. Leonard went on to win the decision and in their next meeting, a year later, outpointed Lew easily.

Mickey Walker and Tiger Flowers were the best middleweights with Harry Greb. Walker, the Toy Bulldog, was a scrapper every inch, who fought with all the zest of Greb. He won both the welterweight and middleweight titles and got a newspaper decision over light-heavyweight champion McTigue. Also, he fought a draw with heavy-weight Jack Sharkey. Flowers outpointed Greb to win the middle-weight title and beat him in a return match before losing the crown to Walker.

Battling Siki, the Singular Senegalese, won the light-heavyweight championship in Paris, in 1922, by knocking out Carpentier and paraded the boulevards with a lion on a leash. He made the mistake of fighting McTigue, in Dublin, Ireland, on St. Patrick's Day, 1923. McTigue got the decision and claimed the title. In turn, Mike made the mistake of fighting W. L. (Young) Stribling, at Columbus, Georgia. That was the famous "three decision" bout. Harry Ertle, brought along as referee by McTigue's group, found himself in a quandary, as the Associated Press reporter put it, at the end of the fight.

After making an unintelligible gesture, he then awarded the bout to Stribling. Upon retiring to his hotel he rendered his final decision —a draw—and angry Georgians booed him. Ertle found it advisable to get out of town, and fast.

McTigue lost the title to Paul Berlenbach in 1925 but made a comeback and scored a sensational four-round knockout in 1927 over Punching Paul, who had lost the light-heavyweight title to Jack Delaney of Bridgeport, Connecticut, in 1926.

Delaney, one of the cleverest men in the ring, had knocked out Berlenbach in 1924 in the fourth round. Berly won their second bout the next year but Delaney beat him easily on July 26, 1926, at Ebbets Field, Brooklyn, to lift the crown. A year later, almost to the day, Delaney surrendered his title to fight as a heavyweight.

McTigue was then recognized again as the champion by the New York State Commission, but the National Boxing Association named Jimmy Slattery of Buffalo as top man. In October of 1927, Tommy Loughran of Philadelphia ended McTigue's claims by defeating him in 15 rounds. The stage was now set for a natural between the good-looking Philadelphian and Slattery.

Here were two of the cleverest boxers to step into a ring, and their meeting in December, at Madison Square Garden, was a superb exhibition that thrilled the crowd all the way. Loughran won the decision by a shade, to become the light-heavyweight champion. When Tommy gave up the title in 1929 to fight as a heavyweight,

Slattery and Slapsie Maxie Rosenbloom were rival claimants. Clever Slapsie defeated Slattery in 1930 to take the crown.

Loughran and Slattery were two of the most publicized operators of their time. Of Loughran, Tunney said: "No one has possessed conscious physical courage to a higher degree than Loughran. No fighter has ever gone into the ring worse equipped than Tommy. Lacking size, strength, speed, endurance, and punch, Loughran takes on all comers regardless of size and strength."

Slattery took New York by storm when he first came down from Buffalo as a youth of nineteen to fight Delaney, the "Rapier of the North," who had a spearlike left and a terrific punch with his right. Handsome, graceful, and possessed of marvelous skill, Slattery was called by Hype Igoe "the darling of the Gods." He was looked upon as one of the greatest ring prospects in many years, but his career ended prematurely. Jimmy liked the bright lights of Broadway.

Max Schmeling of Germany came in near the close of the Golden Decade. The Black Uhlan bore a certain resemblance to Dempsey and had a bobbing, weaving style somewhat similar. In 1929, he gave Johnny Risko, the baker boy of Cleveland, a bad beating and stopped him in the ninth round in one of the most savage fights seen at the Garden. This was the same Risko, a big, powerful hitter, who in 1925 gave Tunney a rough time of it for 12 rounds in Cleveland and later trounced Berlenbach in New York.

Schmeling also beat Paolino Uzcudun, the Basque, in 1929, and as the decade closed out, in June of 1930, he was crowned the world heavyweight champion by winning from Jack Sharkey on a foul in the fourth round. Sharkey had knocked out Loughran in 1929, and he and Schmeling were matched to set up the successor to the title after Tunney had retired. Later, Schmeling was to knock out Joe Louis and to be annihilated by Louis after the latter had won the championship.

A few incidents of the time remain to be recalled. There was, for instance, the occasion when Pete Herman, as world bantamweight champion, was matched with Jimmy Wilde in England. They were to meet in January 1921. There was nothing in the contract compelling Herman to fight Wilde as world titleholder. So, in December 1920, Herman lost his crown to Joe Lynch from New York's West Side.

The absence of the title was resented by London promoters as detracting from the Wilde match's appeal. Herman went over and knocked out Wilde in 17 rounds. Returning, he regained the bantamweight crown from Lynch the following July at Ebbets Field, in a bout conducted by the International Sporting Club. The talk was that Herman, being of the conviction that Willie Ritchie had been robbed of a decision which gave Freddy Welsh the lightweight crown in London in 1914, was taking no chances of exposing himself to similar treatment.

Then there was the Criqui-Dundee situation. A war-shattered hero, Criqui came over here to lift the featherweight title by knocking out Johnny Kilbane in six rounds at the Polo Grounds in 1923. I recollect at the time an organized protest that swamped the New York State Commission over this match. Boxing followers generally held that Johnnie Dundee was the outstanding challenger and that he was being sidetracked in favor of an international bout.

The Commission permitted the Kilbane-Criqui fight only on the condition that Criqui post a substantial forfeit agreeing to defend the title against Dundee within sixty days in the event the French fighter won. Criqui was champion less than two months, for Dundee boxed rings around him to take over the title. The sportsmanship of this compulsion was questioned by some. But the majority agreed that Dundee was entitled to his chance at the championship, and his victory carried its own vindication.

The first two Tunney-Greb fights, mentioned previously, went down in ring history as unexcelled for fury among light-heavyweights. I can still see Greb swarming all over Tunney in the first battle, roughing up Gene as he had never been roughed before and in a manner he never experienced afterward, inflicting upon Tunney the one defeat in his record. Vividly I remember Gene's declaration that the fight taught him he was Greb's master. Tunney had his revenge in the return bout.

I have often been asked about my favorite fighters. The answer always has been that I never have seen a lightweight as good as Leonard, I never hope to see another heavyweight as good as Dempsey. They were my standouts.

After the record Dempsey-Tunney fight, Rickard was to go on to the greatest failure a promoter ever encountered. He tried to induce

Tunney to accept Jack Sharkey as his opponent in a 1928 battle that was to be the champion's farewell. Gene rejected Sharkey and insisted on Tom Heeney, a New Zealander, whose one recommendation was his strength. The match was held on July 26, in New York. Heeney's style was made to order for Tunney to appear at his best. Tunney knocked out Heeney in 11 rounds. Rickard lost a sum publicly estimated at $250,000 on the venture. He told me privately afterward that it more nearly approached $400,000, all things considered.

Tunney retired following the Heeney bout, married, and took up a business career.

With the heavyweight title vacated, Rickard launched an elimination series with the sanction of the New York State Athletic Commission. Sharkey and Young Stribling were principals in this tournament. Rickard was engaged in promoting a Sharkey-Stribling bout in Miami, Florida, in January 1929, when, a few days after the Yuletide holidays, the wires carried news of his death from appendicitis.

"I've lost the best pal a man ever could have," was Dempsey's solemn declaration at the death of the promoter, whose body he accompanied from Florida.

Boxing lost a promoter of immeasurable stature. Indeed, the world of sport lost a figure whose equal is not likely to be seen again.

An era ended—the Golden Era!

HORSE RACING

by Bryan Field

Vice-President and General Manager of the Delaware Steeplechase and Race Association; former Turf Editor, The New York Times

The thoroughbred race horse found the Golden Twenties his period of transition from exterior darkness to the family circle. Entering World War I, Americans knew racing as a society pastime, limited in scope, hidden in a technical argot, and stigmatized by the reformers as gambling at its worst. The breadth of view and general tolerance that followed the war still did not immediately include horse racing.

It remained for a horse to break the spell—a thousand thundering pounds of bone and muscle, to arouse the United States to a new pride. The horse was, of course, the aptly named Man o' War, carrying with him an aura of the patriotism so lately at fever heat. As he swept to victory after victory, the man in the street first learned there were races like the Belmont Stakes and the Lawrence Realization.

"Realize what?" asked the man on the subway. "I don't know," replied his companion. "It's the name of a race that horse just won that they can't beat." Meanwhile, turning in his grave at such continued ignorance, was J. K. L. Lawrence, whose sporting conception of years before few remembered—the Futurity, at a sprinting distance for a horse at two years, and the Realization, a long haul, a twelve-month later, for a mature racer, a horse of three years. In the first, an owner looked forward to the future; in the second, he realized his dreams.

Of such pleasantries was racing made, but few knew aught of that—only the sordid side was heard, until along came Man o' War. He led by the nose a great sport and a vast industry that was to do emotional and financial things to a hundred million people that never before had been done by any sport or industry. For the first time a man could ask his wife to go to the race track without having her feel she was insulted and the family savings were in danger.

Man o' War was a gusty, lusty horse who was made to do his feeding with his bit in his mouth so he wouldn't eat too fast and become such a thorough glutton as to founder himself. He swept his owner into the exclusive Jockey Club and made him a rich man. More, he made Americans rich in the feeling they had something as good as the French and English, particularly the latter, whose King had had horses for generations, and who felt they were pre-eminent.

He made people think that possibly horse racing wasn't so bad. He was the first horse in this country to win over $200,000 when that much money was bigger sounding than now. He cracked record after record for sports followers who were just beginning to have money and leisure to find out all about sports and records and who made them.

The son of Fair Play raced in 1919 and 1920, attaining his climactic fame in the latter year when he won the match race with the Canadian star, Sir Barton, first winner of racing's "Triple Crown," in 1919; and for $80,000, a sum which put in the shadow the money figures of all sports except boxing. This was new stuff to Americans, and it was new in horse racing on this side of the pond.

Man o' War being the horse he was, and having captured the imagination of the public, it was only natural that he would fall heir, in his one defeat, to the implication of skulduggery. From all the facts of the case, nothing was more unwarranted. The sport of racing, however, is beset with thousands of touts who solicit so-called respectable businessmen with tales of a fixed race. The businessman, having in his soul the potential spark of larceny mankind has inherited, is all too prone to fall for such tall tales, until bitter experience teaches him that they are merely part of the tout's sales talk.

On August 13, 1919, Man o' War ran second at Saratoga in the Sanford Stakes in what was the seventh race of his career, after having been made a 7-to-10 odds-on favorite in a field of seven. He was ridden by Johnny Loftus, and the result caused that jockey to be in a defensive position the remainder of his life as to whether he had pulled Man o' War, whether he had run him into an open switch, and so on, all of the insinuations being unpleasant and uncomplimentary to Loftus as both man and rider.

The truth of the matter is that Mars Cassidy, the regular starter, was sick. One of the placing judges, C. H. Pettingill, was pressed into service to double in brass as starter. Needless to say, he not only did not do as well as the regular starter; he did far worse than had been expected of a substitute with his experience. Only two of the starts that day earned the description "good."

The first note of the chart caller's description of the Sanford was: "Start poor and slow." Man o' War was off badly and was promptly interfered with. Whether it was Loftus or any other jockey, the horse could not be quickly extricated from the tangle that frequently prevailed in those days, when only a one-strand webbing was used to make the starts. Golden Broom, second choice in the race and a noted speed star, was off flying. Upset was well placed, right behind the leader.

By the time the field approached the top of the stretch, Man o' War was third, but still well back of the leaders. In the stretch, Upset, who was a pretty keen horse himself, made his bid to go past the tiring Golden Broom. Like Man o' War, Golden Broom was weighted at 130. Upset was in with 115. The final drive to the wire saw Upset out to the last notch to stand off Man o' War, who was gaining steadily but was not capable of doing the impossible.

The race was a keen one, Upset finishing the six furlongs in 1:11 1/5, which was within four-fifths of a second of the then prevailing track record. Among sound judges who saw the race, there was general agreement that Man o' War was the best horse but no thought whatever that there was anything off color in the performance. It was only in later years, when the legend of Man o' War's invincibility grew, that people looked back and asked: "How was he ever beaten that day?" Had Man o' War not had a stainless escutcheon thereafter, but instead had suffered a defeat or two, there doubtless never would have been any whispering as to "What happened that day in the Sanford at Saratoga?"

Man o' War ran and won twice more that August and had only one more 1919 test, the victorious one in the Belmont Futurity that September. Throughout the Winter he was a much discussed thoroughbred, and when he began his three-year-old career with a triumph in the Preakness, in 1920, the ball of fire was rolling again.

Man o' War's whole three-year-old competition consisted of 11 races, and it has been said that the hardest test of his whole career was the brush with John P. Grier in the Dwyer Stakes. This may be so, but there are other opinions. In the Dwyer the thrills were great because the two horses ran head and head for so long. And it is possible that John P. Grier was momentarily in the lead as they came down the then long Aqueduct stretch, running almost head on at the customers. However, the Dwyer was an easy victory for Man o' War; he absolutely conquered John P. Grier, and drew off to score by a length and a half.

Possibly the Potomac was Man o' War's hardest race. Sam Riddle once said that it was. However, Mr. Riddle has been known to say different things at different times. The facts are as follows: In September, at Havre de Grace, Man o' War was assigned 138 pounds, and his owner didn't like it. Of course, no owner likes heavy weight on his horse, and Mr. Riddle was not slow to say just that, particularly as this was the greatest impost ever assigned the superhorse.

However, the opposition was slight, and Man o' War was considered able to beat what was against him carrying the Flatiron Building. Thus it was decided to start Man o' War in what many assumed would be the final race of his career. It was well known in informed circles that Mr. Riddle wanted to retire his horse undefeated for the year.

The twist of fate came with the downfall of the rain. This left the track heavy, and it is one thing to carry 138 pounds over a fast track, and quite another to do the same when the footing is bad. However, the change in track conditions knocked out still more of the opposition, and Man o' War went to the post. He came home a winner, by a length and a half, but probably a more weary horse than at any time since that day, more than a year before, when he failed to catch Upset at Saratoga.

The Potomac would have wound up Man o' War's career had it not been for the staging of the Canadian match race against Sir Barton the subsequent Columbus Day. As most now know, Sir Barton was not at his best. The race was no contest, and the Glen Riddle star romped as he pleased to a hollow victory. One school of thought has long maintained that the race should have been canceled, but, regardless of Sir Barton's condition, Man o' War was his powerful, gallant, flashing self that Fall day at Kenilworth when he lifted America's hearts.

Tolerance had an electrifying effect on racing in the Twenties. For years, only a half-dozen states had enjoyed the sport, and in several of those it was on a sort of "unofficial" basis. In 1922, racing was reopened in Illinois, one more year and the spark of revival was kindled in California. Three more years and Florida was having racing. After the span of a decade the pound of hoofs was to be heard in half the states of the nation, and on a scale never before seen in any country.

Stupendous as are the business figures of racing, running into the millions for investments, and billions for wagering, it was not to these things that the public quickly turned. The flesh-and-blood horse, striving and winning, could be understood by the most casual, and Zev and Epinard were almost immediately to bring the international touch. The royal trappings were supplied by the Prince of Wales, then a bearer of glad tidings and good will, and salesman to the world of the British Empire.

Zev was a horse that very few knew was named for the widely known attorney, Colonel Zevely. That knowledge was to come years later, in the Teapot Dome oil scandal, when Harry F. Sinclair, owner of Zev and the Rancocas Stable, was in the news pages. Zev put Mr. Sinclair in the sports pages. Papyrus had just won the Epsom Derby, and the new-found boldness of American racing would be content with nothing less than bucking the English at their own game.

Most of the British wanted none of that, but Ben Irish, owner of Papyrus, was willing to bring his horse here. It was a $100,000 match race at Belmont Park, with $80,000 to the winner. That Zev won under Earl Sande earned Mr. Irish new criticism in the London clubs and Zev new honors everywhere except with the late Admiral Cary Grayson.

Admiral Grayson felt his My Own should have been selected to oppose Papyrus and wanted to race Zev. Feeling ran higher and higher. Zev subsequently was shipped to Latonia, and the Championship there was billed as a grudge battle between Zev and My Own, who, up to that race, had been undefeated during the season.

The result was a surprise when In Memoriam won, with Zev second and My Own up the stretch.

Growing out of this came the match race at Churchill Downs between Zev and In Memoriam, where the former got the verdict and In Memoriam experienced a fate similar to that of presidential candidate Charles Evans Hughes. Chart callers and others flashed In Memoriam as the winner in what was a tight and bristling nose finish. It was before the days of the finish camera, and the official verdict of the judges, when it came, was in favor of Zev, calling for a correction by those who had announced In Memoriam as the winner.

The excitement of the months in 1923 before and after the Belmont race did not abate, for the statement came from the other side in defense of Papyrus that he should have been shod with different racing plates so as to grip the mud better at Belmont. Ben Irish had been warned to use such shoes, especially in view of the dirt track, quite different from the grass of England. He feared to try new devices with Papyrus and sent him out smooth shod to defeat.

Zev for many years stood at the head of the American money-winning list, and his total earnings were $313,639. There were a good many in those days who were claiming everything for the United States on all fronts, and likewise they claimed that Zev was entitled to the world's leadership. However, the French list included a horse named Ksar, whose earnings were given as just in excess of Zev's figure.

In assessing a horse's winnings there are very strict rules on this side, especially as relates to including or excluding the value of trophies or plate. The accusation was leveled that Ksar's earnings included trophies and plate. The reply from the other side was: "What of it, the horse won the trophies, didn't he?" The argument took a new turn when it was stated that the Ksar total was swollen because of the distortion of foreign exchange.

This was a horse of a different color, and since Ksar raced after World War I, when the fluctuations of the French franc were frantic, there was more than a little to the new angle. However, there were some statisticians with a sporting twist who felt that Zev should hardly be boosted into the top spot by any such paper work and international currency flummery.

The problem in foreign exchange was solved by Sun Beau. The late Willis Sharpe Kilmer, who always had an eye to good advertising, also had a crack handicap star in Sun Beau. In the good old American way, Sun Beau skyrocketed to the head of the list by winning race after race and purse after purse.

Sun Beau went past Zev to lead the American list, and then he swamped even Ksar's doubtful total by finishing off with $376,744. Nowadays the record books, taking due account of foreign exchange, carry Ksar's total at only about $135,000, but the discussion was keen during the years it lasted. In the Thirties, with Sun Beau's eminence threatened, Mr. Kilmer boasted he would bring the chestnut from retirement to stand off Seabiscuit's bid. This was a virtual impossibility and never happened.

What these thoroughbreds and these things had begun to do to American racing is shown by the fact that there were about 4,000 horses racing when Man o' War made his great sweep. A decade later this figure was doubled. Stake money had gone up from less than a million and a half in 1920 to more than three million in 1930. And the general money distribution had jumped in the same ten years from something above $7,000,000 to much more than $13,000,000. American racing was on a march and a surge such as had been known by no other sport, doubling its size in all departments in ten years.

Public opinion had been the main factor in this advance, and public opinion was much too interested in international racing to let matters rest. In France, Pierre Wertheimer, owner of Epinard, felt the same way. This horse was the French champion, and Mr. Wertheimer, wanting to give Papyrus another chance, proposed a three-cornered international battle to be run off in either France or England. Sinclair promptly said he'd run abroad.

It was another story with Britishers, however, and finally matters switched around to Wertheimer shipping Epinard to the United States for a series of three races. The first was at Belmont Park, scene, the previous year, of the duel with Papyrus. The new plan called for three events at different distances, Epinard in each case to meet the best American horses that could be mustered against him.

The Prince of Wales was on hand for the first Special, as it was called, when Wise Counsellor defeated Epinard at six furlongs, with the French champion coming on like a whirlwind. It was a gallant effort, quite as brave as the effort Papyrus had made the year before. But this time the French horse was to have another chance, and at a distance where possibly he would show to better advantage—one mile.

Aqueduct was the place, and again Epinard lost, this time to Ladkin, by a nose, after a rough and stormy journey. There was no complaint from Wertheimer, and no claim of foul by Epinard's jockey. Everyone wished the invader better luck than ever in his trip to the West, where he was to go a mile and a quarter in Kentucky. So powerful had been Epinard's finishes that the extra distance was supposed to favor him.

Here enters the foible of geldings and improving the breed. Eastern racing had long held the fort as to keeping geldings out of the classic races since they could make no contribution to improving the breed. However, Matt Winn, who had bested the Jockey Club twenty years before, in the fight over Empire City dates, tossed such niceties to the wind. He wanted a big field and big betting, as he had the mutuel machine working for him at Latonia.

Admitted, therefore, to the third International Special was a gelding, Sarazen, named for a champion golfer of the period. Not only was the equine Sarazen a gelding, he was to prove a bit of a freak, since he was to become the only staying son of a sprinting sire, High Time. In any event, Sarazen ran against Epinard and he won, strongly and decisively, in 2:00 4/5.

Winn, wanting to make another little stab at what some in the West considered the effete Jockey Club, claimed the mark as an American record. This was a slap at the 2:00 flat made at Belmont Park when the horses used to run the wrong way of the track—the English way, or clockwise. The timer at Belmont presumably mistook the post and snapped his watch too early, giving Whisk Broom II a record which still stands in the books but which has frequently been questioned.

Kentucky racing, while it could not match New York either in class or in devotion to the ideals of the sport, was making great strides in other directions. Even in the days when reformers had closed most of the nation's tracks, in 1911 and 1912, the breeding industry in the Bluegrass of Kentucky carried on. It carried on none too affluently, but it held together substantially enough.

Now the new expansion of the sport and the widening public interest had their effect on the breeding market. The foal registration in 1920 was less than 2,000. Ten years later, with men and women clamoring to get into race tracks, the Stud Book showed foal registrations of above 5,000. Likewise the salesring showed the golden flood sweeping on. When Zev was foaled there were about 400 yearlings sold for a total value of less than $700,000. Ten more glittering years and the yearling market had skyrocketed to more than 1,000 head under the hammer, and more than $2,000,000 in breeders' pockets.

While this was going on, the noble experiment of prohibition was continuing, and several humble men who had acquired millions entered the racing game as track owners. Perhaps the most colorful of these was William Vincent (Big Bill) Dwyer. Bill had been a longshoreman on the Chelsea docks in lower New York in the days when schooners loaded with whisky from Nassau had lain under reefed sails in Rum Row outside the three-mile limit. Dwyer was among the first, if not the first, to take a small boat down the Hudson and out through the narrows and the bounding billows to load whisky for the night-club circuit.

In addition, Big Bill had a brewery or two, and pretty soon he had a race track, Rockingham Park. Next he took over Coney Island in Ohio, where the sport had recently been revived, and he capped it all by adding Tropical Park in Florida, where Joseph E. Widener was cutting a swath in buying, expanding, and gilding Hialeah.

Bill also added a few night clubs, both North and South, and sought to put his Stork Club on the map by inviting jockey Earl Sande to sing there. Reversing the process, Bill took a hoofer out of a night club and put him to training his string of race horses, which carried on under the name of Montalvo Stud.

It wasn't very long before Dwyer had to pull in his horns and sell out at Rockingham, and then at Coney Island, concentrating his interests in Florida and New York. Bill made the point to the moguls at the Jockey Club that racing was the people's sport and that he had as much right in it as those who thought it was the sport of kings. This sentiment might have been brushed aside with not even a sidelong glance had it not been for the fact that Dwyer had his anchors down and well lodged in Florida politics. And Joseph E. Widener, vice-chairman of the Jockey Club, had a bill in the Florida Legislature seeking to legalize the sport there so it would be respectable for Palm Beachites to go racing in Miami. The old maxim, "All men are equal on and under the turf" came to the fore here, and Bill was admitted to the racing family although there were a good many who did not like it.

Dwyer was entering the racing picture just when one of the sport's greatest figures was leaving it. August Belmont died in 1924, after having ruled the Jockey Club for thirty years, beginning soon after its organization in 1894. Under his regime, the Stud Book had been purchased so that breeding and racing were controlled. In the early years of the century, he had established Belmont Park on Long Island, moving the Westchester Racing Association from Morris Park in Westchester.

It was Belmont who fought for the revival of racing in 1913 through the loophole of oral betting and bookmakers. It was he who had managed the international races, and it was he who had established what many considered the greatest stud in America. He was the breeder of Man o' War and, at the time of his death, was the head of both the Jockey Club and of Belmont Park. F. K. Sturgis, and then William Woodward, succeeded him at the Jockey Club.

On the operations side in racing, Joseph E. Widener succeeded Mr. Belmont as the head of Belmont and, by acquiring stock interests in numerous other race tracks, soon was talked of as the czar of racing. Judge Landis having been installed in baseball, talk of a racing czar prevailed but never crystallized.

Meanwhile, on the racing strips and in competition, names such as John P. Grier, Grey Lag, Exterminator, and Morvich were fading. Yellow Hand, owned by Charles Stoneham, head of the Giants, was retired, to be followed by Mad Hatter and Black Servant. The last named was a color-bearer for a comparative newcomer, E. R. Bradley, a gambler who had entered the sport on the advice of his physicians to find an outdoor hobby.

The Kentucky Derby, instead of being just another Western race, was being built up by Matt Winn, who had hired O'Neill Sevier to do the tub-thumping with an eye to the East. Sevier was later to be the publicist who represented many of the leaders of the turf and who took over Arlington Park at its renaissance in 1928. Bradley started Black Servant in the Derby of 1921 and is asserted to have made a tremendous wager in the Winter books, only to have his plans upset by the victory of the stablemate, Behave Yourself. The eagerness of the latter's jockey cost Mr. Bradley his Winter-book wager, which had to be on Black Servant alone.

That was to start the Bradley dominance of the Derby, and his purchase of stock in such courses as the Fair Grounds at New Orleans, Hialeah, and other tracks. Despite his coolness in gambling, which won him a great fortune, Bradley was superstitious and believed in the Bradley B's, even corrupting the Biblical name Abimelech, into the name of his famous racer, Bimelech, so as to maintain the alliteration.

There were other gamblers coming into the sport, some of them not nearly so savory as Bradley. The latter was accepted on all sides, his place at Palm Beach being the rendezvous of the cream of society at the time concentrated there. Never a party-goer, Bradley nevertheless could pick and choose what house he wished to enter.

Quite a different type, at least in the opinion of August Belmont and many others, was Arnold Rothstein. He raced horses in the name of Redstone Stable, which is the English version of Rothstein. At one time he was kept off the New York tracks and, subsequently, he fought for the privilege of entering. This was permitted, but he was followed at all times by a private detective who kept tab on his every move.

Rothstein is credited with bringing off the biggest betting coup of all, a transaction involving hundreds of thousands of dollars on the horse Sidereal. These were the days of the bookmakers, and invariably their word was their bond. Once a man got a price from a bookmaker, he could rely on getting paid. Johnny Walters was the titan of the ring in those days and carried a satchel on a strap around his neck.

Betting was done by the player marking a small card. Many of the richest men in America would bet Walters from $1,000 to $20,000, and he would accept the betting card and slip it into his bag with a nod and a "thank you" without even looking at it. Rothstein was aided in getting down his bets by friends who went to various bookmakers at almost exactly the same moment, on a carefully timed plan, so that no bookmaker would have an opportunity of "laying off," i.e., betting with another bookmaker a portion of the bet he did not want to hold.

The Jockey Club at this time had in the regulations a rule which read: "The Jockey Club takes no cognizance of bets." Many felt this was ostrich-like, and so it proved on at least one occasion.

Tom Healey at the time was one of the best-known of trainers and he handled the horses of Walter J. Salmon and Richard T. Wilson, among others. One day he saddled Display for Mr. Salmon, and African for Mr. Wilson, the two being coupled as a betting entry; and they were so recognized by public and bookmakers, whatever the rule might read. Display, although he later was to sire a fine horse in Discovery, was a mean post horse and frequently gave trouble and delay, as this was before the days of the starting gate.

The field was comparatively small, and the entry of Display and African, either of which could have won, was heavily odds-on. The nearest thing to stern opposition was offered by Upset Lad, a son of the same Upset who scored the only victory ever to be gained over Man o' War.

Display cut up and misbehaved at the post, with the start right in front of the grandstand. As the starter gave the word for the break, Display gave a terrific lunge and barged into African. Pete Walls, rider of African, was knocked out of the saddle. The public groan was enormous, since there broke one string to the bow. Not only that, but the collision so badly impeded the other string, Display, that he was away very slowly, indeed, almost a sixteenth of a mile behind the field. Upset Lad was off flying and soon was winging, far in front.

Amid groans from the crowd, Display took up the chase. It appeared hopeless. Yet he was called an iron horse, and that day Display proved himself one. On he came, passing horse after horse, until in the stretch it appeared he could do no more. Only Upset Lad was in front, and, gallant though Display had been, it seemed beyond the power of the horse to win. Yet win Display did. He got up in a roaring finish, winning cleanly and squarely by a small margin, and saving the backers of the entry.

On the lawns and in the stands the thousands of backers were congratulating themselves at such a turn of fortune. Plunged to the depths, now hauled back to the heights, they formed in lines as usual in front of the bookmakers' cashiers, awaiting merely the red board signifying that the result was official. But no red board was posted.

After a few minutes, Display's number was taken down and, amid astounded silence, Display was disqualified. Upset Lad was placed first. Walter Vosburgh was at the time the steward appointed by the Jockey Club. Other stewards were nonstipendary, or almost honorary.

Mr. Vosburgh's primary function as the only paid steward was to protect the racing public. There was a rush to question him as to the reason for the disqualification. He replied: "Mr. Salmon's horse at the start interfered with Mr. Wilson's horse and knocked the jockey from the saddle, preventing African from having any chance to win the purse."

The rebuttal was instant and quick: "Yes, of course, Mr. Vosburgh, but the two horses were coupled as an entry; what about the public which loses its money because of such a disqualification?" Mr. Vosburgh calmly replied: "The Jockey Club takes no cognizance of bets!" The result stood in obedience to the rules.

Vosburgh, like Belmont, had served many years and witnessed the great growth and expansion of the sport. He was the official handicapper, and an official of extreme meticulousness. So infrequent were his errors that when he made them they stood out more sharply. One of the best known resulted in a new track record in the Metropolitan Handicap at the close of the Golden Decade. Set in 1930, the record still stands.

Weights are assigned considerably ahead of the Metropolitan, on the basis of age, and also on the basis of the handicapper's opinion of the speed of the various horses. In 1928 and 1929, a horse named Jack High was very nearly a champion. He came up for the Metropolitan of 1930 as a four-year-old. Out the same year, but only a three-year-old, was a comparatively obscure horse named Hi-jack.

In assigning the weights, Vosburgh confused Jack High with Hi-jack, the latter not being named for the Metropolitan, and gave the good horse the light impost of 110 pounds. Balko, who was later to head A. G. Vanderbilt's stud, then raced in the Sagamore Stable colors of Mr. Vanderbilt's mother. A crack sprinter, he was assigned 120 pounds. When the weights were announced, horsemen at once saw the obvious error, and Bud Stotler, trainer of Balko, lodged a protest. This was disallowed on the grounds that no mistake had been made.

In a sportsman-like manner, Balko was sent to the post under 120 and, of course, so was Jack High under his gift weight of 110. Balko forced the pace for all he was worth but could not concede 10 pounds to a horse practically his equal. The result was that Jack High finished first in 1:35 for the mile, which was a track record at the time and still stands as a stake record in the Metropolitan.

Bud Stotler was one of the group hailing from Maryland, a state which once had racing under the bookmaking system and then switched to machine betting. The pari-mutuels were popular with the public, as many wished to bet as little as $2 and felt they were getting scant attention from bookmakers, who preferred catering to $50 or $100 customers. Maryland saw Man o' War in competition, not only in the Preakness of 1920, which he won, but also at Havre de Grace, where he ploughed through deep mud and won, as related previously.

Retired to the stud, he became as great a factor as a sire, and as the dizzy Twenties waxed dizzier, his get came to the races. Crusader was among the first and, in the opinion of some, his greatest son. Others in those years were American Flag and Mars, and the fillies Bateau, Florence Nightingale, and Edith Cavell. Later there were to be many others equally famous.

It was in Maryland and in a race with Bateau that Sande, then the rising hero, was set down and denied the privileges of the course. He was caught grabbing a saddlecloth and, despite the intercession of as powerful a figure as Mr. Widener, his suspension was not lifted until he had served out his time on the ground. Sande was contemporaneous with Clarence Kummer, rider of Man o' War, and with Laverne Fator, Linus (Pony) McAtee, Alfred Johnson, Bill Kelsay, Andy Schuttinger, Steve O'Donnell, Johnny Maiben, and Mack Garner.

Sande and Fator were the two big riders for the Rancocas Stable and, together with Frank Catrone, now a trainer, did the riding for that great establishment. Sande, from Idaho, was very quiet and an idol with the public, who felt he did no wrong. Fator, a terrific finisher, was usually accused of being the bad boy of the stable.

Yet Sande was known as "Big feet Sande" among his fellow riders, and not because he had very large feet. Presumably he could give a nudge to a rival rider, when alongside in a rousing finish, that would throw the boy or horse off rhythm just enough to decide the issue. Credited with saving his money, Sande retired in 1928, and there was a unique demonstration when he was called from the unsaddling enclosure to Mr. Widener's box. His retirement from the saddle had long been discussed in the press.

As the jaunty lad in bright scarlet and white silks made his way across the lawn and up the steps to the box, applause burst out from all quarters. A great jockey was through, he was going to put his money into a racing string, and into a famous horse, Nassak. Yet, within two years, Sande was back riding, disillusioned to a great extent on the money to be made by racing one's own horses. Nassak went wrong and proved rather a lemon.

Sande made a new fortune as the trainer for Colonel Maxwell Howard, who always admired his high courage, especially after his accident at Saratoga which nearly cost him his life. But it was on his return to the saddle in 1930 that Sande put new jewels in his crown as a premier rider. He was aboard Gallant Fox when that star swept all before him in 1930, and it was there his "big feet" again that got him into trouble—this time with a brother jockey, Raymond Workman.

In Man o' War's sensational career he could garner only $249,465, yet, approximately ten years later, Gallant Fox and Sande were to roll up $308,275 in one season of competition. As a two-year-old, Gallant Fox had been good but not sensational. Whichone had filled the eye as a two-year-old that year of 1929. When both were three, in 1930, Gallant Fox came to hand early and, with Sande aboard, he swept through the Kentucky Derby, Preakness, and Belmont Stakes to become the second Triple Crown winner.

Whichone had not been sent West for the Derby, and he was made ready for the Belmont, in which admirers of the colt felt he would lower the colors of Gallant Fox. Workman, a powerful whip rider, and the leader when Sande left off, was on Whichone. Gallant Fox took that Belmont, but the Whichone camp wasn't satisfied, especially as Workman felt he had gotten a little the worst of it from Sande.

The return meeting was to be in the Travers at Saratoga in August and Workman determined ahead of that race that Sande would get away with nothing—absolutely nothing! So far as the public was concerned it was a two-horse race, although Jim Dandy and Sun Falcon were also entered. Jim Dandy was 100 to 1, and accorded no chance. The same for Sun Falcon.

At the break, Workman was off best and immediately took the rail position, Sande having to lay alongside and on the outside. It was a deep and muddy track, but a hot sun was burning down, making for a light crust over the slippery gumbo. At the very first turn, Workman allowed Whichone to drift wide so as to carry Gallant Fox and Sande wider still. Going into the backstretch turn, the same thing happened, and now they were in the middle of the track —in the backstretch. Sande attempted to take back and go inside. Workman took back and prevented this. Sande attempted to put on speed and go up on the outside. Workman went with him and, at the far turn, again the two charging horses and intent riders lost much ground.

All this time no one was paying any attention to the superior mudder, Jim Dandy, who was saving ground all the while, skimming along the rail. At the top of the stretch, Workman and Sande came into the home lane boot to boot, Gallant Fox on the outside, Whichone on the inside, but many feet off the rail. It was all or nothing now, and when Workman asked for all Whichone had, the horse was seen to falter and stagger. He was through. A tendon sheath had been burst and he broke down.

But Gallant Fox did not go on to victory. Jim Dandy, seizing his opportunity while the two were busy with each other, had saved more ground and dashed home to a sensational upset victory, with Gallant Fox second. More than ever, that made Gallant Fox the outstanding horse, as Whichone had to be retired.

However, Workman was far from through with Sande. That Fall in New York was to be run the Lawrence Realization. Gallant Fox was in it. So was a horse named Questionnaire, who had done comparatively little but was rated a racer of the top class. Workman went to the lad who had the mount and offered him a bonus to relinquish the chance to ride him. He still wanted to humble Gallant Fox and Sande and his "big feet," although Sande had had time for little or no shenanigans in his stormy journey in the Travers.

The Realization of that year went down in history as one of the most bristling finishes of all. It was a nose on the post, Gallant Fox the winner. Sande didn't get caught on the outside this time. He watched and warded, and in the final run for the wire it was the two horses, throatlatch to throatlatch, and the two boys, boot to boot. Whatever happened in the final driving eighth of a mile, the judges saw nothing. But Workman threw a punch at Sande immediately after the finish in the jock's room! The boys subsequently made up and are good friends today.

Sande's fall at Saratoga was on the backstretch, soon after the start of a two-year-old race in 1924, when the field folded in toward the rail. When picked up, he had many broken bones, a fractured skull, and internal injuries. His life was despaired of while he lay in Saratoga Hospital. It was his courage throughout that appealed to Colonel Howard, who took him on as trainer when he hung up his tack after the great year with Gallant Fox.

Sande, when he was riding for Rancocas, was very close to Sam Hildreth, veteran trainer, called by his admirers the greatest of them all. Others favored the first James Rowe, and down the line the opinion goes through such giants of the Twenties as Tom Welch, Scott Harlan, and Jack Joyner. Hildreth and Rowe trained on both sides of the Atlantic, the latter for Harry Payne Whitney, who was the outstanding owner and breeder during many of these years.

In 1920, Mr. Whitney was the leading money-winning owner, with a very powerful string and earnings of $270,000. So great was the expansion of the turf and the increase in stake and purse values that ten years later C. V. Whitney, son of Harry Payne, was the leader with a more modest string but with earnings of $385,000. Tryster was Harry Payne's juvenile money leader in 1920, with about $49,000, while Equipoise was the son's star, ten years later, with two-year-old winnings of more than $156,000.

Saratoga was the resort of the wealthy and the obscure, but for all classes it was a place to which ailing horsemen went. They were wont to say that the air was good for their horses, so why not for them. Perhaps it is not unnatural, then, that many veterans passed their declining years there. One who left the Spa when he was depressed, to finally pass away in New York, was a man who made his mark in Kentucky.

John E. Madden was for many years the nation's outstanding breeder. He had an insight for a horse that perhaps never has been rivaled. The European maxim: "No foot, no horse" was a guiding phrase in Mr. Madden's career.

Such an able trainer as Max Hirsch credits much of his own great skill in dealing with the hoofs and legs of a horse to his training under Madden. Born in Pennsylvania and a professional foot runner and boxer in his youth, Madden first got interested in trotting horses. He soon switched to the runners, and he dominated the Twenties from a horse-breeding standpoint. From 1918 through to the year of his death in 1927, he was the leader in breeding each season.

Madden sold many of his horses in the East but was one of the most alert to the things that were happening in the West, especially in the Chicago area. After the tentative revival at Hawthorne in 1922, matters went along steadily in Chicago until in 1928 Arlington Park took its place as a course to rival any in the East.

John D. Hertz took over at this time, following the death of H. D. (Curly) Brown, a track builder and operator little known in New York, since his activities were mainly in distant parts. Brown built tracks on the Pacific slope and raced horses there. He erected the Laurel course in Maryland and was active in Louisiana and Florida, his work culminating in the monster plant at Arlington Park, which was the showplace of its day.

However, Havana, where he built the race track, is remembered as the area that very nearly brought Curly Brown's career to a premature end. In prohibition days Havana was the rendezvous of many who liked a more liberal atmosphere but who did not want to stoop to trafficking with bootleggers. Also, Cuba was sort of terra incognita for many in the baseball fraternity, notably John McGraw and Charles Stoneham.

Brown, in addition to building the Havana plant, assisted in its administration. Chris Fitzgerald, veteran racing official, who presided for years at Havana, used to say: "The Cubans do not understand a disqualification—if the horse gets home first, they want him to stay there, and no changing the numbers."

To take some cognizance of the hot Latin blood among the Cuban riders, a tacit understanding was later arrived at in Havana that there were no disqualifications, but the jockey was suspended for keeps. However, this was before the incident concerning Mr. Brown. Endeavoring to have fair racing, the stewards, on an occasion, disqualified a horse. An excited crowd immediately gathered around the stewards' stand and knives and guns were flashed.

This was a long way from sport as the North Americans knew it, but Brown had been in a few revolutions himself and was not a whit abashed. Who fired the first shot history telleth not, but down went an excited Cuban, badly wounded. Brown was arrested. While he was incarcerated at Morro Castle, red tape wound on and on. When the trial would come up was a matter of guesswork. Legal processes were intricate, sedate, and involved.

The long Havana meeting wore on, days drifted into weeks, and weeks into a waning Winter. Mr. Brown's address was still Morro Castle. Influence was brought to bear and availed nothing. The Cuban who had been wounded was quite important, and also influential. Friends of the track builder feared that if the racing group moved out with the end of the meeting in the Spring, Brown would be left alone without adequate witnesses to the affray and might suffer an unjust penalty.

At this juncture, a horse trainer who had been in Cuba for years went to a man who had been a young officer with Major-General Leonard Wood when Cuba was occupied in the Spanish-American war. That officer had spent his life in Cuba and become a large figure in the Island's affairs. Told the story, he shook his head and said: "There is no escape from Morro Castle; the only men who come out of there come out in a coffin!" That sounded discouraging, but it was hint enough to an able horse trainer. Two days later, Curly Brown was smuggled out of Morro Castle in a coffin and crossed to Florida by boat the same night.

After his Cuban adventure, Brown launched the Arlington Park project, which was the most elaborate thing of its kind in the West. The aim was to build a course for July racing, as in the Twenties there was a dip in the New York schedule during the Empire City session. After Brown launched the project, John D. Hertz was drawn into the group and pushed the enterprise to fruition.

Mrs. Hertz also was deeply interested in horses, and soon the

yellow silks with black circle were being carried by such as Anita
Peabody and Reigh Count, the latter winning the Derby of 1928
from the biggest field ever to face the starter at Churchill Downs.
Later a titan in finance, Mr. Hertz never was ashamed to talk of
his humble beginning when he was striving on the streets of Chicago.
His first big advance was in the yellow taxi business.

Asked how he came to choose yellow as a color, he answered: "I
got hold of a few second-hand autos and fixed them. Wanted to make
them look neat with paint. The cheapest paint was yellow." The
racing silks which later were to be made famous by thoroughbred
horses were yellow in memory of the yellow taxis, and the black ring
signifies the circle of a black rubber tire.

The growth of the sport showed itself in another way that, at first,
the breeding fraternity hailed with delight. Prices for yearlings
skyrocketed, and the money that changed hands at the Saratoga sales
began to run from the hundreds of thousands past the million mark.
It was in 1927 that $70,000 was paid for Hustle On, a well-bred son
of Hurry On. But, well bred or not, it was quickly found out that
Hustle On had difficulty. If he was trained hard enough to get him
ready for a race, his legs failed. And if he was trained lightly enough
to keep his legs from failing, he was too fat to win a race. Hustle On
never won, despite his name.

The next year, the record price of $75,000 was paid for a yearling
to be named New Broom. He, too, never won a race. In some cases
extraordinarily high prices were arrived at through an understanding
between buyer and seller. The price didn't "go" in cash, despite the
announcement that a sale had been made. There was a secret con-
tingency that only a certain portion was to be paid at once. The
balance was to be paid if and when the horse won the money as a
competitor on the race course.

The tactics soon proved a boomerang and were not practiced by
reputable breeders. The aim of the breeders in establishing high
prices was to stimulate prospective purchasers to bid strongly. However, unfavorable publicity, resulting from very costly youngsters who
failed to win, put a stop to the device.

Radio, toward the end of the decade, became a companion to the
press in reporting races, the first job of the actual running being
that staged by Credo Harris, of Station WHAS, Louisville. The late

Graham McNamee was used for this initial job at Churchill Downs, and since techniques were crude, he was stationed at the start, a quarter of a mile from the finish. There the word picture was exploded syllable by syllable—the start and finish being considered the crucial parts of the event. In subsequent broadcasts there was a change, of course.

No sooner were the horses off in a cloud of dust than Mr. McNamee and his police escort were off in another smother of confusion, being under the compulsion of running the quarter of a mile from the starting point at the head of the stretch to the finish line. Meantime, the horses were running not only that same quarter of a mile on the track but the additional mile circuit of the oval. Needless to say, McNamee and escort were supposed to do a quarter of a mile before the Kentucky Derby field did a mile and a quarter.

Since the broadcaster's route was partly through the dense Derby crowd, this was rather heavy going. The interim period was planned to be filled by the thrilling thunder of hoofs from microphones placed at appropriate places on the rail and around the track. Human nature being what it is, the radio being still a very new-fangled gadget, few adjacent to those microphones could resist the temptation of talking or yelling the equivalent of "Hello, Mom!" etc.

The broadcasting group got to the finish slightly ahead of the horses, but rather more breathless than usual. Radio wasn't noted for accuracy in those days. Eventually the name of the winner was conveyed to the listeners, who had been treated to as rare a group of impromptu "hoofbeat interrupters" as ever has been heard. Never after were microphones placed at track level unless under proper guard.

There has long been current a report that radio "covered" one of the international races in what was asserted to be the first connection of horse racing and radio. If so, none of the persons to whom I talked knew of the job, and it has always been Credo Harris' proudest boast that his station in Louisville was the first to stage an actual horse-race broadcast. It is possible that the international race job was what we today would consider a news mention of what went on, and not a broadcast at all of the contention in the race.

Clem McCarthy was the first to achieve wide fame on the radio in horse-race broadcasts, gaining it largely through his knowledge of the sport, and the fact that he was so superior to previous broadcasters. Clem, steeped in racing, had been doing the loudspeaker work in Maryland and thus was well equipped to win a large following over the National Broadcasting Company network, which was far the biggest available at the time.

Later, I came tagging along, when the Columbia Broadcasting System felt it had to have an offset to National and McCarthy. Herbert B. Glover, then in charge at Columbia, hired me at the Empire City meeting in July of 1931, and we planned to make a big splash in August at Saratoga. The broadcasting point was in a tower over the finish line, where the engineer and I were stationed.

At the time, Franklin Delano Roosevelt was Governor of New York. Endeavoring to build up the job, Columbia's Glover made arrangements with the Governor to broadcast from his table on the dining terrace. Ted Husing also was assigned to the production and was to introduce the Governor. Roosevelt was to speak for ten minutes or so, and then there was to be a switch to the tower where I would give the sports side, including the race.

Hundreds of feet of cable were laid to connect the two points, and all was in readiness, the cable winding down stairs, across roofs, through kitchens, and under table legs. Since neither party was visible to the other, the time schedule called for me to open the broadcast, set the stage, and then, after one minute, switch to Husing. After a few words of introduction—or thirty seconds—the Governor was to go on for ten minutes or until the horses appeared on the track. Then Husing would throw back to me in the tower. The entire program was to fill thirty minutes.

In the tower, and on signal from the engineer who was alongside of me, the initial minutes were filled. Then I threw the job to Husing. At his end, Husing made his half-minute introduction, and on went the Governor for his ten or fifteen-minute stint. But something was wrong in the tower! After I had ceased speaking, the engineer gave me a frantic signal to continue talking. Through his earphones the engineer could hear nothing coming from Husing or Governor Roosevelt. To keep the air from going dead he did the only thing possible, directed me to continue.

The thirty minutes that ensued were among the most difficult I had run into up to that time. New on the air, unprepared to do other than a job on race calling, I was thus on several second's notice told to keep going. I did not expect that the fill-in would be for more than a half-minute or so, or until the engineer got his feed from the Governor; it lasted for the whole broadcast!

Down at the Governor's table, Mr. Roosevelt was surrounded by a throng, impressed that one in such a high place should deign to come to racing. On went his speech, but no single word ever went into the ether. Somewhere along the line the cable was cut. Meantime, Columbia's new racecaster was doing as well as he could in his tower, filling the entire thirty minutes with racing chatter and gossip and, I fear, much of the history of Saratoga and the Saratoga battlefield.

Needless to say, all kinds of apologies went forward to the executive at Albany, who was to play such a large part in subsequent world history. It was found that the cable, in threading its way along, had been pushed into the hinge of a kitchen-door jam—a door that swung both ways with hurrying waiters and bus boys. The back-and-forth action of the door and hinge had worn through the cable.

While the flat racers were going blithely on to new heights and glories, the steeplechasing game was steadily forging ahead. In what are called "the dark days of 1911 and 1912," when racing was stopped by law, sport continued among the jumpers at private clubs. Many well-known owners first entered racing by having a jumper or two and then branching out into the flat runners.

The best-known example of such an owner is the late Mrs. Payne Whitney, who raced her horses as the Greentree Stable. Later it came to include flat horses, and many famous ones carried the pink silks with black stripes on sleeves. Twenty Grand, contemporary of Equipoise, Mate, and Jamestown, is still the favorite Greentree flat runner of many. He was big and powerful, won the Derby in record time, and was later sent to England.

However, it was with jumping horses that Greentree excelled for years. Vincent Powers, a crack rider, later trained these horses for Mrs. Payne Whitney. Thomas Hitchcock, Sr. and Joseph E. Widener were other prominent owners, and among the three establishments there were Jolly Roger, Fairmount, Bangle, and Arc Light, each a top horse.

Jervis Spencer, Jr., later to be famous as the chairman of the

Maryland Racing Commission, carried over as a gentleman rider in these days. F. A. Bonsal, Dolly Byers, and R. H. (Spec) Crawford were other steeplechase riders who are unrivaled today. Many remember the polo playing G. H. (Pete) Bostwick as a steeplechase jockey of the first grade, but much of what he showed was learned from his elder, A. C. (Brother) Bostwick, who now is a member of the Jockey Club.

In the late Twenties, there emerged in Wilmington, Delaware, a young man with a famous name who was to have a large influence on steeplechasing. This was William du Pont, Jr., whose Foxcatcher Farm silks subsequently have been flown by many famous stars, including Rosemont. But in the Twenties, Will du Pont was a competitor and was winning his laurels by personal skill rather than possession of horses.

As a boy he had spent much time in the Virginia hills and was skilled in all the usages of field and stream and farm. Wiry and strong, he was a natural rider and soon became a star in the steeple-chasing ranks. Later he was to become an excellent club tennis player and to marry a woman champion, Margaret Osborne, but the Golden Decade saw him as a grim and determined rider in the amateur ranks.

Steeplechasing at the time took much of its leadership from two such well-known men as Thomas Hitchcock, Sr. and F. Ambrose Clark. It is axiomatic that, no matter how sporting they may be, steeplechasing devotees rarely agree on the details of how a jumping course should be built. Du Pont joined that duo in building courses, surpassed them in his willingness to work with his own hands, and soon was the leading light on what was right and not right in a steeplechase course, or among fences in point-to-point events.

As the decade drew toward its close, and just before the stock-market crash frightened many, there was one of the pleasantest eras of good sportsmanship in the British-American rivalry in the Liverpool Grand National. The Irish lottery had excited world-wide interest, and for the first time the formidable length and difficulty of the Aintree course became known to the man in the American street.

The war clouds of World War I were far in the background, those of World War II not yet on the horizon, even so small as a man's hand. In Maryland, in 1926, Billy Barton captured the Maryland Hunt Cup. In 1927 he swept through for the Meadow Brook Cup and other races. Grand National talk was on many a lip each Spring. For the race of 1928 it was decided to send him abroad for the great four-and-a-half-mile Liverpool test.

John Hay (Jock) Whitney and many other Americans made up parties, and the trans-Atlantic liners found their choice staterooms taken to the last one. Billy Barton ran gallantly and well to be second in a monster field, beaten by the 100-to-1 shot, Tipperary Tim. Later, American horses, Battleship and Kellsboro Jack, won, but the high point of good feeling, the time of freedom from the worries of war and money, came in 1928 when a country horse, Billy Barton, carried the good wishes of more Americans than ever before.

Other years followed on, the depression struck, but racing expanded still more because of the need of state governments for tax revenues. Today the figures in the Forties dwarf those in the Twenties, but the growth has been largely due to the need for revenues, and less and less is the stimulus to enter racing a sporting stimulus. And never before did the sport double itself in a few short years —primarily because the American people awoke to a sport which long had been present but never a part of their lives.

THE FOOTBALL PANORAMA
and
FOOTBALL IN THE EAST

by STANLEY WOODWARD
Noted Football Authority

In the days of Walter Camp, American football was a game that was confined exclusively to the play pens of the colleges. Following its institution on an intercollegiate basis by Princeton and Rutgers, it developed slowly and painfully into a social event. It provided an excuse for the assemblage of old classmates and for a display of new Fall gear by their consorts. It was jolly and at the same time manly. The hairy-chested heroes of the era struck attitudes and made a high masculine appeal to the limited galleries that attended.

The time came, however, when an unidentified curmudgeon decided: (a) that there was gold in the revelation of masculinity; (b) that the performance of the heroes in the accepted amateurish and posturing vein would lead to no material gain.

Then the colleges started to play each other for what was in it— glory, yes, but also gold. They discovered that winning the game this Saturday would lead to bigger crowds on the ensuing weekend, particularly if the second adversary also had won. It got to be a race. West Point and Annapolis, which started football late and played it to no good effect and before a complimentary crowd invited by the superintendent, began to charge admission.

The back regions of the country took it up, discovered that it was a thing to enrapture the populace and produce revenue while developing manly combativeness among the students. It grew into the general United States autumnal amusement in the years before World War I and was ready to go into high when the boys came back from France.

In the years between the end of the war and the collapse of the stock market, October 29, 1929—overlapping slightly at either end—it burst its bonds and became an all-engrossing sport and business. People who had learned to love it before the war now demanded to see it weekly. They battled each other for tickets. They neglected their businesses to talk about it in the office. They remembered academic loyalties they had almost forgotten and started taking on interest in the old U., its gridiron successes and failures.

The demand for football was universal, and the academicians could have done nothing to quell it even if they had wanted to. A few of the big Eastern colleges, and some in the Middle West, had built stadia before the war. Now concrete was poured on every campus harboring a respectable football team. Coaches were engaged at salaries exceeding those of the university presidents. Agents of the universities scuttled around the farms and mine adits, scouting up potential tackles and backs, and before you could say John Roosevelt Robinson, the game had taken its place in the Golden Age of Sports.

It is just possible we are entering a similar age now, following another war. We may not have the naïveté, but returns accruing from athletic contests indicate that the American public is in much the same frame of mind as it was in the Twenties.

However, herein we are dealing with the past, with Knute Rockne, Pop Warner, Red Grange, the Four Horsemen, and hundreds of other figures who made football in their day one of the most popular, one of the most stirring, perhaps the most loved and criticized sport of all.

The Golden Decade had a most unprecedented preamble, for, in the year 1919, the Eastern titans, who were still supposed to be the dominating forces in football, were largely a bedraggled lot. The outstanding teams were Notre Dame, then just beginning to attract reluctant national attention, and Centre College, which had been lifted to heights of glory by a hard-bitten delegation from Texas, which included the spectacular Alvin (Bo) McMillin.

Both Centre and Notre Dame went through unbeaten. The renowned George Gipp, who died of pneumonia after the 1920 season, first came to prominence in Notre Dame's game with Army, when his kicking, passing, and running produced a victory for the Irish.

Other colleges which were not defeated in 1919 were Harvard

and Stevens Tech, or so Ray McCarthy proclaimed in his review of the season which was printed in the New York *Tribune* of Sunday, December 28. Harvard, he pointed out, had an easy schedule and was tied by Princeton. Of Stevens Tech he wrote nothing except the bare fact that it did not meet defeat. The Engineers of Hoboken, New Jersey, who have long since withdrawn from the football lists, may point with pride to Mr. McCarthy's notation. As for Harvard, it went on to the Rose Bowl and beat Oregon, 7 to 6, due principally to the line bucking of Arnold Horween, who later returned to coach at Cambridge. Natick Eddie Casey played on that Crimson team.

Football in 1919 in some ways was comparable to that of the first postwar year of the current era, i.e., 1946. The people rushed en masse to the stadia, and all records for attendance were broken. Graduate managers caught a glimpse of the golden harvest and started arranging games with what are now known as "attractions" and giving an eye to the material strength of their own football teams. Bigtime football was born and the powerful teams of the year were based principally on returning doughboys and gobs, the fathers of the GI's who resumed play in 1946.

The Dartmouth and Colgate elevens were typical. Reinforced by veterans back from the war, they were among the strongest in the East, the Green losing only to Brown by a point, and the Maroon to Syracuse by a touchdown. The meeting between Dartmouth and Colgate this year, 1919, was one of the unforgettable games of modern times. In the snow and mud of Hanover they waged a battle of giants that ended in a 7-7 deadlock. On that Colgate team were Belf West, one of the great tackles of all time, Gillo, Oc Anderson, Barton, and Watkins. Playing for Dartmouth were Swede Youngstrom, a demon at blocking kicks, and All-America guard; Cuddy Murphy, Dynamite Gus Sonnenberg, Jack Cannell, Bill Cunningham, Jim Robertson, Holbrook, Shelburne, and Jordan.

It should be noted that the forward pass was still a matter for pro and con discussion at this time. There existed a group of football masochists who maintained that the play was both cowardly and unsportsmanlike. They thought it should be thrown in the ash barrel for the greater glory of the dental and orthopedic professions. Opposition to the forward pass hung on for several years, and if it hadn't been for a young pioneer named Knute Rockne, the discussion might have lasted even longer. But Notre Dame's celebrated Norseman took an immediate lien on the play, and the success he had with it, through the agency of Gipp and others to follow, helped greatly to convert the rest of the football world.

In 1919, Pop Warner, who first became noticed as coach of the Carlisle Indians long before World War I, was promulgating his single and double wing back formations, and for years football scientists talked almost exclusively about the comparative merits of the Warner system and the Rockne shifting attack which was being enacted by the teams of Notre Dame.

Until 1919, Warner had gone four years without defeat at Pittsburgh. The football world was startled when Syracuse, led by All-American Joe Alexander, upset the Panthers. On that same day in October, Boston College, coached by the redoutable "Iron Major," Frank Cavanaugh, performed an unruly and iconoclastic act by beating Yale, 5 to 3. Such things were not done in those days.

Interlopers who had been invited to play in the sacrosanct New Haven precincts were supposed to succumb with grace and speed to the horrendous longhairs who wore the Blue.

It should be noted that George Gipp, Notre Dame's first renowned back, is better known in history than in the writings of the recreation authors who were present during his brief career. The season of 1920 was his last. He died of pneumonia at South Bend, Indiana, on December 13, and was told just before his death that he had been selected on Walter Camp's All-America team. Gipp played a good part of the Indiana game of that year with a broken collarbone and was instrumental in winning it, according to the vague historians of the day. The Gipp lore had not developed at that time. It sprang up in years that followed, in stories related by his teammates, and most particularly in those told by the master storyteller, Rockne. Gipp is painted as a slashing, swashbuckling player who had the gift of relaxation and almost never failed to come through when the stakes were high, either in football or kelly pool.

He was dying when Walter Camp picked him on his first All-America team. It was pretty daring of Walter to go out as far as South Bend to find a football player, for in those days the East was supposed to be supreme. Of the 33 players selected on the 3 All-

America teams in 1920, 21 were from Eastern colleges, 7 from the Middle West, 3 from the South, and 2 from the Pacific Coast. In justifying the selection of Gipp, Camp had this to say:

"In the backfield, Gipp of Notre Dame gets the first place on account of his versatility and power, able as he is to punt, drop-kick, forward-pass, run, tackle—in fact, do anything that any back-field man could ever be required to do, and do it in a well-nigh superlative fashion. He drop-kicked on his freshman team 62 yards. When a man who has been taken out with a badly injured shoulder can go in in a pinch and carry the ball over the goal line to get his team an absolutely necessary touchdown, something of the man's power can well be understood."

Notre Dame was undefeated also during the 1920 season, when Gipp was at his best. It won all of its nine games and scored 251 points to 44 for the opposition. Still it made compara-tively little impression on the Eastern writers, who seemed to be unanimous in nominating Princeton as the best team of the year—better than California's "Wonder Team," and Boston College, which won every game and defeated Yale for the second time in succession. Walter Camp selected two Princeton players, Don Lourie, quarter-back, and Stan Keck, tackle, for his All-America team.

Callahan was the captain of that Princeton team, and he had a brother at Yale who was on the All-America team and was called the best defensive lineman of the year. The Callahans got a big play, particularly when they squared off in the Yale-Princeton game. Garrity, Legendre, and Murray were other able operatives on that Tiger eleven, which won every game except for a tie with Harvard.

Pittsburgh—with one of the best running backs of the year in Tom Davies and an All-America center in Herb Stein—and Penn State were two other strong teams of the East. Hinkey Haines, Glenn Killinger, and Way were the hatchet men for State.

Notre Dame kept doing pretty well in 1921, '22, and '23, beat-ing Army twice and tying once, but it didn't really get into its post-Gipp position of prominence until the Four Horsemen were unveiled in 1924—they being Harry Stuhldreher, quarterback; Jim Crowley, left halfback; Don Miller, right halfback, and Elmer Layden, full-back. In 1921, the football chroniclers gave the Irish rather scant notice, though they were listed among the leading teams of the Middle West in the reviews of that season.

The East continued to dominate the All-America teams and to get most of the notice. Sports writers of the era had concluded that the Yale Bowl, seating seventy-odd thousand, was too small and should be doubledecked. The clients poured in their money, and graduate managers acquired an hauteur toward their alumni bodies which has never since been reproduced. Mr. McCarthy, still writing for the *Tribune*, didn't get around to Notre Dame and Iowa in his annual review until the second-last paragraph. Then he pointed out that these two had achieved a balance between running and passing that made them almost impossible to stop. That was the Iowa team that had the great Duke Slater at tackle and Aubrey Devine and Gordon Locke in the backfield and was coached by Howard Jones.

Mr. McCarthy had nothing whatever to say about Washington and Jefferson, small Pennsylvania college which had been selected to play the mighty Bears of California in the Rose Bowl. For that matter, neither did he mention the Bears themselves, the second edition of Andy Smith's "Wonder Teams," which went undefeated for four successive seasons, 1920 through 1923. In the annual New Year's Day game at Pasadena, which was later to be called "the fabulous Rose Bowl" by Bill Stern, master of the airborne garble, W. and J., coached by Greasy Neale, tied the formidable Bears and Brick Muller, 7 to 7. Lafayette, piloted by Jock Sutherland, also added to the glory of the Keystone State that season and placed Frank Schwab on the All-America team, and Cornell now was launched on one of its greatest periods.

The year 1922 was the one in which Princeton's long-remembered "Team of Destiny" was produced, though we fail to find the term in the sports writing of the day. Apparently it was a posthumous appellation. Bill Roper's Tigers, with Captain Mel Dickenson at guard, Herb Treat and Pink Baker at the tackles, and Johnny Gorman at quarterback, had a clean slate, beating their Eastern rivals, and also Chicago, which was cochampion of the Big Ten with Iowa and Michigan. Iowa, however, beat Yale. Army went undefeated in 1922, and Edgar Garbisch was All-America center. West Virginia was one of the elite, too.

This was the year that the modern place-kicking method of try for point after touchdown was introduced. The pioneers in the new method almost invariably employed the drop kick. Incidentally, Herb Covington of Centre set a drop-kicking record by scoring six field goals in a single game, against Louisville.

Notre Dame, a little below par in this pre-Horseman year, was tied by Army and beaten by Navy. All in all, in reading over the stories of games and reviews of the season, contributed to the press in this year, it is obvious that confusion reigned. The idea still was extant that the East only was important, and the All-America selections of the era gave scant notice to the heroes of the hinterlands.

In 1923, everyone had built or was building a stadium. There seemed to be no end to the dollars people were willing to spend on the game. Only cowardly educational institutions refrained from launching million-dollar bond issues, and none too soon, either, for this was the first year of Red Grange. It was the year of Yale's ascendancy, by transfer, the redoubtable Blue having scoured the intercollegiate brush and come up with such operatives as Mal Stevens, the fabulous Century Milstead, Widdy Neale (Greasy's brother), and others of their ilk; also Ducky Pond, of Torrington, Connecticut, a more normal acquisition, and Memphis Bill Mallory, Lyle Richeson, and Winnie Lovejoy.

Bolstered by this group, Yale had an undefeated season, thus rendering itself virtually unapproachable in the writings of the more insular Eastern scribes of the day. It was noted, however, that Cornell, which had started rising to power in previous years, under the dour teaching of Gil Dobie, also was unbeaten, for the third successive season. George Pfann was the big gun for the Ithacans, following in the footsteps of Eddie Kaw and Swede Hanson, and abetted by Sunny Sundstrom. Syracuse and Maryland were tough this year, too.

Painfully and reluctantly other Eastern gridiron experts recognized that the ascendancy of the Atlantic seaboard was no longer the whole story. Notre Dame came East and beat Army, Princeton, and Carnegie Tech. In the far and inaccessible fastnesses of the Corn Belt, Grange was galloping about 150 yards a game, leading Illinois to a tie with Michigan for the Western Conference title. He had yet to become known as the "Galloping Ghost" or the "Wheaton Iceman." Nobody wanted his signature. In short, he was just a football player and not the phenomenon he later became after the laggard press finally sought him out.

In this year of 1923, this department, a rosy-cheeked boy on the staff of the Boston *Herald*, got its first look at Notre Dame and was transported into paroxysms of admiration. The Boston *Herald* had a sports editor named Burt Whitman (who still reigns), whose vision was more pronounced than that of others of his time. It was not sufficient to cause him to send one of his first-string football writers to Princeton, New Jersey, to see Notre Dame take its expected beating from Princeton, but strong enough, in the face of a blanket of sea-coast uncomprehension, to cause him to jerk your reporter off the copy desk for a day and give him a chance to write.

It was a tremendous adventure traveling from Boston to Princeton. It was necessary to go to the steam-car depot and take a train to New York, then cross that city, through all the wild hurly-burly and the cacophony of taxi bulbs, and catch the train to Princeton Junction. We shall spare you the further accounts of the difficulties of the trip. We got there three hours before the game and, for the first time, encountered that pillar, the *Daily Princetonian*.

This organ had interviewed the virtually unknown man who was coaching Notre Dame. As we recall it, his name was spelled "Rochne." He was described as a friendly man with a broken nose and Norwegian ancestors. He discoursed to the *Princetonian*, in effect, as follows:

"While we do not expect that our little university can win a game against so powerful a team as Princeton, we do think this opportunity to come to this Revolutionary site and to see this great University will be a benefit to us. I believe firmly that our boys will get a good deal out of their contacts with Princeton men."

Mr. Rockne did not say in the interview that he had been in the habit of thumping the whey out of some of the best teams in the land for a number of years, both as player and as coach. He just made it nice and let his boys speak for him.

Among them were such as Stuhldreher, Crowley, Don Miller, Layden, and sundry rugged linemen, such as Rip Miller. They certainly benefited from their contacts with Princeton men. They upended the Tigers in rows all over the field and, but for the forbearance of their coach, they might have made it pretty drab for the Princetonians. As it was, they won only by 25 to 2.

The horsemen were not Horsemen yet. Grantland Rice had not yet had his brainstorm, caused by a view of the motion picture, *The Four Horsemen of the Apocalypse*, with Rudolph Valentino. At this point they were just members of the Notre Dame team.

The football played at Notre Dame in those days probably would not get a team far in these. In fact it would not any longer be considered kosher. At that time the rule provided that a team which shifted must stop momentarily after the shift before putting the ball in play. Rockne considered that "momentarily" was a vague word which specified no measurable expiration of time. Consequently, when Notre Dame moved from its T formation to its box, there was scarcely any delay before it started knocking the brains out of the opposition.

The Irish shifted and started in one motion, running over tackle or around end mostly, inserting passes where they counted, and occasionally opening up the middle for the lightning rushes of Layden. But they had no shortside attack except a cross-buck over guard, on which Layden carried. As long as "momentarily" remained in the rules, Rockne, with rare perception, saw no sense in developing a weak-side attack. When the rulemakers caught up with him, he did it at once and effectively.

Grange was All-America halfback in 1923, '24, and '25. His discovery by that part of the country which lies beyond the city limits of Champaign, Illinois, did not occur until late in the 1923 season, when he ran wild against Nebraska. He was rather slow in arriving. As a high-school halfback in 1921, he made a spectacular reputation in Wheaton by averaging five touchdowns a game. This attracted the attention of numerous football coaches but earned him bare mention in the newspapers outside his immediate area.

Grange was the son of the Wheaton police chief. His mother died when he was young, and his father was determined to get him educated. The old man had to order him to attend high school, for Red was ready to abandon academic life as soon as he finished ninth grade.

Bob Zuppke of Illinois admired Grange's work, discovered that Red was one of his own admirers, and helped him enter the university. He had been attracted to football in high school principally because the uniforms were free. He'd enjoyed it and the acclaim he had received. When he got to Illinois, however, he found himself in a group of 200 freshmen candidates and almost decided to quit.

Zuppke, however, took an interest in him (and who could blame him?) and assigned him to the seventh freshman team. Within a week he was the regular freshman left halfback. The elevation excited him so that he forgot about everything but football and did a noble job of flunking his studies. He was so popular with his teammates and the freshmen in general that he was elected captain of the track team, even though the university wouldn't let him compete because of his low academic standing.

He made up his work in the Summer, no doubt because he couldn't bear not to be on the football team, and never was in difficulties with the academicians again until he had completed his last college season and jumped school to turn professional after his final game.

He arrived all of a sudden, following the Nebraska game of 1923. In the first quarter he sprinted 35 yards for a touchdown, ran 65 yards for a second before the half was over, and scored another in the third period in a 12-yard burst.

The next morning he was famous nationally. One encomium stated that he "instilled such confidence of scoring that it made the Illinois team indomitable, paralyzing opponents by the most feared things in football—touchdown runs."

Though the Nebraska game is rated by the chroniclers as his first big one, he did other things in 1923, which are practically forgotten in the light of subsequent operations. He ran 175 yards against Iowa and scored one touchdown, playing 60 minutes. Against Chicago he played 59 minutes, running 160 yards and scoring one touchdown. He went sixty minutes against Ohio State for 184 yards and one touchdown. He played briefly against Butler, Northwestern, and Wisconsin, running respectively for 142 yards and two touchdowns, 251 yards and three touchdowns, 140 yards and one touchdown. In the 295 minutes he played in his first varsity year, he gained 1,260 yards, scoring 12 times.

The Grange legend started to grow between the time that the 1923 season ended and that of 1924 began. It developed that Red had taken a job delivering ice, and he was photographed weighing ice, chipping ice, cutting ice, and carrying ice throughout the Summer of 1924. When he started to operate in the Fall, everybody in the country knew his name, and promoters of one kind or another were laying plans to capitalize on him.

At the end of the year, Grantland Rice, who had christened the Four Horsemen, was still calling Grange the "Flying Terror" although the "Iceman" and "Galloping Ghost" motif was supposed to have been launched at this time. The next year, Mr. Rice, who customarily invents names for important athletic persons, had adopted the "Galloping Ghost" and was using it freely. One felt, on reading Mr. Rice's review of 1925, that he was more or less unnerved by Grange's departure from the amateur ranks into the professional, a move which was supposed to have netted Harold a sheer $500,000, and perhaps netted him an eighth of that.

The movies claimed they paid him $300,000 for playing in a picture. His postcollege football tour of December 1925, made under the direction of the celebrated C. C. Pyle, may have produced more headaches and backaches than mazuma for the Galloping Ghost, but it was publicized as a bonanza and it put more people into the New York Polo Grounds than have ever been there since.

It is necessary now to return to the season of 1924, when Grange was supposed to have made the greatest football performance of all time. The feat was described by Zuppke, coach, artist, and pragmatic philosopher, in an article written for the Hearst press. Mr. Zuppke was a little mixed as to dates and seasons, but it should be taken for granted that his story of the Michigan-Illinois game (score —Illinois 39, Michigan 14) is the truly authenticated one.

The first time [writes Zuppke] he [Grange] took the ball on our five-yard line and then, running down a field strewn with Michigan tacklers, he outwitted them and ran past each—ninety-five yards for a touchdown. Please, however, do not forget the splendid interference—especially of Wallace McIlwain and Art Hall, the quarterback.

The second time he handled the ball was when he took it on our own thirty-three-yard line and then—in that snake-like way he had of running—raced sixty-seven yards, describing a huge figure eight down the field, side-stepping one tackler and another, twisting and squirming and never halting—or being halted—until he had loped across the goal line.

The third time Grange handled the ball, he carried it fifty-six yards for a touchdown, and the fourth time he scored for us from the forty-five-yard line, a total of 263 yards and four touchdowns in four runs in the first twelve minutes of the game.

I kept him out of the second half until nearly its end. I wanted to have his record stand, but Grange was not the kind who cared for records. His whole heart and soul was in that game—football. He loved the game as few men I have known ever loved it. And so I hearkened to his pleas and sent him back into the game in the final half.

Grange carried the ball only once, ran it fifteen yards, and scored his fifth touchdown on five plays in a game against an eleven then rated as one of the greatest ever welded together in America.

Red Grange was just about as easy a man to handle as I have ever known in my coaching years. When he climbed to stardom and became the most talked-of halfback in the United States, it never affected him. Conceit was foreign to his makeup. He was always modest, quiet and unassuming, and he was as strict in his obedience to the rules then as in his earlier years when he was trying to make the team.

Mr. Zuppke gave this gem to the Hearst press more than two years after Grange had quit Illinois to turn pro. He was under the impression that 1924 was Grange's last season, whereas actually Red played through 1925 and made his only appearance in the East, completely desolating Pennsylvania with three runs for touchdowns, which set the pace for a 24-2 victory over the Quakers. A crowd of 62,000 impassioned Philadelphians saw the game in Franklin Field and hardly believed it after they had seen it.

The field was wet and muddy, but it didn't slow up the Iceman, according to W. B. Hanna, celebrated football writer of the time. After a column devoted to a variety of descriptive phrases, and having given the readers an inkling that Grange was pretty good, Mr. Hanna finally got around to what he did. In the first period he ran 55 yards off tackle for a touchdown. The Illini hammered to a second touchdown before the half was over without employing Red for anything much except a 50-yard kick-off return.

In the third period, on a lateral which developed from a fake place kick and forward pass, he ran 30 yards for another touchdown at long range. In between, he got around end for a brief run and scored. His yardage total for the day, including run-back of kicks, was 360 yards. This he performed against a team which had beaten all its Eastern rivals prior to the game, played on October 31.

Illinois had a bad season in 1925, during which Grange was incapacitated, wholly or in part, much of the time. He concluded his college career at Columbus, Ohio, November 21, when 85,200 spectators saw Illinois beat Ohio State, 14 to 9. Grantland Rice was one of those who covered the game. He found that the redhead was "not at the top of his brilliant peak," having been worried and harried for a couple of weeks over what he was going to do following his last game.

Rice says Grange's runs and passes beat Ohio State, but Red didn't score either of the touchdowns. He gained plenty of ground and built up his intercollegiate yardage to a final figure of 3,637 yards or, as translated by the writers of the day, two miles plus 117 yards.

Grange didn't go back to Champaign after the game. He delivered himself into the hands of Mr. Pyle and was soon playing against the professional teams in the East, South, and Middle West. The fabulous amounts he was supposed to have made were printed in large headlines, and the devotees of amateurism concluded that he wasn't such-a-much after all.

Tad Jones, the Yale immortal and coach, was trapped into an interview in Norfolk, Virginia, where he had gone to hunt ducks.

"Grange is a beautiful player," Tad was accused of having said. "but he is not the all-around player he is reputed to be. He does not rank with players of a few years ago, such as Thorpe of Carlisle and Heston of Michigan. Oberlander of Dartmouth, Wilson of Washington and Nevers of Stanford easily rank with the Illinois Flash."

The mawkishness of the times may be fully comprehended when one reads a story in the Brooklyn *Eagle*, which apparently was picked up from the Boston *Post*. With tears in our eyes, we give it to you. It is as follows:

"That mystic '77' which once adorned the back of Red Grange's dark blue jersey is not destined to be gazed at admiringly by future generations of Illini. Instead of reposing in a glass case in the trophy room of the university, it is now lying in some corner with rubbish, the symbol of an idol whose feet have turned to clay.

" 'The famous number 77 may next year adorn the back of some sixth-string substitute,' says Bill Cunningham in a special dispatch to the

Boston *Post.* 'It was destined to go down in history as Red's number. But it's anybody's number now,' says the Boston writer.

"The attitude of the Illinois University officials towards Grange appears to be 'the least said about the matter the better.' They had seen the thing coming and in an effort to prevent it had called upon alumni as far West as Denver and as far East as New York. Grange had been offered splendid business connections by certain members of the alumni, one of the offers, Cunningham relates, calling for an annual salary of $15,000 with a ten-year contract.

"But Red became sort of a lone wolf on the campus and took advice from no one. He signed the contract with Pyle, his present manager, before a district judge, after that official had informed him that it was vastly unfair to his (Grange's) interest. But Grange preferred to accept the advice of Pyle and another student named Cooley, who, it is said, has become quite unpopular since the incident, and affixed his name to the professional agreement.

"After the victory at Ohio State, Red slipped off the famous jersey and handed it to Bob Zuppke, the Illinois coach, with tears in his eyes. Zuppke took the sweat-stained shirt and folded it tenderly. The famous coach brought the trophy back home as if it were a prize of considerable importance, moved perhaps by sentimental regard for Grange, the greatest player he had ever developed. But now the jersey that once flashed down the cross-barred field to bring victory after victory to Illinois, and which had been destined to hold down a place among the treasures of the university, reposes in a heap of dust waiting for the next call of the rubbish man."

It is remarkable to note in retrospect how completely Grange eclipsed the Notre Dame team of 1924, which was the year the Horsemen jelled. They had been unobtrusive substitutes in 1922, played only occasionally together in 1923 when such interlopers as Dutch Bergman were considered superior football players. But in 1924, Rockne pitched all or nothing on them and they came through for him, uninterruptedly walloping outstanding teams of East, South, and Middle West, and finishing with a brilliant victory over Stanford, coached by Pop Warner and manned by Ernie Nevers & Co., in the Rose Bowl, 27 to 10.

The Horsemen were little guys, as football players go today. The biggest of them was Miller, who weighed a little more than 170 pounds. Crowley and Layden were in the 160's, and Stuhldreher weighed about 164. Notre Dame had a big line, secondarily publicized as the Seven Mules, and it was this wall that took the brunt of Nevers' pounding and stood off Stanford sufficiently well so that the Horsemen could outslick the Warner entourage.

The game was billed as a contest of systems, the Rockne shift against the Warner double-wing, but it turned into a race. Notre Dame made only one march, scoring a touchdown on a three-yard slash by Layden over guard. However, Layden intercepted two passes for touchdowns, and Huntsinger, Notre Dame end, scooped up a fumbled punt and ran for a fourth touchdown. You could do that in those days.

There is some doubt that the Horsemen ensemble was Rockne's greatest team, though it was the most thoroughly publicized, particularly in the years following the graduation of its members. The name Rice thought of was the greatest factor. It was considered strictly left-wing to write a football story for ten years after the Horsemen without referring to them at least five times.

Notre Dame didn't make a perfect record again until 1929, when it won nine without losing or tying. The following year it won all ten of its games. That was Rockne's last season. He was killed in the crash of an airliner at Cottonwood Falls, Kansas, March 31, 1931.

In the realm of football he was the dominant figure of his day, a tactician who reached beyond his time, a psychologist and persuader of almost unparalleled ability.

Born in Voss, Norway, in 1888, he was brought to Chicago by his parents in 1893. He went to school there and enrolled at Notre Dame in 1911. He played four years at end on the Notre Dame team and excelled in pole vaulting as well. He was selected football coach in 1918. He attracted attention when his teams of 1919 and 1920 went through undefeated, scoring 626 points in 18 games to 68 for the opponents.

Following the great year of 1924, Notre Dame's fortune waned, reaching a low in 1928, when it lost four of nine. That was the year Rockne brought back the ghost of George Gipp to inspire his players to beat a favored Army team in Yankee Stadium. The story was that Rockne promised Gipp when the latter was dying, that someday he would ask a Notre Dame team which seemed down and out to rally and win one for him.

Well, this is the one they won for the Gipper, or so the story goes, 12 to 6. Jack Chevigny, who was killed leading a company of Marines on Iwo Jima, was the Gipper's principal executor, scoring one touchdown and getting the ball in position so that "One-play" O'Brien could score the other.

Getting back to our continuity and starting with the year 1925, where we dropped Red Grange safely into professional sport, it should be noted that the avidity of the nation for football was still keen. It was whipped to new frenzies in 1926 when Gene Tunney won the heavyweight championship from Jack Dempsey; Gertrude Ederle swam the English Channel; Bill Tilden got beaten by Rene Lacoste; Tris Speaker, George Sisler, and Eddie Collins were removed as baseball managers; Ty Cobb gave up the game; and Princeton and Harvard broke athletic relations, snooting each other fearsomely in the process. It was reported by one Harvard authority that Al Miller came out of the Princeton game with the imprint of a seal ring on his nose.

Dartmouth was the pride of the East in 1925. In 1924 it had gone unbeaten and stood with Penn, Yale, and Army as a leader of the section. Now Jesse Hawley's Indians established a strong claim to national leadership. They ran up 340 points to 29 for the opposition, in 8 games, and shocked the Big Ten out of its stuffy self-sufficiency by giving Chicago a frightful belting. Only Alabama, Michigan, Texas A. & M., and Washington compared with Dartmouth that year. Michigan and Texas A. & M. each lost a game on a field goal— the only points scored on the Wolverines all season.

Swede Oberlander, a tremendous passer and a stampeding runner, was the big man on that Dartmouth team. Dutch Diehl was possibly the best guard in the country, and Nate Parker was an outstanding tackle. Bob MacPhail did a fine job in filling in at quarterback for Eddie Dooley, who was writing poetry that season, and Tully and Sage were an inseparable couplet at the ends. Princeton this year had two of its ablest operatives of the modern era in Ed McMillan and Jake Slagle, and Colgate, led by one of its most famous backs, Captain Eddie Tryon, went through undefeated.

Navy was regarded by writers of the time as the best team of 1926, though it was tied by Army, 21-21, in Soldier Field, Chicago, before a crowd supposed to have comprised 110,000 people. The counters were pretty reckless in those days. Tom Hamilton played in the Navy backfield, and Frank Wickhorst was great stuff at tackle. Bill Ingram was serving his first year as head coach at Annapolis.

That was the year that Rockne decided to go and scout a future opponent the day Notre Dame was playing Carnegie Tech with its celebrated Howard Harpster. The result was a severe beating for the Irish. New York University, drilled by Chick Meehan in the military huddle and the unrelieved off-tackle play, was undefeated until its last game at Nebraska, where it took a lacing in a snowstorm.

The Brown Iron Men, a team that abjured substitutions in most of its major games, introduced Tuss McLaughry as a bigtime coach, he having moved from Amherst to take over what was generally supposed to be rag-tag material in Providence. This team won nine straight and was tied by Colgate, 10 to 10, on Thanksgiving Day, when Dave Mishel's attempted drop-kick for a game-winning field goal hit the crossbar. Lafayette, coached by Herb McCracken, was another fine team and defeated every opponent, scoring 327 points to 37, and Army lost only to Notre Dame.

The chroniclers of the era, mostly syndicated out of New York, seemed to think that Pittsburgh, Illinois, and Yale were the best teams of 1927. However, Stanford trimmed Captain Welch's Pittsburgh Panthers in the Rose Bowl on January 1, 1928, which introduced the possibility that Stanford, after all, might have been the best of them, and Texas A. & M. was unbeaten. Yale had three All-Americans in Dud Charlesworth, Bill Webster, and Sid Quarrier, and a famous pair of ends in Dwight Fishwick and Stu Scott. Bruce Caldwell, however, stole most of the headlines, particularly when he was dramatically barred on the eve of the Princeton game.

A renowned coach withdrew from the lists after the season. Tad Jones of Yale announced early in the Fall that he would retire at the end of the year, and did so. Chick Meehan, who had raised N.Y.U. to national prominence, said that he was considering laying down his portfolio. Ultimately he was re-engaged, but the rub between him and the athletic purists, who were attempting to reproduce Oxonian amateurism on the far-flung campi of the New York institution, was beginning to come into the open. Army and Navy broke off relations this year over a disagreement on eligibility rules.

We note, in a sum-up story about the 1928 season in which Boston College, Army, N.Y.U., Navy, Carnegie, and Penn were the strong teams of the East, that Ken Strong of N.Y.U. was the leading scorer in the country, with 160 points. That was just before he launched one of the longest professional football careers in the country. In 1947, the same Strong was a member of the New York Giant professional team, though used only as a specialty kicker. Boston College, under its new young coach, Joe McKenney, only a year out of school, beat every opponent.

Notre Dame was below its customary standard in 1928, but Rockne even then was making preparations for his two greatest seasons. Georgia Tech was invited to play in the Rose Bowl and won from California, 8 to 7. That was the game in which Roy Riegels, California center, ran the wrong way, sprinting nearly three-quarters the length of the field, to within six inches of his goal line, where he realized his mistake and was finally tackled by his teammate, Benny Lom. A blocked kick on the next play gave Georgia Tech a safety and ultimately the victory.

Knute Rockne, who had been ill off and on and more or less down from his pinnacle of football attainment in the years following 1924, came back to the wars in 1929 with a team that won nine straight. The Irish beat Army in Yankee Stadium on the coldest football day of this department's remembrance when Jack Elder intercepted a pass thrown by Army's celebrated Chris Cagle and ran the length of the field for the only touchdown of the game.

Pittsburgh, Colgate, and Fordham were the strong teams of the East. Donchess, Parkinson, Montgomery, and Uansa excelled for Jock Sutherland's Panthers. Macaluso, Orsi, Huntington, and Hart were Andy Kerr's chief executors at Colgate, and Tony Siano was captain of Fordham.

That year Albie Booth, Yale's Little Boy Blue, had a day of glory reminiscent of Grange's against Michigan when he came in the Bowl as a sophomore and scored three touchdowns to beat an Army team that was giving the sons of Eli a whaling. Later, Big Ben Ticknor, Harvard's all-America center, made the headlines by collaring the little gadfly in blue and all but jerking him out of his jersey.

This was the last tremendous year of sports until after the depression. The stock-market crash came in the Fall, and breadlines had been formed before the Notre Dame team of 1930 was called out for practice. This team won 10 straight and attracted as much attention as that of 1929, inasmuch as sports followers apparently prefer to give up necessities before amusements.

A high for attendance was set in 1929, but this was nothing unusual, for new figures were established each year throughout the era of wonderful nonsense. This was the first season that the defense was denied the privilege of running with the fumbled ball, and much talk was given off by the experts about the sanity of the rule.

The Western Conference convicted Iowa of making illegal arrangements with some of its best football players, and the Carnegie Foundation conducted an investigation which tended to prove that some of the colleges, including one or two of the more illustrious academic institutions, were hiring their players in one way or another.

With the collapse of business, the Golden Era of Football, or the one that preceded the one that started in 1946, was definitely over. The sag had commenced, though the big teams continued to draw full houses. Incidentally, football was more or less a minor sport in 1930 because Bobby Jones perpetrated his grand slam, winning the amateur and open golf championships of both the United States and Britain. It was Rockne's last year in football, and his team was up to the best he produced, particularly in its blocking, though it barely beat Army in Chicago—7 to 6—for one of its ten victories.

A retrospective glance at the decade brings into the sharpest focus Rockne, Grange, and the Four Horsemen. There were others who left their marks in football—Jock Sutherland, who launched his Pittsburgh football dynasty; Tad Jones, who resurrected Yale; Percy Haughton, who quit Harvard and made a reasonably spectacular comeback at Columbia, where he had an All-America back in Walter Koppisch; Gil Dobie, the dour man of Ithaca, and many players. These included the redoubtable Benny Friedman and Benny Oosterbaan of Michigan; Nevers, Bronk Nagurski, Wilbur Henry of W. & J.; Wes Fesler of Ohio State; Ed Weir of Nebraska; Jack Cannon of Notre Dame; Peter Pund of Georgia Tech; Herb Joesting of Minnesota; Johnny Mack Brown of Alabama; George Wilson of Washington; Joel Hunt of Texas A. & M.; Rags Matthews of Texas Christian; George Owen of Harvard; Light Horse Harry Wilson of Army; and Lynn Bomar of Vanderbilt.

In the late years of the decade the rules were changed to an approximation of what they are now, and the short-side attack was developed when coaches started to over-shift defenses to meet such maneuvers as the Rockne hop and the Dobie off-tackle play.

It was great stuff while it lasted, and, so help me, I think we're launching ourselves into a comparable sporting era.

FOOTBALL IN THE
MIDDLE WEST

by ARCH WARD
Sports Editor, Chicago Tribune

There was a Golden Age in Middle West football long before the terrific 1920's arrived with their superstadia and superheated press agents. Walter Eckersall of Chicago's Maroons had run his course as the most spectacular athlete under the aegis of that kindly sports despot, Amos Alonzo Stagg. Fielding H. (Hurry Up) Yost's point-a-minute Michigan elevens were in the gridiron history books. Chic Harley had finished his devastating career as the boldest of all the Buckeyes from Ohio State. And that great forward-passing combination from Notre Dame, Gus Dorais to Knute Rockne, long since had made its last dazzling pitch-and-catch play.

These spectacular characters were forerunners of tremendous things to come in the football palaces of the Midwest—an amazing crop of players, tacticians, and wonder teams. No other period is so rich, not only in the midlands, but in any other section of this broad land of ours. It was almost as if the gods of the gridiron had deposited all these performers between the Alleghenies and the Mississippi and said: "Here they are!" If this seems effervescent, forgive me. I was there.

When the 1920 season unfolded, giant stadia were rearing their steel and concrete contours high into the sky in the prairie cities and towns which were seats of the great universities. On these stages, Notre Dame would move into national dominance, Harold (Red) Grange, a darting redhead from Wheaton, a Chicago suburb, would electrify a sports-loving nation, and other schools in the Western Conference would have their sensational athletes.

That was the year of tragedy, too, when perhaps the greatest of them all, Notre Dame's George Gipp, died from an ailment contracted on the football field. There's a monument to this monumental athlete in his home town of Laurium, Michigan, built of boulders from the shores of Lake Superior and the copper-bearing formations from the mines of Calumet. It says simply:

GEORGE GIPP, All-American, 1895-1920.

How better to begin a saga of the Twenties than to dwell briefly on this incomparable athlete? Rockne saw him idling one afternoon, nonchalantly booting drop kicks farther and more accurately than his varsity boys kicked punts. In 1917 and 1918 he led the Irish to undefeated seasons, lifted them to national recognition with great victories over Army. He was the first Notre Dame player picked on a Walter Camp All-America team. That was in 1920, when George was on his deathbed and the news of his selection was still a cold mass of type in a magazine print shop. "That's jake," he said when told of the honor.

The Gipper played his final game against Northwestern in Evanston, and only the wild exhortations of fans and alumni broke Rockne's resolve to keep him on the bench. The previous week against Indiana at Indianapolis, Gipp had suffered a dislocated shoulder in the third period. Notre Dame had gone into the final quarter of that one behind, 10 to 0. Then the Irish scored and soon were on the one-yard line. His players were so excited and tense that the coaching master feared disaster. This was the spot for a steady, dependable clutch halfback who could be trusted to hold the ball. With his crushed shoulder heavily padded, Gipp went in, slashed off tackle, and nearly crashed through a fence at the end of the field for a 13-to-10 triumph.

Now they were playing Northwestern's Wildcats and far out in front. From the stands came the steady chant, rising in volume as the minutes ticked off: "We want Gipp!" George, disconsolate at inactivity, sat on the bench, covered with blankets and coats, his shoulder taped and bandaged. With only six minutes left, Rockne heeded the frenzied pleas. Gipp hurled six passes, one to Roger Kiley for 30 yards and another to Norm Barry for 45 and a touchdown.

The next day Gipp visited Loyola University on Chicago's north side, where Grover Malone, an old teammate, was coaching. He gave the players kicking and passing pointers. It was on this field that he contracted the throat ailment that was to prove fatal twelve days hence.

Gipp, a rangy athlete, weighed 175 pounds. He was a clever runner, great passer, and superlative punter. He was adept at faking plays. After taking the ball from center, he would grip it in his right hand, simulating throws until the defense started to run back to cover receivers. As soon as he saw an opening, he would tuck the ball under his arm and skirt end or drive off tackle. In the huddle he improvised plays which sometimes caused the great heart of his coach to skip a beat. But they usually clicked for long gains.

Rockne was only one of a great number of geniuses who left an imprint in these hectic Autumns. Illinois had its wily Bob Zuppke; Iowa, its Howard Jones; Chicago, its A. A. Stagg; Michigan, its Hurry Up Yost; Minnesota, its Dr. H. L. Williams; and Ohio State, its Dr. John Wilce. It is not provincialism to suggest that here was a concentration of coaching brains unequaled at any one time in any one section of the nation. The Big Four, of course, included Rockne, Stagg, Yost, and Zuppke. Here is a table of their all-time coaching records at their famous four schools:

	Won	Lost	Tied	Years
STAGG, Chicago	243	104	28	40
ZUPPKE, Illinois	141	81	12	29
YOST, Michigan	176	33	10	27
ROCKNE, Notre Dame	105	12	5	13
Totals	665	230	55	109

So here you have the backdrop of those exciting years when football was building up to its tremendous crowd appeal and giving college ticket managers the shakes as they opened all those stacks of envelopes.

Walter Camp, guiding genius of football in the years preceding the Big Boom, came West in 1920 to watch the Ohio State–Wisconsin game. Word finally had seeped through to the Atlantic seaboard that the sport was being played out in the great Midwest. He couldn't have chosen a more appropriate game. At the finish, Camp voted it the most exciting one he had seen in years, and those sixty minutes did much to impress him with the knowledge that here was a new, vital football territory.

In this contest, the Badgers rushed into a 7-to-0 lead, and that was the score with four minutes left. Then the Hoge Workman–Pete Stinchcomb forward-passing act jelled for the first time, and the Buckeyes had a touchdown. When the kick for the extra point was missed, the Badgers breathed easier. But not for long. With a minute left, Ohio State was on its own 20-yard line when a pass from Workman to Stinchcomb moved the ball to midfield. From the same formation, Stinch fielded another pass and raced 20 yards for the winning touchdown.

That was the year the Irish sped through their schedule without defeat, showing great offensive power. As a tribute to his skill, Rockne allowed Gipp to pass in his own territory, even with Notre Dame ahead or on even terms. He maintained that the passes were covered in such a manner that if intercepted they would serve the same purpose as a punt, with the added chance of gaining yardage. This, indeed, was daring thinking in those days. This was the season Rockne's forces whipped Army, 27 to 17, with Gipp at his best.

The Rockne coaching story was just opening to its brightest chapters for the Norwegian-born lad who had learned to love the game while playing with the Tricky Tigers in the Logan Square district of Chicago. It had been seven years since Knute, the end, and Dorais, the passer, had stunned the East with a 35-to-13 upset of the mighty West Point Cadets. That day Gus threw passes all over the field, and his associate caught many of them. After his graduation in 1914, Rock remained as an assistant coach. In 1918, he took over the top job while retaining his duties as a chemistry professor. As all football fans know, Rockne, while at his peak, died in an airplane crash on the Kansas plains, in 1931.

Rockne favored a system which stressed speed, power, shock, and the highest deception the sport had known to that time. It was frequently said of his teams that opponents half the time couldn't locate the ball. He was an expert on fundamentals, was close to his men, and gave personal attention to their physical welfare. He built up a strong football psychology, was a driver, but never abusive. Here was a man who could inspire his players and keep them tingling.

The wizard of Notre Dame had unbeaten elevens in 1919, 1920,

1924, 1929, and 1930, his final campaign. He opened up the game so that the spectators knew what was going on. He and his teams caught the fancy of the fans on the street, producing the largest group of synthetic alumni football has known.

On his deathbed, Gipp had whispered:

"I've got to go, Rock. It's all right. I'm not afraid. Sometime, Rock, when the team is up against it, when things go wrong and the breaks are beating the boys—tell them to go in there with all they've got and win just one for Gipp. I don't know where I'll be then, Rock. But I'll know about it and be happy."

Sure, it sounds like something out of a movie script. But it's so, the most dramatic true-to-life scene in football history.

Eight years later, Notre Dame was in the throes of its darkest season. Wisconsin had won a surprising victory in that drab '28 campaign. Georgia Tech had taken picks on the Irish the following Saturday. Now they were getting ready as best they could for the Army. It was just before this game that Rock called for a victory for the Gipper.

The result: a 12-to-6 triumph over the Cadets, the most tremendous upset of the season. Walter Eckersall, the referee, pronounced it the greatest demonstration of inspired football he had ever seen.

In 1921 the crush of fans was terrific and few stadia were adequate for the crowds. This was the glory year for Howard Jones and his Iowa Hawkeyes. This fine athlete from Yale had coached Ted Coy and fellow Elis in 1909. In 1910 he taught the game at Ohio State and returned to Yale in '14 after taking a vacation from the sport. That Fall, his Eastern forces had walloped Notre Dame, 28 to 0. He had gone out to Iowa in 1916, remaining for eight years for a record of 42 victories, 16 defeats, and one tie. His team of 1918 lost only to the wartime powerhouse at Great Lakes and to Illinois.

Led by Captain Aubrey Devine, Gordon Locke, and Duke Slater, giant Negro tackle, Iowa took the 1921 crown in the Big Ten, its first since 1900. But it reached the zenith with a 10-to-7 victory over Notre Dame, one of the unforgettable battles of this spectacular decade.

Iowa scored in the first half, sparked by the plunges of Locke and Devine's darts around the flanks. Locke was sprung loose by the gigantic Slater, who that day was playing against Heartly (Hunk)

Anderson, one of the Irish all-time guards. Time after time, Duke opened up the hole or secured just enough of a charge so that Locke could squeeze through for precious yards.

The Irish came right back with the tying touchdown when Johnny Mohardt flipped a long pass to Roger Kiley, who sprinted 30 yards. They struggled on almost to the point of exhaustion, with the Hawkeyes stopping one rally after another. Then Iowa somehow gathered enough strength for a final surge, which brought it close enough for Captain Devine, a great leader and versatile player, to kick the winning field goal.

Iowa's winning streak reached 20 games before it was stopped in the fourth contest of the 1923 season by Illinois, 9 to 6, and you may be certain Red Grange had a hand in that one. Jones, who later won fame at the University of Southern California, died in 1941 at the age of 55 after a rich contribution to intercollegiate athletics, stretching over twenty-nine years.

In 1921, the Midwest took four out of five from Eastern opponents. Chicago won at Princeton, 9 to 0, for the first victory of a Western eleven on the Tigers' home field. Notre Dame beat Army and Rutgers. Nebraska whipped Pittsburgh, 10 to 0, but Indiana cost its area a sweep by losing to Harvard, 19 to 0.

Seventy-two thousand slightly insane spectators greeted a new football era at Ohio State in 1922, when its handsome million-and-a-half-dollar stadium was packed to the brim for the traditional game against neighboring Michigan. Outside the vast structure fans were offering fabulous sums for tickets. This was gridiron hysteria at its wildest. The Wolverines won from the Buckeyes in that historic meeting, 19 to 0. They were led by Harry Kipke, who later was to succeed Yost as Michigan's coach.

But the greatest game that year was on Stagg Field, between the Old Man's Maroons and the Tigers from Princeton. As the final quarter opened, it was: Chicago 18, Princeton 7. Maroon partisans were preparing for another victory celebration and saw nothing of dire import in the three points after touchdowns which their favorites had flubbed.

Then Chicago fumbled, a Princeton player grabbed the ball and sped for a touchdown. The goal was kicked, and now it was 18 to 14. Both teams were dog tired but that unexpected break brought the

Tigers back to life. Finally, Crum blasted over for a touchdown, the kick was perfect, and Chicago trailed, 21 to 18.

Back roared the Maroons after the kickoff, with John Thomas, strong man of the backfield, straining every muscle for those vital yards. Now it was fourth down on Princeton's one-yard line and only seconds left. Thomas surged into a wave of defenders but could advance only one foot, and the game was over.

That was the year Howard Jones took Iowa East to down Yale, 6 to 0; when Army and Notre Dame dueled to a scoreless draw; and when Michigan and Iowa tied for the Western Conference title. Harry Kipke, who could sweep the ends, strike off tackle, execute passes with finesse, and punt beautifully, was the heart of the great Michigan squad. Illinois, always a troublemaker for contenders when not in the race itself, knocked out Wisconsin, 3 to 0, and had Iowa on the ropes, 7 to 6, when the Hawkeyes pulled it out on a safety. Captain Locke again was Iowa's tower of strength in the backfield, an end-running fullback who gathered speed quickly and also could batter a line. One of the grand upsets in 1923 was Nebraska's 14-to-7 thriller over Notre Dame.

Several new trends were apparent—a swing to rangy linemen, widening the base in the backfield from which plays radiated, swinging linemen out for interference as against the old close formation, and utilization of more players in the game. Also prominent was the substituting of specialists for kicks or long passes, and a more artful concealment of aerial plays. Brute strength was taking a back seat.

This was the year of Red Grange's first appearance on the gridiron stage. A total of 738,555 spectators were to see him dashing around and weaving his way past bewildered rivals in three seasons on the Illini's home grounds. Here was a two-threat man, passing and running, this Galloping Ghost who never was in focus long enough for opponents to learn for themselves whether his jersey number actually was 77. In 20 appearances with the Orange and Blue he scored 31 touchdowns, gained 3,637 yards, and completed 42 passes for 643 yards.

It was fitting and proper that Illinois' Memorial Stadium was opened in Grange's introductory varsity campaign. The opponent was Chicago, on October 20, 1923, with 60,232 folks present. And it was just as fitting and proper that a touchdown scored by the redhead was good for a 7-to-0 decision. Fullback Earl Britton and half-back McIlwain gave Grange wonderful blocking support to embark him on his dizzy scoring excursions. The Illini tied Michigan for the conference title with a string of shutouts over all opponents.

Memorial Stadium at Champaign-Urbana was formally dedicated in 1924 against Michigan, and those living among the 66,609 spectators never will forget that explosive afternoon. Grange fielded the opening kickoff and rambled 95 yards for a touchdown. Within twelve minutes he had barged into the Wolverines' end zone four times, all on long runs. He returned in the third period and scored again, besides pitching a touchdown pass. At game's end he had romped for 402 yards and passed for an additional 64 in a 39-to-14 rout.

At the same time, Stagg was in his thirty-third season at Chicago and the Old Man, who had come to the home of the Maroons in 1892, led the team to a championship with three victories and three ties. The Maroons' hero was little Bob Curley, son of a famous Hearst editor, whose field goals beat Northwestern and Ohio State. A loss to Minnesota eliminated Grange and his Illinois colleagues. This is as good a time as any to report that the mild and high-minded Stagg never uttered a stronger expletive than "Jackass" to an erring player, unless it was "Double Jackass," just for emphasis.

This, too, was the climactic year of Notre Dame's Four Horsemen —Harry Stuhldreher, Jim Crowley, Don Miller, and Elmer Layden —the most storied backfield in all football history. The Irish downed every team they met from coast to coast and nailed down their first solid claim to a national college championship.

They weren't giants—this foursome—but they were fast, smart, and tricky. All went on to the heights after graduation. Stuhldreher, Layden, and Crowley became famous coaches and sports executives, while Miller won signal success as a lawyer. In that final year at South Bend, Notre Dame bowled over Army, 13 to 7; Princeton, 12 to 0; Georgia Tech, 34 to 3; Wisconsin, 38 to 3; Nebraska, 34 to 6, and had a narrow squeak with Northwestern, 13 to 6. The Wildcats had little to offer except Ralph (Moon) Baker, who wasn't far behind Grange. The Irish wound up their glory season by whipping Stanford in the Rose Bowl on New Year's Day of 1925 by a 27-to-10 count.

Yost called his 1925 team the "greatest I have ever seen in action." That is a broad statement, considering the almost unbelievable scoring power of his juggernauts of the early 1900's. His point-a-minute teams of 1901, '02, '03, '04, '05 had won 55 games, tied one and lost one! They had scored 2,821 points to 42! The spell had been broken in the last game of 1905 when Chicago won, 2 to 0.

Old Hurry Up had been among the first to stress the pass. Of his famous plays, Old 83 held front rank. This was a hidden-ball beauty in which the power was thrown to the right side of the line while the Michigan quarterback held the ball out of sight of his opponents. After the play apparently was stopped, the quarterback passed the ball rearward to a halfback who ran around left end. With variations it was used sucessfully for more than thirty seasons.

This 1925 Michigan eleven was fortified in every department of play, but it took a sportsmanlike gesture from Northwestern to clear its way to a Big Ten title.

A week before the Wolverines and Wildcats were scheduled to take the field, few gave Northwestern a chance. Then the elements intervened. It rained all night before they were to battle it out on Chicago's Soldier Field. At kickoff time, the downpour was continuing and it never let up. With puddles of water covering the field, open tactics were impossible. Early in the struggle, Northwestern's Tiny Lewis propelled the waterlogged football with his toe for three points.

After the Wildcats had grimly held for downs on their five-yard line, they gave the Wolverines a safety, and that was the ball game —a 3-to-2 upset Northwestern triumph. The victorious team's adherents claimed a tie for the championship. But in the midst of these claims, Northwestern's athletic officials declared the title rightfully belonged to Michigan—that on a dry field the result would have been reversed. In the season Michigan had won five and lost one, Northwestern three and one.

The celebrated Grange was still running for the Illini, and this was the year of his biggest collegiate thrill—the 24-to-2 victory over mighty Pennsylvania at Philadelphia. Illinois was out of the Big Ten race, and Zuppke had pointed his team for this Eastern invasion. Penn had already sideswiped Brown, Yale, and Chicago.

Years later, Grange credited the crafty Zuppke for the upset.

"In all our games," said Red, "I always had run toward the strong side, that is, behind the strongest side of our unbalanced line. Penn scouts noted this, and our operatives advised us that the Quakers were prone to overshift in meeting an unbalanced line. So Zup told me to run toward the short side of our line. I was giving the signals that day, too. I called for an unbalanced line and, sure enough, our opponents overshifted. Bob Reitsch, the center, passed the ball to me. I hesitated until my interference came around, then I ran inside Penn's left tackle. The boys cleaned out a path beyond the scrimmage line and I kept going until reaching the goal line, 55 yards away."

Red scored three times in gaining 360 yards and also completed one pass for 13 yards.

An anonymous statistician has figured that in Red's 232 games as a prep, college, and pro star, he gained 32,820 yards, equivalent to 18.6 miles, scored 531 touchdowns, and carried the ball 4,013 times for a lifetime average of better than 8.1. And he was an uncanny defender against passes, this son of a small-town police chief.

That Fall, Notre Dame traveled the rocky road—for Notre Dame —losing to Army, 27 to 0; Nebraska, 17 to 0; and getting only a scoreless deadlock with Penn State.

With such greats as Benny Friedman and Benny Oosterbaan, Michigan came back in 1926 to tie Northwestern for the Big Ten title, each boasting unbeaten records in its own competition. But Notre Dame edged out Northwestern, 6 to 0, and the Wolverines fell before Navy, 10 to 0.

Notre Dame had another characteristically strong eleven, but met defeat when Rockne, the guiding genius, was elsewhere. The meeting with Carnegie Tech was not taken too seriously, and the Rock wanted to see a game on the same afternoon in Soldier Field between Army and Navy, two of his favorite playmates. So while Knute watched this one, his Irish took a 19-to-0 shellacking from the Pennsylvania eleven. The next week, Notre Dame nosed out Southern California, 13 to 12. This was the year that Northwestern, led by Moon Baker, an All-America back, began operating in Dyche Stadium, which seated 47,000.

Before the Carnegie Tech shock, the Irish had taken the measure of Army, 7 to 0, on Christy Flanagan's 63-yard run. They also whipped two other conference teams, Minnesota and Indiana.

Perhaps the most powerful runner in the Midwest that season was Herb Joesting, one of a long line of outstanding Minnesota full-backs. The Gophers gave Michigan one of its two scares. They looked like certain winners until Oosterbaan recovered a fumble late in the game and scampered 50 yards for a score, with Captain Friedman kicking the goal. The other close one was a 13-to-12 decision over Ohio State.

The mighty Joesting and his backfield buddy, Shorty Almquist, were the headline hunters of the 1927 campaign. Both the Gophers and Illinois were undefeated. Zuppke's stalwarts won from North-western, Michigan, Iowa, Chicago, and Ohio State, but were held to a tie by Iowa State outside the conference. The Golden Gophers were handcuffed into a deadlock by Indiana but took decisions over Wisconsin, Iowa, and Michigan.

Minnesota, with the fabulous Bronko Nagurski making his debut, had perhaps its best eleven since 1919, and Clarence W. (Doc) Spears, the Gophers' expansive coach, was unable to account for that tie with Indiana. The Gophers walloped Iowa, 38 to 0, and nailed down identical 13-to-7 verdicts over Wisconsin and Michigan, even though the Wolverines were very stubborn, holding a 7-to-0 half-time edge. Then Joesting and Almquist darted off tackles for gains which put Minnesota close, whereupon aerial attacks did the business for two straight touchdowns. Nagurski went on to win a place among the all-time immortals, getting All-America recognition as both tackle and fullback.

Old Zup had a well-balanced team, well drilled in all the funda-mentals and with plays well adapted to his players. The consensus was that the Orange and Blue was deserving of a championship edge over Minnesota. Illinois' toughest victory was over Northwestern, 7 to 6. The Wildcats were first to tally but missed the extra point. Then the Illini marched 72 yards with runs and passes and kicked the decisive point.

Notre Dame split with the service teams, shellacking Navy, 19 to 6, but absorbing an 18-to-0 crusher from the Army.

The year 1928 saw Illinois' banner waving majestically at the top of the conference. And for the first time in years, Rockne's Irish had no claim on the Midwestern championship. Notre Dame had a dismal time of it, losing to Wisconsin, 22 to 6; Georgia Tech, 13 to 0; and to Navy, 7 to 0. That season marked the passing of Coach Wilce at Ohio State, a gentleman who had brought signal success to the Buckeyes.

Chicago's Maroons were on the way down as de-emphasis started taking its toll. Time was running out for Stagg too. The conference crown was determined on the final day in as zestful a race as the Big Ten had experienced. They came up to the final afternoon with Illinois, Wisconsin, Ohio State, and Iowa still having a chance. The Badgers were unbeaten but had been tied by Purdue. Illinois had lost to Michigan, 3 to 0. Ohio State had submitted to Iowa, 14 to 7, and the Hawkeyes had fallen before Minnesota, 13 to 0.

The Badgers needed only a tie or victory over the Gophers, who failed to co-operate and scored a 6-to-0 upset. Michigan, thrice beaten in the circuit, straight-armed Iowa, 10 to 7. The Illini took the title by dropping Ohio State, 8 to 0.

It was a season of closely contested battles, and there was no truer pattern than Iowa's 7-to-6 victory over Minnesota. There was no score until the fourth quarter, when Minnesota's Hovde dashed back for a punt which had sailed over his head, picked it up on the 8, and raced for a touchdown. The kick for the point was missed.

Shortly thereafter, Coach Burt Ingwersen of the Hawkeyes invited a fleet halfback, Pape, into the contest, with the Gophers' goal 42 yards away. He thereupon broke loose over guard and sprinted for a touchdown. Nelson, a goal-kicking specialist, hammered home the winning point.

When the last year of the Golden Decade came up for decision, Rockne's pupils were spreading his gridiron gospel from coast to coast. One of the most gifted was Jimmy Phelan, a sharp-witted Irishman who brought Purdue's Boilermakers into the limelight in 1929. Eight straight victories added up to a Western Conference flag and more than a press agent's claim to the mythical national championship.

Phelan had Ralph (Pest) Welch and Glen Harmeson as spark plugs of a great backfield, not to mention Fullback Yunevich, who was every bit as tough as his name sounds. It was he who blocked for those hell-for-leather backs. Michigan crumbled, 30 to 16; Chicago was routed, 26 to o; Wisconsin took a 13-to-o whitewashing; Iowa fell, 7 to o; and Indiana was soundly thrashed for the Old Oaken Bucket, 32 to o.

Rockne was ill most of the season, but one of his bright men, Tom Lieb, line coach at Wisconsin the preceding Autumn, filled in admirably. While Knute was treated for a leg ailment at Mayo Brothers, the Irish went on their triumphant way with victories over Indiana, Navy, Wisconsin, Carnegie Tech, Georgia Tech, Drake, Southern California, Northwestern, and Army.

Notre Dame introduced new gridiron strategy by opening up with "shock troops." This was a combination of a second-string backfield and first-string line. Up front were such as Captain Johnny Law, Jack Cannon, Tim Moynihan, and Ted Twomey. Of more than a little help to the Notre Dame cause were fleet Jack Elder and Marty Brill in the backfield. A reserve fullback was Jumpin' Joe Savoldi, who later was to bring joy to Rockne and Irish adherents.

Ten golden, glorious years! Midwestern football had surged to the forefront, a measuring stick for true greatness on the gridiron. What a parade of players on the field and brilliant masterminds roaming up and down the sidelines while mass hysteria reigned from bottom to upper tier among the fanatics!

FOOTBALL IN THE
SOUTHWEST

by WELDON HART
Sports Editor, Austin American-Statesman

Southwestern football, which flexed its growing muscles in relative privacy until well after World War I, suddenly thrust itself upon the outside world with a burst of brash exhibitionism on October 6, 1928.

It is possible to be specific about the time, and about the place, which was the hallowed plains of West Point. That was the afternoon Christian Keener Cagle and his Army mates found themselves in unexpectedly deadly combat with Southern Methodist University's "Flying Circus."

Army won the ball game, 14-13, but not before a bewildering diversity of forward passes and single, double, and triple laterals had "made the hair stand straight up on the heads of 1,200 frantic cadets," as one chronicler put it.

"Passes such as Eastern football never saw before flew from the hand of Redman Hume, a Texas version of what Red Grange should have been," he further declared, with the sanction of the staid Associated Press.

The game ended with a heart-wrenching fillip when S.M.U.'s Sammy Reed caught a pass in the clear but fell on his face, exhausted, on Army's 16-yard line. Texans culled some satisfaction out of the fact that the winning extra points had been kicked by an old Dallas boy, Bud Sprague, a former University of Texas tackle.

Until the Mustangs swept up from Texas with their "razzle-dazzle" attack, their bright red and blue uniforms, and their prancing, tootling jazz band that was eternally promising to come fully loaded with Peruna, the elite East and the hard-bitten North hadn't paid much mind to Southwest football. A preliminary flash of enlightenment had come late the preceding season when four ignited Texans ran amuck in one of the early East-West games. For that performance the names of Gerald Mann of S.M.U., Joel Hunt and J. V. Sikes of Texas A. & M., and Raymond (Rags) Matthews of T.C.U. had been briefly in the spotlight, and the attending sports writers belatedly labeled Hunt the "Forgotten All-American."

Of scarcely more than regional prominence, however, had been still-great Southwest football names like Carl Reynolds of Southwestern, Puny and Mule Wilson of A. & M., Oscar Eckhardt and Hook McCullough of Texas, Logan Stollenwerck and Gene Bedford of S.M.U., the Underwoods of Rice, Jack Mahan of A. & M., Herman Clark of T.C.U., and Rusty Blailock of Baylor. These worthies and their cohorts committed aggravated assault on one another, Autumn after Autumn, with few persons the wiser outside the Lone Star State.

For development of a certain attack-mindedness that eventually turned national attention on the section, contemporaries credit wily Frank Bridges, who tutored championship teams at Baylor in 1922 and 1924. Bridges was forever trying something new and tricky; he pioneered the return kick, the quick kick, the tackle around, and other innovations or revivals of the era.

Some prominence was becoming attached to the classical name of bull-voiced Dana Xenophon Bible, who had hard-running championship teams at Texas A. & M. in 1921, 1925, and 1927 (likewise 1917 and 1919).

But the one man most responsible for putting more eyes than those of Texas on Texas football was Ray Morrison of Southern Methodist.

In the chest of this scholarly-looking ex-Vanderbilt quarterback there beat the heart of a football adventurer. He was a gridiron dreamer, schemer, and innovator—the first coach in the Southwest, and one of the first in the land to use the forward pass as a basic weapon of attack.

Morrison's championship team of 1923, with Stollenwerck throwing to ends Gene Bedford and Jimmie Stewart, was the pilot outfit. Jerry Mann, in 1926 and 1927, offered further refinements, and the rest of the conference was a long time catching up in the aerial department.

The Southwest Conference's greatest player of the Twenties (and some say of all time) was not, however, a Morrison protégé. S.M.U.

had its greats in that decade, and so did the others, but the name of Joel Hunt led all the rest.

Hunt came to Texas A. & M. in 1924 from Waco, where he'd been a one-year high-school sensation on a team that scored 636 points to opponents' 3. Aggie coaches took Hunt's arrival with notable self-possession. He was a good high-school boy but too small to draw a freshman uniform. He finally got one when Blackie Williams, a big tackle, quit the squad and went to Texas Christian. Three years later, they were to meet as captains of their teams, which played a memorable 0-0 tie.

When halfback Taro Kishi hurt his shoulder in the first game of 1925, the 145-pound sophomore Hunt went in. During the next three seasons he rarely came out, except for meals and the Summer vacation. He was all-conference three years in a row, and two of these were championship years. The first was 1925. Fay (Mule) Wilson, a great fullback, was captain of that team. Ox Dietrich at tackle, Norman Dansby at guard, and little Bob Berry at quarterback were some of Bible's best boys.

The 1926 season wasn't a bright one for A. & M., but Hunt continued to develop. His weight went up to 155. Bible put him in charge of the team on the field. As a sample of his versatility, against T.C.U. he scored a touchdown, kicked the extra point, place-kicked a field goal, and finally notched a 46-yard drop kick to deadlock the game, 13-13.

Hunt really blossomed out in 1927. Grown up to 168 pounds, he scored 128 points—high in the conference and second in the nation. He did all of A. & M.'s punting, passing, place-kicking, and drop-kicking; he kicked off, ran with the ball three out of five times, called signals, was captain of the team—and played all except three minutes of the schedule.

A game-breaking 97-yard kickoff return against Arkansas was Hunt's most spectacular single feat that year. But his big day was against defending champion S.M.U.

Piloted by the great Jerry Mann and accompanied by trainloads of confident fans, the Mustangs invaded College Station as heavy favorites. The score was 39-13 for A. & M. Hunt directed his team to touchdowns on all six scoring opportunities, scored three times himself, passed for two touchdowns, and punted eight times for an

LOU GEHRIG AND BABE RUTH

GENE TUNNEY AND JACK DEMPSEY BEFORE THEIR FIRST FIGHT

TUNNEY DOWN FOR THE "LONG COUNT" IN THE DEMPSEY FIGHT AT
CHICAGO IN 1927. THE REFEREE IS DAVE BARRY

A HIGHLIGHT OF BOXING'S GOLDEN AGE: DEMPSEY TUMBLING INTO THE
WORKING PRESS ROW AFTER BEING HIT BY FIRPO

MAN O'WAR, CLARENCE KUMMER UP

EARL SANDE AFTER RIDING ZEV TO VICTORY OVER PAPYRUS
IN FAMOUS MATCH RACE

NOTRE DAME'S FAMOUS "FOUR HORSEMEN" AT A REUNION IN CLEVELAND IN 1942. LEFT

Photo by The New York Times

KNUTE ROCKNE

Photo by The New York Times

RED GRANGE

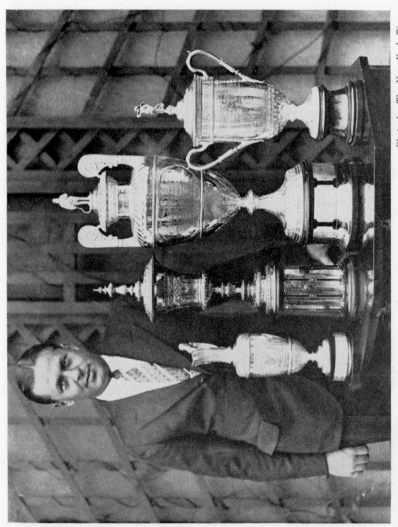

Photo by The New York Times

GENE SARAZEN

Photo by The New York Times

WALTER HAGEN, AFTER RECEIVING THE BRITISH OPEN
TROPHY FROM THE PRINCE OF WALES IN 1928

BILL TILDEN AND BILL JOHNSTON

Press Association, Inc.

HELEN WILLS

Photo by The New York Times

MLLE. SUZANNE LENGLEN

TOMMY HITCHCOCK

PAAVO NURMI

WILLIE
HOPPE

*Photo by The
New York Times*

Press Association, Inc.

RALPH GREENLEAF

JOHNNY
WEISSMULLER

*Photo by The
New York Times*

Photo by The New York Times

GERTRUDE EDERLE BEING WELCOMED IN NEW YORK AFTER HER
SUCCESSFUL CONQUEST OF THE ENGLISH CHANNEL

BASKETBALL'S FAMOUS ORIGINAL CELTICS. LEFT TO RIGHT: JOE LAPCHICK, CHRIS LEONARD, DUTCH DEHNERT, PETE BARRY, NAT HOLMAN, JOHNNY WITTE, JOHNNY BECKMAN AND ERNIE RIPLEY.

average of 44 yards without any punt being returned so much as a foot.

A flaming competitive spirit drove Joel Hunt to greatness, but he was a natural player as well. Football was easy for him. He liked practice, loved scrimmage, looked forward to games with real zest. And his never-flagging zeal carried others to heights with him. He possessed a congenital elusiveness that led a contemporary to muse: "He ain't so fast, but you couldn't catch him in a telephone booth."

The only man who had the Indian sign on Hunt was Rags Matthews. During their three years of battling, Hunt's Aggies never defeated Matthews' Horned Frogs. There was one T.C.U. victory and two ties.

In the 1927 game, A. & M. made a first down a yard or two from a touchdown. Matthews helped rack up Aggie ball carriers on three straight plays. On fourth down Hunt called his own signal and made up what the others had lost. The game ended scoreless.

Matthews was a smashing, slashing, laughing end with a great nose for the ball. He loved to taunt the opposition, invite them with gestures to "run it around this way." Coach Matty Bell didn't think much of that and tried to discourage it but found Rags couldn't play without talking. It was as natural for him to pass pleasantries with the other side as it was for him to throw his six-foot-one, 185-pound frame into the thick of every scrimmage.

In Matthews' first season, Bell played him at guard alongside Bear Wolf, an earnest workman who thrived on a different brand of inspiration. Said Coach Bell: "I'd look out, and there'd be Matthews laughing and Wolf crying, and both playing fine football."

There is little or no argument against the flat statement that Rags Matthews was the toughest defensive end in Southwest Conference history. Most quarterbacks tried to keep the ball away from him. Mann of S.M.U. had a contrasting theory. He always figured it was better to run at Matthews, because then at least there'd be someone assigned to block him. If the play went another way, Matthews was so smart and fast he'd likely wind up in the middle of it. He could play off blockers as well as crash, and he was a capable pass receiver.

Matthews didn't play on a championship team; Texas Christian didn't win its first title until 1929 under Francis Schmidt, with quarterback Howard Grubbs, tackle Mike Brumbelow, center Noble Atkins, and the flying halfback Cy Leland, in the saddle.

Jerry Mann managed to sandwich a winning year, 1926, between two Hunt-inspired all-Aggie seasons. As a sophomore, the year before, he stamped himself a comer. He started out running interference for Chris Cortemeglia, a burly fullback. Ray Morrison tossed him in at quarterback against Texas, and he staved off a threatened defeat, got a tie for S.M.U.

Fatherly Coach Morrison saw "the Little Red Arrow" was headed for the headlines. He sat down that night and wrote Mann a six-page letter urging him not to let football fame change him from the quiet, modest youngster he was.

The Little Red Arrow never had to buy a bigger hat. His coach never heard him use an oath. Mann once instructed Cortemeglia to step over and call some rough-playing opponents "what they are. . . . I can't use the proper language," he explained. The story stops there, but presumably rugged Chris carried out one of the most unusual orders a quarterback ever handed down.

Mann's best show that first year was in the Baylor game, when he sprinted through the whole team five times. Each time, though, the Bear safety, Bennie Strickland, ran him down.

S.M.U.'s championship team of 1926 must have set some sort of record for tenacity and mental stamina. It came from behind in every conference game to win. Mann's inspiring example and his disinclination to believe any game lost until the final whistle were largely responsible for the Mustangs' amazing rallies.

These were typical scores: S.M.U., 9, A. & M., 7; S.M.U., 21, Texas, 17; S.M.U., 14, T.C.U., 13. In the Aggie game, the Mustangs were backed against their own goal with the score 7-6 against them. Mann faked a punt and passed down the middle to Cortemeglia, and this daring maneuver sparked a fourth-quarter drive that the Aggies finally halted. On fourth down, from a difficult angle, Mann kicked the winning field goal—the only field goal he ever attempted.

Texas had S.M.U. down, 17-0, at one time and 17-7 in the last quarter when Mann passed to Ross Love for a second S.M.U. touchdown. Figuring the Longhorns wouldn't pass with a three-point lead and only a few plays left, Mann came charging up from defensive right halfback just in time to scoop up a Texas fumble and race for a touchdown that won the game, 21-17. Texas fans were left to wonder forever and a day how he happened to be across the line of scrimmage on that play.

In the last game of the year, with the championship up, S.M.U. trailed T.C.U., 13-7, late in the last quarter. Boring into a terrific headwind from his own 35, Mann passed over the safety's head to Co-captain Stanley Dawson, who went to the one. S.M.U. scored on the next play, and Mann kicked the winning point.

In addition to his individual passing and ball-carrying—he worked indefatigably at two things, his throwing and his starts—Mann was one of the shrewdest signal callers this section has produced. He never weighed more than 157 pounds, thus being another of the many little men who have played big in the Southwest Conference.

The three immortals of the Golden Age's Texas heyday—1925-27 —finally got on the same team at San Francisco, December 26, 1927. Along with Siki Sikes, the Aggie end, Hunt, Mann, and Matthews became the first Southwestern players to participate in an East-West game.

The East had Bruce Caldwell of Yale, Herb Joesting of Minnesota, and Glen Presnell of Nebraska, and was a heavy favorite on soggy turf. On the first scrimmage play, the East fumbled on its 19 and Rags Matthews pounced on the ball. A moment later, Hunt was slashing over the goal on a 12-yard cutback.

The West's margin climbed to 9-0 in the second quarter when Matthews and a teammate nabbed an Easterner for a safety. At this stage, Mann entered the game, helped carry the ball to the East 18, and then caught a sideline pass for a touchdown. Half-time score: 16-0. Final score: 16-6.

The middle years of the decade produced other fine backs in the Southwest Conference. Besides Hume of S.M.U. and Clark of T.C.U., already mentioned, there were Mack Saxon of Texas, a mighty linebacker and plunger, and George Cole of Arkansas, a stocky 158-pound speedster with an educated toe. Homer Hazel, the old Rutgers All-American, called Cole the greatest halfback in the South after he ran over Hazel's Ole Miss team in 1926. In 1925, Cole kicked seven field goals, including three against Oklahoma A. & M., in a 9-7 victory. His best year, however, was 1927, when he ran, passed, and punted in top-shelf style, scored 22 points against a respected L.S.U. team, and wound up in the all-conference back-field with Mann, Hunt, and Hume.

The early Twenties are remembered best for dramatic moments in which D. X. Bible's Aggie teams figured. Bible had come back from the air corps in 1919 to find almost intact his undefeated, unscored-on team of 1917. They continued a perfect record through that season, and down to the final game of 1920.

That game was with the University of Texas at Austin, also undefeated but an underdog before A. & M.'s impressive lineup and 287-0 total score for the season. The going was slow, but Bugs Morris kicked a field goal and the champs were riding out a 3-0 decision when fourth-quarter lightning struck. Texas' Tom Dennis, on a "tackle eligible" play, made an unbelievable leaping catch of a pass near the Aggie goal. To Coach Barry Whitaker of Texas it always seemed Tom fairly hovered in the air, waiting for the ball to arrive.

Francisco Domingues, a substitute fullback, bucked the ball across and, for the first time in their collegiate careers, famous Aggies like Big Jack Mahan—Olympic javelin tosser, fleet Roswell Higginbotham, fiery Puny Wilson, and the fine guard, Cap Murrah—stood with their backs against their own goal posts and watched an extrapoint kick float over the bar.

That 7-3 victory gave Texas its first conference title. Quarterback Grady (Rats) Watson, end Hook McCullough, and center Swede Swenson, along with Dennis, were stars of that team. The Longhorns were not to win the title again until 1928, when Clyde Littlefield's team, powered by Rufus King and Dexter Shelley and having the colorful Gordy Brown at tackle, rumbled home ahead in spite of a 6-2 defeat by S.M.U.

Texas A. & M. came back in 1921, led by Murrah, Wilson, and halfback Sam Sanders, for Bible's third championship. This Aggie team scored an unexpected victory in a postseason game at Dallas that was the predecessor of the modern Cotton Bowl.

Little Centre College was the victim. Undefeated, and a widely heralded conqueror of mighty Harvard, Centre was a 20-point favorite. Two All-Americans from Texas, quarterback Bo McMillin and end Red Roberts, were in the lineup.

On the morning of the game, the entire Centre squad went over to Fort Worth for the wedding of McMillin and his hometown sweetheart. After a leisurely wedding breakfast, the Praying Colonels motored back to Dallas, took the field, and almost immediately found themselves trailing, 2-0, when Puny Wilson threw one of their backs for a safety.

Centre forged ahead briefly in the third period, but A. & M. came back with a scoring pass, racked up another touchdown, and finally intercepted one of McMillin's desperate heaves for the clincher. It wound up 22-14 and, as the Colonels left the field, to an anonymous reporter of the conflict, "they presented a rather jaded and dejected appearance."

Sanders, Murrah, and Wilson were the Aggie stars, but a lad who didn't even get in the game received more lasting recognition. As injuries began taking a heavy toll, Bible remembered that a substitute back named King Gill was in the crowd. Gill hadn't made the traveling squad, but now Bible called him out of the stands and bade him put on a uniform. And that was the origin of A. & M.'s famous "Twelfth Man" tradition, which implies that if the Aggies on the field can't make it, somebody will climb out of the grandstand and help them.

The 1922 Aggies, while losing the championship to Baylor in a 13-7 game (Baylor's first conference victory over A. & M.), had the satisfaction of winning their first game from Texas at Austin. Texas returned the favor in 1923 by winning its first game on Kyle Field (and its last for eighteen years). In 1924 was launched Texas' valued "Memorial Stadium tradition" of superiority over A. & M. that not even such distinguished Aggies as Joel Hunt, Dick Todd, and John Kimbrough could dint down through the years.

Baylor's title-winning 1922 team had fleet Wesley Bradshaw as quarterback and captain, John Tanner as a ripping fullback, Guy (Cop) Weathers at guard, and a pair of big ball-carrying tackles, Russell Blailock and Roy (Country) Williamson. In 1924, when the Bears and Bridges won again, the stars were Captain Ralph Pittman at halfback, William Coffey at quarterback, Bear Walker at center, Jack Sisco at guard, and Sam Coates at tackle.

The "uncrowned champions" of this early era—in the minds of balding University of Texas grads—was the Texas team of 1923, which went through unbeaten but was tied by Baylor. S.M.U., which didn't meet Texas that year, licked Baylor, 16-0, and was awarded the title at a conference meeting in Dallas. Die-hard Longhorn fans still scoff bitterly at S.M.U.'s "Oriental Hotel champions."

Powerhouse of the 1923 Longhorns was a rangy, rawboned, 190-pound speedster with a great stiff-arm, by name Oscar Eckhardt. He was to earn a reputation as a fine minor league hitter. Eckhardt ranks with the best running backs of the Southwest, and some say he was the best. The story is still told of his gaudy day against Vanderbilt, when he repeatedly circled All-America end, Bomar, and led Texas to a 16-0 triumph.

There are many more remembered and revered names on the dusty record books around the Southwest Conference—names such as Bull Johnson, Aggie guard; Smack Reisor, S.M.U. fullback; Bennie Winkelman, Arkansas fullback; Eddie Dyer, Rice halfback; Ed Bluestein, Texas tackle; John Mac Brooks, S.M.U. guard; Buddy King, S.M.U. center; Ox Higgins, Texas tackle; Babe Watts, A. & M. center; Glen Rose, Arkansas end; W. S. Lister and A. C. Sprott, A. & M. tackles; Ike Sewell, Texas guard; Nig Bralley, Texas center; Jake Williams, T.C.U. tackle; Weldon (Speedy) Mason, S.M.U. back, and three of the conference's first widely recognized All-Americans: Wear Schoonover, Arkansas' superb end of 1929; Choc Saunders, S.M.U. guard of the same period; and Bochey Koch, Baylor guard, who didn't reach his peak until 1930.

As for the best teams, it depends on the class and the school of the selector. Probably the favorite is A. & M. of 1927. One will find loud support for S.M.U. of 1926 and '23, Baylor of 1922, and Texas of 1920 and '23.

For the smaller colleges, the 1920-29 period was one of transition from the old Texas Intercollegiate Athletic Association to their modern alignments. At one time or another, the T.I.A.A. fathered nearly all the colleges in Texas, including those that formed the Southwest Conference in 1915 and later. T.C.U., for example, was in the T.I.A.A. as late as 1922. It was always an unwieldy organization because of its large membership, and it was finally drained to death by the formation of first the Texas Conference and finally the Lone Star Conference.

Texas Tech, later to rank right along with the best in the section, was just getting started in the late 1920's. One of Tech's first major stars was a flashy halfback, Ransome Walker.

Howard Payne College was a consistent power in the Twenties, enjoying the best ten-year record among the smaller schools. The 1924 team, under "Dad" Amis, great Georgia Tech center, was perhaps the best of the decade. Other standout teams included: North

Texas Teachers of 1920; Southwest Texas Teachers of 1921, 1926, and 1929, coached by O. W. Strahan; Barry Holton's Trinity team of 1925; St. Edward's, under Jack Meagher, in 1927; Lefty Edens' Southwestern eleven of the same year, and McMurry, coached by R. M. Medley, in 1927 and 1929.

Making Howard Payne tick in its big seasons was Joe Bailey Cheaney, a low-slung 160-pound ball of fire. Cheaney was fast enough to tie Charley Paddock's then world record of 10.2 seconds in the 100-meter dash at the Olympic tryouts in 1924. That Fall was his senior and best season at Howard Payne, which he brought to a proper climax against Simmons College (now Hardin-Simmons) by running the kickoff back 105 yards. In 1922 he beat D. X. Bible's Texas Aggies with a 68-yard sprint on a pass play.

A scourge to fleet safety men like Cheaney was a grinning, vicious Southwestern University end, Carl Reynolds. Big and fast, he was one of the most versatile athletes ever to attend a Texas college. He was a star in football, basketball, track, and baseball, and he later became a well-known major league outfielder.

A veteran observer of the Texas "minor college" scene recently selected this all-star team for the 1920-29 period: Cheaney and Nig McCarver of Howard Payne, Lyons McCall of Southwest Texas Teachers, and Ted Wright of North Texas Teachers, backs; Wright of Howard Payne, center; Lou Hertenberger, St. Edward's, and Boggs, Trinity, guards; Ed Kallina, Southwest Texas Teachers, and Dell Morgan, Austin College, tackles; Williams, North Texas State, and Reynolds, Southwestern, ends.

FOOTBALL IN THE SOUTH

by FRED RUSSELL
Sports Editor, The Nashville Banner

That college football in the South was entering a flourishing stretch was evident as early as 1920. As the fires of World War I embered into ashes, veterans returned to swell university enrollments—and varsity squads—to new highs. Schools that had abandoned football resumed the sport on a scale bigger than ever. It was the beginning of the most colorful and lively gridiron period Dixie had known.

Reported H. J. Stegeman, of the University of Georgia, in Spalding's Football Guide: "The 1920 season was without doubt the greatest that this section of the country has ever enjoyed. Interest in the sport, as shown by the crowds that attended the games, was greater than ever before."

It was an era of stadium building, of replacing wooden stands and roped-off playing fields with large concrete structures. In Atlanta, Georgia Tech enlarged its Grant Field to seat 25,000. Vanderbilt was soon to follow with a horseshoe holding 20,000. From Virginia to the Gulf Coast, architects, engineers, contractors, and the steel and sand and gravel and cement people became highly conscious of the new business possibilities in college athletics.

Through the war years, Georgia Tech had been one of the nation's football powerhouses. Employing Coach John Heisman's famed shift, the Golden Tornado stormed through 33 games without defeat, won 18 straight and, behind the spectacular ball carrying of Joe Guyon, Everett Strupper, and Buck Flowers, averaged 48.6 points per game against opponents' 3 points. The 1920 season found Tech with a new backfield sensation in David Irenus (Red) Barron and a new coach in Bill Alexander, the University of Pennsylvania having recalled Heisman. Yet the South's football headlines were being swiped by an unknown little school at Danville, Kentucky, called Centre College.

The man who designed the Centre dream team was R. L. (Chief) Myers, who returned to his alma mater in 1918, carrying with him the best players of his Fort Worth (Texas) high-school squad, including Bo McMillin, a bold and brilliant quarterback, and Red Weaver, a rugged center. Around this nucleus he added talented Kentuckians and Red Roberts, destined to become, along with the Fort Worth products, an All-America choice by Walter Camp. In 1919, Centre had the best offensive record in the nation, scoring 485 points, and had caught the public's fancy by flashing across two touchdowns in the last two minutes of play, to upset Indiana, 12-3.

Myers retired to the athletic directorship in 1920, brought Uncle Charlie Moran in as head coach, and scheduled games with such mighties as Harvard and Georgia Tech. The three games prior to the visit to Cambridge saw Centre roll up totals of 66-0, 120-0 and 55-0 against Morris Harvey, Howard, and Transylvania, respectively. Though Bo McMillin scampered for two touchdowns and was hailed by Eastern critics as one of the great players of all time, the Praying Colonels bowed to Harvard, 31-14, their first defeat in 21 starts. The very next week they headed for Atlanta and the South's top clash of the season against a Georgia Tech unit that had walloped every Southern foe, including stout Vanderbilt, by overwhelming scores.

The struggle attracted 17,000, a record for the South. "Grant Field, scooped out like a giant saucer, presented a spectacle beside which the barbaric splendor of a Roman circus must have shrunk to insignificance," raved one Atlanta journalist of the day. With Weaver and Roberts injured, McMillin was stopped cold as the Yellow Jackets scored early on a field goal by Flowers and added long touchdown runs by Barron and Ferst and a plunge by Harlan for a rocking 24-0 upheaval.

The season of 1921, however, found Centre capturing the nation's imagination and acclaim in even larger measurements. Its picturesque play, highlighted by a 6-0 upset of Harvard, catapulted the hardy, if not so holy, Praying Colonels to undying fame. In the South's Golden Age of football, they sparkled brightest, if briefly.

Unprecedented publicity accorded little Centre revived and stimulated the South's desire for intersectional competition. Dixie's pioneer in that field, as in many other phases of football, was Dan

McGugin, a guard on Michigan's celebrated point-a-minute team, who came to Vanderbilt in 1904 to remain its head coach for thirty years. While remaining unbeaten in the South those early years, trail-blazing along with Auburn's Mike Donahue, McGugin scheduled, and his teams absorbed, lickings (usually by close scores) from Michigan, Ohio State, Harvard, and others, and waged a 0-0 tie with Yale.

The early 1920's saw Tennessee playing Dartmouth; Georgia Tech playing Pittsburgh, Rutgers, Penn State, Navy, and Notre Dame; Auburn battling Army; Georgia going against Harvard, Chicago, Dartmouth, and Yale; Mississippi State tackling Indiana; Virgina engaging Princeton; North Carolina (1922 was its best season to date) meeting Yale; and little Sewanee taking on Pennsylvania as intersectionalism thrived. In 1922, Michigan made the Western Conference's first visit to the South in an invasion of Nashville, dedicating Vanderbilt's stadium in a 0-0 tie.

Undefeated in the South in 1922 and 1923, Vanderbilt furnished the only Southern All-America player from 1922 through 1924 in Lynn Bomar, versatile end. The great McGugin's genius reached its zenith in 1924, when Vanderbilt upset Minnesota, 16-0, for the South's most resounding intersectional triumph up to that time. On the previous Saturday, Minnesota had shackled the country's No. 1 ball carrier, Red Grange, to down Illinois, 20-7. But all the time, new football dynasties were being fashioned in the South.

An assistant coach named Wallace Wade had left Vanderbilt's staff in 1922 looking for a head portfolio. He sought such a post at the University of Kentucky, but when forced to cool his heels outside a committee meeting for an undue length of time, he stormed out and instead accepted the vacancy at the University of Alabama. Two seasons of thorough effort found Alabama no longer a second-rate power. The Crimson Tide in 1924 defeated Georgia for the Southern Conference championship and, emerging unbeaten again in 1925, became the first Southern team to receive an invitation to the Rose Bowl.

The generalship of Pooley Hubert, a hard-hitting quarterback, the flying feet of Johnny Mack Brown, and the stout, unerring passing-arm of Grant Gillis combined to lift Alabama to a peak against a heavily favored University of Washington team in the Pasadena classic. The Tide's throbbing manner of victory electrified the nation that New Year's Day. Outplayed the first half to trail by 12 points, the Crimsons roared back in the third quarter with an offensive display that netted three touchdowns in seven minutes, one on a 50-yard pass from Gillis to Brown. Although the hammering and heroic Wildcat Wilson slashed to another touchdown for the Huskies, Alabama won, 20-19, and claimed the national title.

The upsurge of the Tide overshadowed two highly successful seasons Tulane enjoyed under Coach Clark Shaughnessy, featuring a spirited and dangerous runner in Charles (Peggy) Flournoy, who starred in upsetting Northwestern, 18-7, in 1925.

What really focused the national spotlight on the South in the Golden Age of football was Alabama's second straight trip to the Rose Bowl after another perfect season in 1926. Wallace Wade had uncovered new stars in a pair of redhead backs, Emile Barnes and Tolbert Brown, to go along with veteran Wu Winslett at end. But it was a substitute, Jimmy Johnson, who scored the touchdown to tie Stanford, 7-7, at Pasadena.

The Tide ebbed in 1927, but Southern football was better balanced and generally stronger than ever. To pit his skill, savvy, and efficiency against such coaching sages as Wade, McGugin, Shaughnessy, Alexander, Greasy Neale of Virginia, and George Woodruff of Georgia, there had arrived at the University of Tennessee a young West Pointer named Robert Reese Neyland. As head of the ROTC unit there in 1925, he served as an assistant coach, becoming head coach in 1926. Thorough and painstaking, a drillmaster from the start, Neyland achieved quick results with an unbeaten eleven in 1927, sharing the Southern crown with Georgia Tech and North Carolina State, the latter beaten only by Furman.

Tennessee's archrival had been Vanderbilt, with the Volunteers taking regular wallopings at the hands of McGugin's men. In 1928, Neyland's charges won, 6-0, for the first Tennessee victory since 1916. Since that day, and up to 1948, a Neyland-coached team has lost to Vanderbilt only once, in 1937.

Edging into the limelight as much as Tennessee was a sensational University of Florida eleven, also under a new coach in 1928, Notre Damer Charlie Bachman. He constructed a smooth machine around such homebred talent as Clyde Crabtree, Rainey Cawthon, Dutch Stanley, Dale Van Sickle, and Muddy Waters. It was a high-class combine that riddled every opponent, including Auburn, North Carolina State, Georgia, and Washington and Lee, until Tennessee tripped it, 13-12, in a snowy, near-zero December thriller at Knoxville.

Southern football had progressed to such an extent by 1928 that it was generally believed that the section's top three or four teams might be on a par with the best in any area. Winning greater national prominence than either Tennessee or Florida was Georgia Tech, which boasted a 13-0 decision over Notre Dame in its perfect season's record. That earned a Rose Bowl bid, Dixie's third in four years. When the crew of Stumpy Thomason, Warner Mizell, Father Lumpkin, Peter Pund, et al, downed the University of California, 8-7, Georgia Tech held as justifiable a claim as any team to the mythical national championship.

Coaching staffs in the South's colleges, now enlarged, had added full-time specialists. Incoming freshmen had received much better high-school athletic training. All equipment was vastly improved over that of the World War I period. Schools were arranging more representative schedules. By 1929, Alabama, Duke, and Georgia had completed new stadia. Georgia's dedication brought Yale to Athens, the first time Old Eli had played a major game in the deep South. Among the three outstanding teams of the season was North Carolina, heralding a grid resurgence among the colleges of the Atlantic seaboard, so powerful in the early days. With 346 points, the Tar Heels were second only to Southern California in scoring. Tennessee, spearheaded by the finest backfield trio in its history in Bobby Dodd, Buddy Hackman, and Gene McEver, again was unbeaten, and Tulane lost only to the Texas Aggies.

Football boomed so in the South that attendance, rather than reflecting the business depression, zoomed to new peaks in 1930. In Dixieland, it was the brightest of football's golden years. Never had the competition been of such high caliber; never were there so many well-manned squads. In the estimation of most experts, Alabama and Tulane were as strong as any two teams the South had produced in a single year. Again Wallace Wade led 'Bama to the Rose Bowl, while Bernie Bierman at New Orleans was to wait one season before skippering Tulane's Green Wave on the South's fifth Pasadena pilgrimage in seven years.

Instead of the Thin Red Line of yore, it was a pack of rampaging Red Elephants that thundered to a 24-0 victory for Alabama over Washington State in the Tournament of Roses feature, January 1, 1931. The Tide backfield of Suther, Campbell, McRight, and Cain was hinged to two tackle bulwarks in Fred Sington and Foots Clement, both of whom rated many All-American selections. It was a fighting farewell gift to Wade, who had announced his resignation to move to Duke University as head coach. Sitting beside him on the Alabama bench, was the new Tide coach, Frank Thomas, later to take his place among the South's leading mentors.

Though Wade was to reign supreme in the Southern Conference after the new Southeastern body (embracing Alabama, Auburn, Florida, Georgia, Georgia Tech, Kentucky, Louisiana State, Mississippi, Mississippi State, Sewanee, Tennessee, Tulane, and Vanderbilt) was formed in 1932, his heyday was the 1920's. In that Golden Age of football, the South had its full share of 24-carat performers in coaches, players, and teams.

FOOTBALL IN THE FAR WEST

by BRAVEN DYER
Football Editor, Los Angeles Times

The Golden Age of Sports on the Pacific Coast properly began with the first great season of California's "Wonder Teams" in 1920. Prior to that decade, the University of Washington had been the big noise for a number of years in the West. Those Huskies, under "Dour" Gil Dobie, had terrorized the territory from 1908 through 1916, hanging up an all-time undefeated string of nine years, which included consecutive wins of 39 games and a record of 63 games without a loss. Then came World War I.

In 1919, a Washington team handed California its last defeat for years to come. The score of that affair was 7-0 in favor of the Huskies, then coached by Claude J. (Husky) Hunt. After that setback, California embarked upon one of football's greatest periods of prosperity.

Starting in 1920 with a 21-0 victory over the Olympic Club of San Francisco, a collection of former collegiate stars, California sailed through an eight-game schedule that included a win over little St. Mary's College by a score of 127-0. Nevada was beaten that same season, 79-7. After the regular campaign was ended, California received an invitation to represent the West at Pasadena in the youthful Tournament of Roses classic.

Until this battle, the rest of the nation had looked down a collective nose at Western football. Ohio State, invited to Pasadena by tournament officials (it was handled differently in those days), was an outstanding team with a reputation far greater than that possessed by the Bears.

All Fall, the Buckeyes had capitalized on a great passing combination, Stinchcomb to Workman, for win after win that added up to an undefeated untied record and a Big Ten title.

Ohio State was given a good chance, that day, of swamping the

Golden Bears with passes. Almost every critic picked the Buckeyes to win. When the final score of 28-0 favoring California was posted, Andy Smith's great eleven was on its way to becoming the toast of the nation. And a new passing combination had been born.

That New Year's Day, Harold (Brick) Muller and Howard (Brodie) Stephens teamed up to complete several passes, one of them a 53-yard aerial for a modern record.

So tremendous was that toss and so demoralizing its effect on Ohio State that few in the stands at Tournament Park realized at the time just how the play was engineered. Archie Nesbit, California's great plunging and punting fullback, feigned injury on the play before, just long enough for his teammates to shoo six other men up on the line of scrimmage. Then, big and blond Archie reached over and, with one hand, flipped the ball back to Pesky Sprott, who gave it, on a backward toss, to Muller. In the meantime, Stephens had raced in behind the skeptical Buckeye safety. Brodie took the pigskin over his shoulder on the dead run as he crossed the last stripe.

Part of the crowd sat in stunned silence, then joined the others in roaring their amazement. That day, January 1, 1921, truly ushered in the Golden Age of Sports in the West.

On California's team that beat the Buckeyes were many stars who are still spoken of with awe whenever fans look back. There, as regulars, were Bob Berkey, Stew Barnes, Cort Majors, Fat Latham, Lee Crammer, Dan McMillan, Harold Muller, Charlie Erb, Pesky Sprott, Crip Toomey, and Duke Morrison.

Partisan Pacific Coast fans claim that Ohio State's defeat so upset the Western Conference that high educational authorities did everything in their power to prevent a Big Ten team from returning to the Tournament of Roses classic. If the Big Ten's policy was to shun the Rose Bowl, it was a pretty thorough job. No team returned until 1947, when the Western Conference gained ample revenge as Illinois smashed the University of California at Los Angeles, 45 to 14.

In 1921, after winning nine straight for a point total of 312 to 33, California came back for another helping of postseason and intersectional honors. This time the "brass" in the Tournament of Roses organization had invited Washington and Jefferson College of Pennsylvania to come West. The choice was far from popular.

The fact that this school was one of the oldest in the land, founded at the close of the Revolutionary War, and had a pigskin past far greater than did California meant nothing to local partisans. The temerity of the visitors in even showing up was questioned.

It had rained hard before the game, but at kickoff time the sun was shining over a swampy gridiron. Without taking a second's time out or making a substitution, W. and J. humiliated California and would have won the game but for an eagle-eyed official who called back a beautifully scored touchdown. It went into the records as a scoreless tie.

Still, that frightening experience did more for Coast football than had the win over Ohio State the year before. It jarred a slowly forming smugness among Western fans to the core and it excited their interest in intersectional competition as never before.

As if to compensate for this temporary setback of sectional pride, the late Walter Camp honored the West by naming Brick Muller to his No. 1 All-America team. Others on the Coast, including Muller, had been placed on a number of Camp's earlier second and third teams, but the famous Brick broke the ice as the first top-flight selection.

Despite an undefeated and untied season in 1922, California declined to play at Pasadena. That decision gave the University of Southern California its big chance. Earlier in the year, these two institutions had dedicated the new Rose Bowl, the Bears winning by a score of 12-0.

The Trojans made the most of their opportunity by downing Penn State, 14 to 3. Hayden Pythian, Norman Anderson, Leo Calland, Chief Newman, Harold Galloway, Roy Baker, Hobo Kincaid, and Gordon Campbell were outstanding that day. Their coach, Elmer C. (Gloomy Gus) Henderson was immediately plummeted into the national limelight.

Only a scoreless tie with Nevada marred California's 1923 season, and that was easily explained away by the fact that Andy Smith had taken his first stringers down to Palo Alto to case the Stanford situation. But again the Bears resisted all Pasadena invitations, and the University of Washington got the nod.

The Huskies had lost only to California, 9-0, in 11 starts, and Enoch Bagshaw's squad was loaded with talent. Great backfield stars, like George Wilson and Elmer Tesreau, had made Washington's season so successful—284 points to 44—that even the approaching battle with Navy in the Rose Bowl failed to disturb the average Western fan. Navy did that on January 1, 1924.

The Middies, who had been tied by Army and Princeton and had been beaten by Notre Dame, were not too highly regarded before the kickoff. All that, however, changed in a matter of minutes, for the future admirals tossed 11 passes for 11 completions in the first half and left the field for a well-earned rest with a 14-7 lead.

Not only did Navy pass Washington into a state of frustration but it left the fans wondering if they had ever before seen any such passing. The Middies threw short and long in the orthodox manner. They also mixed forward and lateral tosses. Sometimes these were thrown two-handed, as a basketball player would. Others were shoveled underhanded. A few were lobbed. Some shot like a bullet to a receiver just a few yards beyond the line of scrimmage.

As the spectators left the Rose Bowl that evening, almost all of them felt that the resulting 14-14 tie was just about right. Everyone there had learned a lot about passing versatility.

Washington's first Rose Bowl team included such name starters as Kuhn and Petrie at tackle, Bryant at guard, and a backfield composed of Abel, Wilson, Ziel, and Tesreau.

As the 1924 season opened, California followers were predicting that Andy Smith would field his greatest Wonder Team. And it came close to being just that. The line was led by that young giant, Edwin (Babe) Horrell, and star of the backfield was a speed burner by the name of Tut Emlay.

An upset 7-7 tie with Washington that year caused a little gloom and was considered a blot on California's five-year record, which was approaching fifty games without defeat. The Wonder Teams still had not known the meaning of the word reversal as the Bears prepared for the finale of the 1924 season, their annual Big Game with Stanford.

The Indians, that season, were playing their first year under the personal direction of the great Glenn Scobie (Pop) Warner. The "old fox" had signed two years earlier and had dispatched Andy Kerr to the Farm, there to install his intricate double wingback system.

Stanford trailed, 20-6, with ten minutes to go, and the crowd began to file toward the exits. Then it happened. Murray Cuddeback, Fred

Solomon, Ted Shipkey, Jim Lawson, Cliff Hey, and others ignited for two touchdowns and 14 points. That finish wrote into the record books just about the most famous of all 20-20 ties. It was still being discussed everywhere when tournament officials selected Stanford and Notre Dame as Rose Bowl rivals.

Stanford's greatest star, Ernie Nevers, did not play in that thrilling stalemate with California. The big all-time, all-Coast fullback had been sidelined by a pair of injured ankles, but he was ready for the Irish. His supporting cast consisted of Ted Shipkey and Jim Lawson at ends, H. Shipkey and Johnston at tackles, Swan and Neill at guards, Baker at center, Solomon at quarter, and Cuddeback and Walker, halfbacks.

Opposing Nevers and Company was Notre Dame's most famous and most opportunistic team—the Four Horsemen and the Seven Mules.

It was one of Pasadena's most sensational and savage battles—Warner wizardry against Rockne resourcefulness. Nevers' plunging was never greater, but Elmer Layden's pass catching was even more telling—regardless of which team threw the ball. In the end, it was the pass interceptions of Layden that downed a great Stanford eleven, 27-10, and preserved the belief in the invincibility of the Four Horsemen. The victory did more. It added to the growing legend of a young coach and placed an indelible stamp of greatness upon him, Knute Rockne.

Far from crushing Western pride in its teams, Stanford's Rose Bowl performance against Notre Dame was stimulating. Many were quick to point out that the Indians had gained 298 yards to 179 for the Irish; had run up 17 first downs to 7.

As the 1925 season opened, the experts automatically looked to California for the best in the West. The Bears had completed 50 games without defeat, scoring 1,564 points to 139 for the combined opposition. Ten times, Walter Camp had singled out some player from the Berkeley campus for All-America recognition.

Then, in his last year at California, and the last of his life, Andy Smith ran into trouble. Three times his team met defeat. The first was by the Olympic Club. Fans shrugged that one off and clung to their faith in the great Andy. That faith was shaken to its very roots when Washington, last collegiate team previously to beat a Smith creation, duplicated its 1919 victory with another 7-0 win. Then Stanford poured it on with a 27-to-14 triumph. It would be years before another Golden Bear eleven would climb to the lofty heights of those Andy Smith teams.

There was no question of who ruled the Pacific Coast during the 1925 season. Enoch Bagshaw came up with his greatest team, headed by his greatest player—George Wilson. The Huskies rolled over every West Coast foe, got a 6-6 tie with Nebraska, for a season's scoring total of 459 points to 39, before accepting the honor of appearing at Pasadena against the first of many fine Southern elevens to play there, Alabama.

The Crimson Tide defeated Washington in that Rose Bowl game mainly because Wilson had to be rested during the entire third quarter. It was during this Wilson-less period that 'Bama bounced back with three touchdowns. One was scored by the crashing Pooley Hubert; the other two on sensational passes by Hubert and Grant Gillis to the amazing Johnny Mack Brown. It was the greatest fifteen minutes of Rose Bowl history.

Yet again, Western fanatics felt that their brand of football needed no vindication. Had George Wilson been able to play the entire sixty minutes, they reasoned, all would have been well. His absence for one quarter, they argued, meant the ball game. While he was in he gained 134 yards for an average just shy of nine yards. While he was on the bench Alabama scored all 20 of its points and won, 20-19.

That one-point victory of the Crimson Tide, however, prevented Washington from going down in football history as just about the greatest eleven ever put together west of the Rockies. Schuh, P. Wilson, Brix, Bonamy, Wright, Erickson, Cutting, Guttormsen, George Wilson, Patton, and Elmer Tesreau were the stars who started for Washington.

Pop Warner's third Stanford team, in 1926, may have been his greatest. At least, it was his only undefeated eleven. And it went to the Rose Bowl to play Alabama.

Before it reached Pasadena it racked up 10 straight victories, including a 41-to-6 triumph over California in the Big Game—or enough to make any Stanford season a supersuccess.

Fans today still talk about the prowess of such stars as Ted Shipkey, Dick Hyland, and Biff Hoffman. Others on that eleven included

Poulson, Swan, McCreery, Robesky, Harris, Walker, Lewis, and Bogue.

Possibly, the strategies of those two masterminds, Pop Warner and Wallace Wade, counterbalanced each other at Pasadena. The resulting 7-7 tie went down in the books as the dullest Rose Bowl game in a decade.

Stanford defeated all of its conference rivals during the 1927 season except Southern California, a constantly growing power under Coach Howard Harding Jones. The Trojans gained a 13-13 tie. Indian supremacy was considerably dimmed by a pair of defeats by upstarts, St. Mary's and Santa Clara.

Since Stanford had failed to impress Alabama the year before, and as most fans felt that the selection of Pittsburgh as Eastern opponent was influenced in part by Pop Warner's fondness for his former charges, few were particularly excited over the Rose Bowl clash on January 2, 1928.

The Stanford cast was much the same as in the previous year's contest. The "Heavenly Twins," Post and Robesky, held down the guard spots. McCreery, as captain, played center. The backfield was composed of Murphy and the three H's—Hill, Hyland, and Hoffman. Frankie Wilton, a sub, was destined to be both the goat and the hero.

Having shown a tendency to fumble all season, no one was amazed when Frankie bobbled to give Pitt a score. But no one was prepared to see him recover a Panther mistake on the five-yard line, which he gobbled up for a touchdown to put the Indians back in the ball game.

The conversion that followed ultimately proved the winning margin.

There were, and still are, many in the West who have insisted that the best team did not play at Pasadena in that 1928 game. Up until the hour of selection, the Trojans had lost only to Notre Dame, by a score of 7-6, had tied Stanford, 13-13, and with that game had gained a claim to half of the Pacific Coast Conference title.

Howard Jones had what many believe was his greatest team at Troy, headed by Morley Drury and Jess Hibbs. Other stars of that era are still recalled with devotion. Anthony, Barragar, Boren, Edelson, Elliott, Heiser, Hoff, McCaslin, Moses, Saunders, Scheving,

Steponovich, Tappan, Thomas, Williams—in alphabetical order—are only a handful of the players the Head Man could call upon.

No one has ever been able to explain successfully why California was selected to represent the West next year. The obvious choice was Southern California. Although the Bears got the nod, their record showed a defeat by the Olympic Club and two ties, with Stanford and Southern California. The Trojans, on the other hand, had won the conference championship and had beaten Notre Dame, 27 to 14.

Out on the Troy campus, however, all was not gloom. Added to many of the stars of previous years were such performers, as Marshall Duffield and Jess Mortensen. The faithful followers, too, were still talking about that great 10-0 victory over a 3-1 favorite, Stanford, when the powers of Pasadena weakly announced that California had been chosen to play in the Rose Bowl. It was the beginning of the end as far as tournament control of the classic went.

The entire football world has heard of the California-Georgia Tech contest in 1929, but only because of a freak happening. It was in this game that Roy Riegels was stunned into running the wrong way on a play that ultimately gave the Ramblin' Wrecks an 8-7 win. Despite their defeat, the Golden Bears were not without a handful of stars —one of them Riegels. Others to be remembered were Schwartz, Bancroft, Phillips, Lom, and Schmidt.

In 1929, the West enjoyed its biggest moment. The Rose Bowl also proved a realization of everything conjured up in Western dreams. The Trojans supplied the opium.

During the regular season, Southern California had run into a surprising defeat by California, 15 to 7, largely because a lad by the name of Benny Lom could run as well as kick. That same season, Notre Dame had taken another one-point victory from the Trojans. In spite of these two setbacks, Troy was generally regarded as the best team in the West and thus won the Rose Bowl assignment.

Pittsburgh came to Pasadena, but not as a challenger, with one of the greatest records ever packed aboard a train. It read: Won 9. Lost 0. Tied 0. Points, 277-43. At least four of its players were bona fide All-Americans. Pregame publicity spread the fame of Donchess, Montgomery, Uansa, and Parkinson.

When the final gun cracked over Rose Bowl sidelines, the scoreboard showed the magic figures: Southern California 47, Pittsburgh 14. Never in the history of the Rose rumpus had there been such a reversal. Never had a team risen to greater heights than did those Trojans with their one All-American, Francis Tappan.

Tappan and Arbelbide at end, Hall and Anthony at tackle, Barragar and Galloway at guard, Dye at center, and Saunders, Edelson, Pinckert, and Shaver in the backfield, started the game. It was of small matter whom Jones substituted as the slaughter continued.

Replacements were many. As the score mounted, in went Wilcox, Jurich, Steponovich, Seitz, Hoff, Ward, Templeton, Bond, Baker, Shaw, Williamson, to spell linemen. Helping out with the backfield chores were Mortensen, Aspit, Brown, Stephens, Hill, Musick, and Moses.

This rout stunned most of the All-America selectors in the Middle West and in the East. It also elated Western fans no end and encouraged the fixation of some that football as played on the Coast was just a fraction better than that played in other sectors. Such a feeling of superiority was destined to last not more than twelve months. On January 1, 1931, Washington State played Alabama, and the Crimson Tide bowled over the Cougars, 24-0.

Pittsburgh's famed coach, Dr. John B. Sutherland, was destined to go almost twenty years before any of his teams took a worse drubbing than that suffered in the 1930 Rose Bowl encounter. It wasn't until 1947, when he was coaching the Pittsburgh Steelers pro team, that bad luck overtook Jock again. Once more it was a Los Angeles team —the professional Rams of the National Football League—who administered a 47-7 trimming, and on Jock's home grounds, too.

That lopsided Trojan win in the 1930 Rose Bowl game was to be followed by other Southern California victories at Pasadena. In fact, under the able leadership of Howard Jones, the Trojans were destined to win their every additional game (four) in the Arroyo Seco saucer. And after his death in 1941, one of his players, Jeff Cravath, came along to run the string of unbroken Rose Tournament wins to eight before Alabama stopped the parade with a 34-14 pasting in 1946.

The Golden Age of the Twenties not only brought to California Andy Smith, Pop Warner, and Howard Jones, it also served to introduce one of the greatest intersectional series of all time.

This was the Notre Dame–Southern California rivalry, begun in 1926 at Los Angeles. The rapid growth of the University of Southern California as an athletic power, first under Elmer C. Henderson and then under Howard Jones, was one reason why city, county, and state officials decided to erect the mammoth Los Angeles Coliseum, with an original seating capacity of 75,000, in 1923. Enlarged to more than 100,000 for the 1932 Olympic Games, this always has been the home field of the Trojans—and the Bruins of U.C.L.A., too. It is not an uncommon thing for both Trojans and Bruins to sell out two or three times a season, which means that outstanding teams all over the nation are eager to get on the schedule of one or the other.

The popularity of football in Los Angeles dates back to its rapid growth in the huge Coliseum during the Golden Age. Prior to the Twenties, the Trojans played on Bovard Field (now their practice grounds), where only 10,000 fans could sit to watch a game.

This Trojan–Notre Dame series has enjoyed such tremendous popularity that it is an annual sell-out whether held at South Bend, Chicago, or Los Angeles. When Rockne and Jones were alive, coaches flocked to this annual classic from all over the country as young doctors would to the Mayo Brothers to see the masters at work.

Rockne's last team, the 1930 outfit, which was unbeaten, scored one of Notre Dame's greatest victories in Los Angeles, beating the favored Trojans, 27-0. The Wizard of South Bend died in a plane crash within four months after this smashing upset.

Outside of the Pacific Coast Conference, the Far West produced only one outstanding team during the Golden Age. This was St. Mary's. In 1920, as related, St. Mary's lost to California, 127-0. That was too much for supporters of the Galloping Gaels.

They hired a young man fresh out of Notre Dame. His name was Edward P. (Slip) Madigan. In due time he got the Gaels rolling. By 1926, they defeated California, 26-7. His 1929 team was unbeaten. He journeyed East of the Rockies for the first time in 1930 and whipped Fordham in New York City, 20-12. His 1931 team opened the season by thumping Southern California, 13-7.

This latter victory is mentioned because it was this 1931 Trojan team, a carry-over from the Golden Age, which scored Troy's greatest triumph—a 16-14 win over Notre Dame at South Bend. This shat-

tered an Irish winning streak that had extended through 25 games
and gained Johnny Baker, who kicked the last-minute field goal,
All-America honors.

In 1947, sports editors of metropolitan newspapers extending from
San Diego to Seattle collaborated on an all-time Pacific Coast Conference team.

Almost without exception, the players honored were products of
the Golden Age.

The ends were California's Brick Muller, 1921 and 1922, and
Stanford's Ted Shipkey, 1924, 1925, and 1926. The tackles were
Washington State's Glenn (Turk) Edwards, who finished his intercollegiate career in 1930, and Ernie Smith of Southern California,
who was a Trojan freshman in 1929 and followed with three years of
varsity ball.

The guards were Aaron Rosenberg of Southern California, following just a year behind Smith, and Bill Corbus of Stanford, who played
his final college game in 1933. Mel Hein of Washington State, a
contemporary of Edwards, was the center.

Only one of the backs completely escaped the Golden Age era.
He is Kenny Washington, Negro ace of U.C.L.A., who was a defensive and offensive standout on Bruin teams in 1937, 1938, and 1939.

The great George Wilson, the great Ernie Nevers, and the great
Morley Drury rounded out the quartet. Wilson and Nevers closed
out their rah-rah careers in 1925, Drury two years later.

Thus, ten of the eleven members of the Coast Conference's all-
time team either played all their college football during the Golden
Age or were freshmen at the tag end of this glorious era.

It would seem to me that no greater tribute could be paid to the
players, teams, and coaches of football's Golden Age.

PROFESSIONAL FOOTBALL

by Arthur Daley
Sports Columnist, The New York Times

The calliope was wheeled stridently through the Loop, brassily proclaiming that the Chicago Bears were playing in Wrigley Field the following Sunday. But George Halas, who served as end, captain, coach, and owner of the now universally acclaimed Monsters of the Midway, reluctantly had to return the calliope to its garage. He couldn't quite afford the $15 a week it was costing him.

Free tickets for pro football games gathered dust in stacks on every sports editor's desk in every town. No one would take them —even for free. Newspapers so scorned printing more than the bare results ·of each fray that Halas once was thrilled to tears when an overzealous reporter tacked on to his mere recital of the score this remarkable extra sentence: "It was a very fine game."

That was the low estate into which professional football had fallen when sport's Golden Decade rolled around. Fallen? Perhaps that's the wrong word. To fall you have to drop from a certain peak of eminence. The play-for-pay sport had never reached it. When 1920 arrived, this particular stepchild of the block-and-tackle pastime was precisely twenty-five years of age. Instead of being strong and vigorous, however, it was a puny, rag-tail, tatterdemalion object of dubious respectability. It was unwept, unhonored, and unsung—and unattended.

Before the Golden Decade was over, though, pro football had gained maturity, respectability, solidity, popularity, and prosperity. It was then that the firm foundation was laid for the towering structure we see today. But all structures need cornerstones. The play-for-pay sport had four of them, one for each corner. They were Joe E. Carr, George Halas, Tim Mara, and Red Grange.

For a quarter of a century the pro game had been a haphazard, hit-or-miss affair. Teams would be assembled on a Sunday, run through signals in a hotel lobby that morning, and play together that afternoon. Teammates one week might be rivals the next. The sport was run on virtually a day-to-day basis.

A feeble attempt at organization was made in 1920 when the American Professional Football Association was formed, but it was not until this was reorganized a year later, and renamed the National Football League that order emerged from chaos. The main reason was the strong man who was put at the helm, Joe E. Carr, of Columbus, Ohio. He ruled wisely and well until his death eighteen years later. A powerful National Football League was to be his enduring monument.

At this same approximate time, a restless seeker for perfection, George Halas, was beginning to grope his way along the pro football paths. He had been a star end at the University of Illinois just before the First World War and he was to become a star end again on the mighty Great Lakes team which won Rose Bowl honors.

The naval station attracted some of the most talented athletes in that branch of the service, and that fact forcibly brought back to Halas' mind a remark which had been casually dropped by his old coach, Bob Zuppke. It was: "Just as a player begins to get good and learn something about this game, he graduates." Halas kept toying with the idea of postgraduate football.

The Staley Starch Works of Decatur, Illinois, gave him his chance when he was named athletic director and football coach of that establishment. Naturally enough, he surrounded himself with the best ex-collegians he could find. More important, though, the hard-working, hard-driving Halas instituted a system of daily practice. No pro team had ever tried that before. So fiendishly thorough was the youthful coach, even in those days, that he actually used a hose to pipe in water to a corner of the field so that his heroes could practice handling a wet ball.

The Staleys of Decatur eventually became the Chicago Staleys and, in 1922, they were rechristened the Chicago Bears. The most glamorous dynasty in professional football thus was created. The famed Monsters of the Midway have won more championships, set more records, and become more synonymous with gridiron perfection than any other team in the history of the sport.

However, the new and sprawling National Football League lacked the one ingredient it needed most. It had as many as 20 teams, including too many whistle stops. But it didn't have the one town that was necessary for major league recognition, New York.

And in 1925 a New York franchise was offered a big, handsome, wealthy Irishman, Timothy James Mara. He loved all sports, but he never had seen a football game in his life when he was given a proposition at what now seems a ridiculous price. "Any New York franchise should be worth $2,500," said Tim with the penetrating shrewdness which has marked his career. So he bought it. That same franchise is worth more than a million dollars today.

Mara has long since handed the direction and control of his team over to his two sons, but he still is one of the elder statesmen of the league, with his sound advice a leavening force in the league councils. Never was a man of his stature more needed than in 1926, when a new rival league was formed to battle the NFL. Less venturesome souls suggested compromise and amalgamation. But Tim said, "We'll fight them." The fight was mainly a pocketbook warfare.

Although Mara lost $70,000 in one season, he killed off the new circuit and thus gave the National Football League the chance it needed to grow and solidify its position. Had he been weak and vacillating, the new league would have survived before there were enough customers for two circuits to share. Inevitably, both loops would have collapsed, and pro football would have been set back a generation.

The fourth key operative was Red Grange. When the Galloping Ghost was a collegiate gridiron scourge for Illinois, he was the most publicized player in the game. His name had become a household word. In that respect he has never had an equal and he was a gate attraction without parallel in the football world.

The night of his final college game, Grange surreptitiously climbed down the fire escape of his hotel, hatbrim pulled down over his eyes, and coat collar turned up. Everything was in the best E. Phillips Oppenheim fashion. Stealthily he crept past the joyously celebrating crowds and into a waiting taxicab for a secret rendezvous with the wily Papa Bear, George Halas.

Grange emerged from the conference a professional, and pro football made the biggest advance in its history. The Roaring Redhead was one of the Chicago Bears, and the play-for-pay sport, which had been avidly welcoming little headlines, suddenly began to get big ones. Grange was a name to conjure with. Maiden aunts who didn't know a right tackle from a wrong one knew all about Grange. His every move and gesture was a front-page story.

The date of December 6, 1925, was a milestone in the annals of pro ball. New York was to be afforded its first opportunity to see in action the Galloping Ghost, whose hysterically worded praises Gothamites had been reading for months.

Being a lucky Irishman to start with, Mara was given a marvelous break for the Giant-Bear clash which was to introduce Grange. The Army-Navy game had been played in the Polo Grounds a week previously, and therefore all the extra stands were still in position, stands which gave the field a larger seating capacity than it ever had before or has had since.

To appreciate fully the magnetic turnstile attraction that lay in the magic name of Grange, two things must first be understood. One is that in those days there was no advance sale worthy of the description, the overwhelming majority of the fans buying their tickets at the park on the afternoon of the game. The second is that the entertainment world has learned from bitter experience that rainy weather seriously interferes with any normal advance sale.

Yet, in spite of the fact that it rained for a solid week before the game, and regardless of the fact that the Giants usually sold no more than a few hundred tickets in advance, the customers practically broke down the doors of the Giant offices in their frantic eagerness to buy ducats. They descended in such numbers that Mara had to yell for help from the police. And all week long drenched and soggy fans sloshed into the Giant headquarters, until more than 60,000 tickets had been sold *in advance*.

As bad as the weather had been all week, however, Mara luck held—as usual—for the day of the game. The sun shone benignly, and a gentle, unseasonable warmth dropped a protective cloak about the Polo Grounds. But that made things all the more uncontrollable. Those cautious citizens who'd been waiting for the rain clouds to clear before even thinking of buying a ticket joyously stampeded out to the park.

As they descended on the field, the bewildered gendarmes first gave way and then sent in a riot call. And about every fifteen minutes they would turn in another alarm for reinforcements. Uncounted thousands upon thousands were turned away, but the official tally on those who contrived in some inexplicable style to jam their way into the park was a quite incredible 73,651.

Pro football, a front page-item for the first time, was made. The game itself, though, was very incidental. The Giants kept watching Grange in such open-mouthed wonder that they completely neglected to keep their eyes peeled on little Joey Sternaman, who did some very unwraithlike running of his own to score most of the points in a 19-7 Bear victory.

Oddly enough, the Galloping Ghost never was as electrifyingly sensational in the play-for-pay sport as he'd been with the college kids. But he did develop into an exceptionally fine all-around player. He learned to block and became one of the best. He learned the defensive side of the game and soon was a top-flight defender. In fact, Halas insists that Grange pulled off the finest defensive play he ever saw—and the Papa Bear has seen plenty.

It came in the final minute of a championship clash between the Bears and the Giants. They'd been locked in a thriller-diller. Six times the lead changed hands, and the count was 23-21 in favor of the Bears as the New Yorkers came roaring downfield in a last desperate drive. There was time for only one play, and it was a thing of beauty.

Harry Newman passed to Dale Burnett, who eluded every Bear except Grange. The redhead rushed up for the tackle and was horrified to see Mel Hein, the Giant center, high-tailing it down the middle and in perfect position to take a lateral from Burnett. What to do? If Grange didn't make the tackle, Burnett was away for a touchdown. But if he did, then Burnett merely handed over the ball to Hein and the big center would rumble on undisturbed.

In a flash Red made up his mind. He sailed through the air at the Giant wingback, but this was not the ordinary or expected ankle-high tackle. Instead, Grange clutched Burnett around the waist, pinioning his arms against his sides and preventing him from throwing the lateral. They rolled over onto the ground together, almost at the feet of the disappointed Hein, and the game was over. Grange had undisputedly saved victory for the Bears with a truly smart and brilliant play.

Although Grange was the greatest headline catcher the pro game had possessed up to his time, he was by no means the greatest star it ever had. Most historians are inclined to agree that the immortal Jim Thorpe, the Sac and Fox Indian from Carlisle, was the finest player who ever lived. But by the time the Golden Twenties rolled around, the big fellow had seen his best days. Yet on occasions he was the Thorpe of old.

Take, for example, the time Stout Steve Owen first played against him, in 1924. Stout Steve now is the coach of the Giants, but then he'd just graduated from Phillips University and was making his first pro start. Owen was at tackle, Thorpe at wingback. The ball snapped, and Steve rudely pushed Jim aside, throwing the ball carrier for a five-yard loss. "I guess the old Indian is slipping," he muttered to himself as he eagerly returned to the scrimmage line. So he took a better angle, pushed the Sac and Fox out of the way, and again threw the ball carrier for another loss. "He's not so hot," he drawled.

For the third time Stout Steve catapulted through. The ground came up and hit him. The grandstands seemingly had collapsed atop him. Dazed and shaken, he lay on the turf until a strong hand pulled him to his feet. It was the hand of Jim Thorpe. Down the field a touchdown had been scored through the hole Owen had left when he was so unceremoniously pole-axed by the grinning Thorpe, who'd finally decided to throw a man-size block.

"Young fellow," said Jim to Steve as he waved an admonitory finger, "never take your eyes off the old Indian."

Owen never forgot that lesson. He forgot very few of them because he's since achieved the reputation of being one of the best and most resourceful coaches in the game. But that opportunity never came to him until the very end of the Golden Decade, when Tim Mara was seeking a field boss for his Giants. One day Mara telephoned his well-upholstered star tackle.

"Steve," he said, "I've finally decided on my coach."

"Who is he, Mr. Mara?" asked the unsuspecting Owen.

"You," said Tim—and hung up on him. Thus did Mara entrust the fortunes of the pivotal team of his league to a man who was to parlay them to undreamed-of heights. There is no doubt about the

New York franchise being the pivotal one, either. The pro game was strictly bush-league stuff for the first half of the Golden Twenties and didn't attain big-league stature until the Giants were organized in 1925.

For most of those earlier years the play-for-pay sport was built along knockdown-drag-'em-out lines. The Green Bay Packers were about the only pass-conscious team in the circuit and they haven't changed to this very day. Curly Lambeau, the first and only coach of the Ponderous Pachyderms, had been a pretty good passer himself and he stressed forwards. Yet the massive Cal Hubbard, the American League baseball umpire and an all-time Packer standout at tackle, once remarked, "Only sissies throw the ball." That symbolized the spirit of the age.

However, Curly was no sissy and he threw it. There even was one Packer-Giant game when Owen, hard bent on rushing the passer, personally knocked down Lambeau 21 of the 22 times he tossed an aerial. After Lambeau, as a star pitcher, came Red Dunn. Then followed Arnie Herber and Cecil Isbell later on, the greatest chain of superb passers the sport has ever had.

But before we get too far away from the active playing days of M'sieur Lambeau, it might be well to mention the final play of his career—or so the legend goes. Curly was near the end of his string, anyway, but he still wore his uniform for every game, just in case he'd be needed. And in the first half of a fray with the Bears, the Green Bay attack went very sour.

Curly stormed and raged in the dressing room during the intermission. "I'll show you fellows how to pass," he bellowed in rising indignation. "I'm gonna play myself. I'll show you."

The Packers were a hard-boiled lot in those days, and many of them resented the tongue-lashing they'd received, because they'd really been trying their best even though everything had gone wrong at once. So when Lambeau jogged onto the field to direct the action, one of the Ponderous Pachyderms—the most persistent rumor has always identified Cal Hubbard as the culprit—offered a suggestion to his mates.

"Let's open the gates on Curly," he whispered.

The ball snapped from center to the waiting Lambeau. Ten Packer blockers dutifully stepped aside. Seven Chicago Bears delightedly rushed in through those yawning portals and hit Curly all at once. He wearily hauled himself to his feet afterward, cast a reproachful glance at his grinning hired hands, and limped to the sidelines, his active days at an end. Curly got the idea instantly.

However, the mahout of the Ponderous Pachyderms is just as important a key figure in pro football today as he was then. He was one of the pioneers, and his contributions to the sport are immeasurable. Not only did he produce a great succession of artful passers but he always bobbed up with uncanny receivers. Everyone has heard of Don Hutson, of course. He holds every pass-catching record in the game.

But too many followers of the play-for-pay pastime have already forgotten the most colorful figure that the Golden Twenties furnished, the fabulous Johnny Blood. Until Hutson came along, Blood had held all of those very same marks. The one he has left, though, is the quite incredible one of performing for fifteen full seasons in the National Football League.

Johnny was something of a paradox to start with. His real name was McNally and he came from a wealthy family. Football was in his veins, and he was not at all adverse to playing professional ball on Sundays under an assumed name. He was searching for a suitable and descriptive tag one day when he and a companion dropped into a movie. It presented Rudolph Valentino in *Blood and Sand*.

"I've got it," said Johnny. "You be Sand and I'll be Blood." Thus was created Johnny Blood. His career was to overlap slightly that of Hutson. As mercury footed as was the Alabama Antelope, however, he and Blood had a race the first season Don joined the Packers. Hutson won by a scant foot. Don then was twenty-two years old, Johnny an ancient thirty-four.

Blood not only was lightning fast in his prime but he had a sure pair of hands and was a will-o'-the-wisp in an open field. If he was not the best halfback in the league for most of those campaigns, he was mighty close to it. They still speak with bated breath in Green Bay about a catch he once made against the Detroit Lions.

The Packers were losing, 18-13, in the final minute of play and they were beyond midfield. The undaunted Blood called for the strong-armed Herber to throw him a pass in the enemy end zone, 65 yards away. Herber made ready to throw, discovered that Blood had three men covering him, searched frantically around, and soon observed that everyone else was covered, too. On the theory that Johnny was a better bet as a receiver with three men on him than the average man with only one, Arnie let go.

The ball arched through the air into the end zone. Three Lions and one Packer leaped for it. But that one Packer was the remarkable Johnny Blood. Naturally enough, he made the catch for the winning touchdown.

It got so after a while that Green Bay began to expect the un-expected of Blood, the Frank Merriwell of his day. There was one set of Packer sequence plays that ran off the same fundamental pat-tern: On Play 69 Johnny was supposed to feed the ball to the fullback and fake to the end on an end-around. On Play 69X he was to fake to the fullback and feed to the end on an end-around.

So Johnny blithely called for 69XX at one crucial moment of a crucial game. It was a marvelous call—except for the fact that the Packers didn't have any Play 69XX in their repertoire. The puzzled fullback faithfully went through his plunge as Blood faked to him. The bewildered end scampered around as Blood faked to him. There-upon, Johnny, who'd fooled the enemy even more than he'd fooled his teammates, gleefully romped by himself to the winning tally.

The orthodox held no attractions for the ebullient Blood. He once broke off tackle, artfully sidestepped his way down the field, and twisted past every rival tackler in a beautiful open-field run of 80 yards for a touchdown. A touchdown? Wait a minute. Once Johnny was in the clear he lost interest. This was much too commonplace. So he paused at the 20, waiting for one of the Packers to come roaring up so that he could toss him a lateral.

However, the enemy got there first, much to the annoyance of Mr. Blood. He dodged and ducked. He was forced on to the 10, then to the 5, weaving and twisting as he looked around to unload that lateral. But no one was in sight. Hence the spectacular Johnny was reluctantly compelled to score himself, dragging four tacklers over the goal line with him.

The escapades of this 195-pound Apollo off the field were just as zany as his feats on it. He thought nothing of leaping in a driving rainstorm across an open court, six stories above the street, in order to press a claim for a salary advance on Lambeau, who'd barricaded himself in his room.

He was a magnificent monologist and entertainer. So brilliant was his mind that he could discourse learnedly on the Malthusian theory. He once wrote a book. On football? Don't be silly. It was a ponderous tome on economics.

The Golden Decade in pro football barely captured on its calendar one of the truly great football players of all time, Bronko Nagurski. The rock-hewed Bronk arrived in 1930 just as the Decade was closing up shop. He won the reputation of being the only fullback in the history of the game who ever "led his own interference."

The Chicago line buster needed no interference. He just crashed through. Even today, Stout Steve Owen will thoughtfully finger his head and remark, "I still got some knobs here from trying to tackle the Bronk." When Nagurski was in his prime, the rival teams devised one certain way of halting him. The first chap to hit him was supposed to slow him down so that the second fellow could spill him and the third one hold him down. That's how unstoppable he was.

There even was one period in the history of the Bears when those archdisciples of the T formation actually abandoned the Terrible T in favor of the single wing. The Monsters of the Midway floundered and sputtered against the Pittsburgh Steelers. And into the Chicago lineup came the Bronk. He'd been late in reporting that season because of his commitments as a wrestler and that single-wing business was all new to him.

"Gosh, fellers," he said in the huddle, "let's use the old stuff."

The ball was on the 22-yard line and there was no score when the Bronk took charge. He plummeted through center from the T. He swept wide. He hit inside. But there's no sense in stringing this out. He carried the ball on every play and slashed his way to the only touchdown of the game. Incidentally, that ended Bear experiments with the single wing, and it's just as well. It was the skillful way the Monsters exploited the T in their famed 73-0 rout of the Washington Redskins that was to revolutionize all football, college and pro.

The game has advanced so far in the not-so-golden-Forties that one can't help but wonder how it ever struggled through those early years—even with such stars as Thorpe, Grange, Ernie Nevers, Benny Friedman, Ken Strong, Dutch Clark, Jack Hagerty, Indian Joe

Guyon, Paddy Driscoll, Jimmy Conzelman, Duke Slater, and scores and scores of former college All-America performers.

Even in the second half of the Golden Decade, when it first started to flourish, there were some mighty disconcerting moments. One such was when the Chicago Bears came to New York to play the Giants. It had snowed all week, and Tim Mara spent hundreds of dollars in paying workmen to shovel off the snow as fast as it fell. It was a losing battle. A full-fledged blizzard dropped from the skies on Sunday.

When Tim arrived at the Polo Grounds, he found that both the Giants and the Bears, hardy souls all, had put in an appearance. But the weather was so discouraging that even the ushers and ticket takers did not show up. The customers? Perish the thought. There wasn't one in sight.

"George," said Tim to Halas, his voice tinged with regret, "it's impossible out there. We can't play. We'll have to call off the game."

But the Bland Bohemian from the Loop was hard put in those days to keep the wolf out of his parlor. Pro football had yet to make him a millionaire—"the nicest rich man I know," as he's described by the nimble-witted Jimmy Conzelman. Halas was willing enough to call off the game, but he demanded his $5,000 guarantee.

Mara flared up. "If you want it," he said heatedly, "I'll give it to you. But first of all you'll have to play for it. I'm not handing over $5,000 for nothing and I want to see a game for my dough. I'll lock the doors and be the only spectator. I suppose I'll be the only man in history to pay $5,000 to watch a football game, but I want my money's worth. Take your choice."

Halas looked out at the snowbanks, as high as the crossbar in spots, and he knew when he was licked. "You win, Tim," he said. "Let's forget the guarantee."

Nowadays the pros would never dream of postponing a game, come hell or high water. And it's the assurance that every fray will be played on schedule which has removed from the sport the element of uncertainty that surrounded it then.

In fact, professional football has come so far since the Golden Twenties that there is just no comparison between the two. Back in that era, the droll Conzelman held the Detroit franchise and sold it. He since has explained the deal with remarkable clarity: "That transaction alone demonstrates what an extraordinary businessman I am. I sold the Detroit franchise for the munificent sum of $50. But when Fred Mandel bought it later on, he paid $250,000 for it. That's Conzelman for you."

Be that as it may, however, the nostalgic days of the Golden Twenties played a vitally important part in the history of the play-for-pay sport. It served as the springboard which was to catapult it to heights it never before had known.

GOLF

by O. B. KEELER
Golf Editor, Atlanta Journal

The Golden Age in golf in the U. S. A. dawned over a burnished horizon in 1920, with a curiously compensatory effect, later realized, for a sun setting on another era of import and greatness, in a game then turning its first recognized quarter of a century over here.

It was in 1920 that Chick Evans won his last major championship and Alexa Stirling her last of three National titles in a row, and Jock Hutchison his only P.G.A. crown, defeating in the final round at Flossmoor the late Douglas Edgar, the most bewilderingly brilliant golfing genius that ever came over to America, playing less than two years on this side and dying tragically in 1921.

And it was in 1920 that Harry Vardon and Ted Ray, the English professionals, came back for another swing at the U. S. Open, seven years after a twenty-year-old amateur named Francis Ouimet had introduced American golf to the front page by tying them for the Open at Brookline and beating them in the play-off.

And this time—this time, Ted Ray finished a single stroke in front of a four-way tie for runner-up, at Inverness; and in that quartet were Jock Hutchison, Leo Diegel, Jack Burke, and the great figure of British golf, Harry Vardon. This is the point: in 1900, Harry Vardon, aged thirty, came over to the States with his famous compatriot, John Henry Taylor, and Vardon won the U. S. Open at the Chicago Golf Club, with Taylor second. And twenty years later, as Dumas père would put it, at the age of fifty, Harry Vardon came back again. Fifty years old—and in the Open championship of 1920, with nine holes left to play, Harry Vardon was leading the field by four strokes.

And he was shooting the card. I know—I was tagging along with the pop-eyed gallery, covering my first U. S. Open. The Old Man was shooting the card. The championship was in the bag as he played

the 10th and 11th with a par and a birdie and stood on the tee of
the longest hole on the course, the 12th, 522 yards.

Well, if you follow this darned game long enough, it will make a
Presbyterian out of you, or anyway a fatalist. I mean, it seems to be
all in the book, before a ball is struck. . . . As Harry Vardon stood
up to drive from the 12th tee of that last round, a gale of wind came
sweeping down the green valley, full in his face, from under a towering black cloud in the northern sky. It required four strokes, all
perfectly played, for Harry Vardon to get the ball on that upland
green, for a dreadful 6. And he lost stroke after stroke on hole after
hole, till his lead was gone, and the gale died away, and the tired
Old Man clicked for his par 4 at the last green.

Statistics or no, I'll show you that final round, my not too humble
nomination for the classic tragedy of major league golf:

Par (out)	....	443	454	435—36	
Vardon	....	443	444	445—36	
Par (in)	....	445	344	444—36	—72
Vardon	....	436	455	564—42	—78

A par 4 at the 430-yard 17th, the 71st hole of the tournament,
would have made Harry Vardon again Open champion, at the age
of fifty. And his second shot, a desperate wood, landed on the fly
in a narrow little ditch in front of the green, a ditch no more than
four feet wide, for the penalty stroke and that second 6. If that shot
had traveled one yard farther, or one yard shorter, and bounded over
the beastly little ditch—as suggested, it makes a fatalist out of you.

Huge Ted Ray won, the 240-pounder who was knocking out drives
of around 300 yards. Did I say it was all in the book? Ask a member
of the Inverness Club of Toledo what they call that 320-yard dogleg
seventh hole today. "Ted Ray's Hole," he'll tell you. Straightening
out the angle, the longest walloper of his era went always for the
green, 290 yards away. He was on it twice; in a pot-bunker beside it
once; and in the fairway, just off the edge, the other time. He picked
off four birdie 3's, at Ted Ray's Hole. And he won the championship
by one stroke.

Quite a tournament, the first Big One in 1920. Besides the bowing
out of the great Vardon and the triumph of his vast teammate, a

number of other factors obtruded. There was young Leo Diegel, soon to be rated in the top rank of the tough-luck competitors. That 6 on the 417-yard 14th hole of the final round cropped up from a mental explosion, touched off, as he waited to play a difficult second shot, by a friend who came racing over to him with the news that Vardon had collapsed, and that Diegel "had it." That 6 left him one stroke out of the championship, just as another 6 at Hoylake a decade later kept him from tying Bobby Jones for the British Open of 1930.

Then there were a couple of promising youngsters, playing for the first time in the Big Show; nineteen-year-old Gene Sarazen, a rugged little professional, finishing modestly in 30th place, and an amateur from Atlanta, Georgia, listed as Robert T. Jones, Jr., aged eighteen, who finished 8th. Quite a lot was heard of these kids later.

And (still staying away from the statistics) one of the neatest little anecdotes that ever emerged from a golfing championship developed in this Inverness affair, in the second qualifying round.

In a gracious gesture to the young amateur, the committee paired Bobby Jones with Harry Vardon, and they had tied at 75 strokes in the first round of qualifying play. Bristling with emulation, Bobby was leading the great man by a single stroke at the sixth green of the second round. They both went for the carry over the dangerous angle of the Ted Ray Hole, the 17th, and both were safely in front of the green, with Vardon away. He played a simple run-up shot, close to the flag.

Not Bobby Jones. He drew the trusty niblick and, with nothing in the way, essayed one of those lovely cut pitches with a lot of backspin, a spectacular gallery shot when it comes off. This one didn't. Half topped, the ball went skittering across the green into a bunker beyond.

After the round I asked Bob what Mr. Vardon had said about his game. He had led the Old Master by two strokes at the end of the qualifying play. Mr. Vardon had said one thing, it appeared.

"Remember that second shot on the seventh?" Bob asked me.

I told him I'd never forget it.

"Well," said he, "as we were walking to the next tee, I tried to use up some of my embarrassment by asking Mr. Vardon if he'd ever seen a worse shot than that. He said, 'No.' And that was all he said."

Walter Hagen was in that field, too, finishing 11th, and Sir Walter had already won his two U. S. Opens, in 1914 and 1919. He was in the role of defending champion at Inverness, but his defense didn't come off. He was never to win another U. S. Open, but in the decade now dawning he won the British Open four times, and the P.G.A. championship of the United States five times—four of them in a row! And the blazing rivalry between Sir Walter and the budding Gene Sarazen became one of the top features of the Golden Age.

Chick Evans won the U. S. Amateur in 1920 at the Engineers Country Club on Long Island, defeating in the final round his traditional rival, Francis Ouimet, who had eliminated Bob Jones in the semifinals. And it was Chick Evans who had won the U. S. Open and the Amateur, back in 1916—a record that stood up until the Grand Slam of 1930, while his score of 286 in the Open was another record, good for precisely twenty years, until Tony Manero and Ralph Guldahl came along.

Now we will present the little redheaded Atlanta girl, true pupil of Stewart Maiden—Alexa Stirling, winner and champion for the third successive time in the Women's National, at the Mayfield Country Club of Cleveland, in 1920. And as Alexa bowed out of the championship picture, though she played top golf nearly a decade more, a demure young lady named Glenna Collett came in at Mayfield to lose in the final round and continue in major league golf until she had won six National championships of the United States, which is more than any other golfer, masculine or feminine, has yet racked up on the amateur scoreboard.

And with the victory of Jock Hutchison, the transplanted Scot, in the P. G. A., and with the hardy Hutch all set to open the ball in this startling era by winning the British Open the following year at Old St. Andrews, the picture seems to be fairly rounded out for the year 1920. Something was in the air at all these tournaments, something that set the gallery blood to tingling, as in the days of the First World War, when the professionals and the top amateurs and at least two of the girls, Alexa Stirling and Elaine Rosenthal, toured the country playing golf for the Red Cross. Something was in the air, along with the sunlight and the touch of Spring and the tang of Autumn, at all those golfing affairs of 1920.

That gallery swarming over the Engineers layout for the final match between Evans and Ouimet in the 1920 U. S. Amateur was

estimated at 13,000. But that wasn't the answer, only part of it.
Americans were beginning to play golf all over the premises. The
clubs were jammed. Public courses were spreading in every direction. The golfing population bounded up from around a quarter of
a million in 1916 to half a million in 1920, and in the next five years
to a peak that inspired me to swipe (with due credit) a line evolved
by O. Henry, who had recorded a classic rejoinder to the snobbish
old theory that there were in New York only four hundred people
who mattered. O. Henry wrote a great book entitled *The Four Million*. And I was struggling away on a little golf book, back in the
middle Twenties, *The Autobiography of an Average Golfer*, and I
headed the introduction "The Four Million of Golf."

It wasn't too flamboyant then. And now?

It still stands, I'd say. But the grand bounce came in the Golden
Age.

That's the way the game was catching on, in those Roaring Twenties. The Winter League was looping it, now, hither and yon,
swinging up to an unprecedented $25,000 open tournament at Agua
Caliente, in Mexico, when Gene Sarazen clicked for a 68 in the last
round to nose out by a single stroke Al Espinosa and Horton Smith,
the Tall Pine (or the Galloping Ghost) from Joplin. There was
money on the line in those days, too.

At Pinehurst, the St. Andrews of America, the North-South
championships were in full and tremendous swing. There was a
boom reported in Florida. Reported? They could hear it from as far
away as California!

The good old U.S.G.A., in 1922, inaugurated a formally approved
Public Links Championship and team match, with Jimmy Standish
of Detroit chairman of the committee about which I should love to
write freely and with unbridled enthusiasm, because I was a member
of it. And the U.S.G.A., with George H. Walker president in 1920,
had previously planned the International Match for the Walker
Cup with Great Britain, and Samuel Ryder of the Royal and Ancient
Golf Club at St. Andrews, five years after the amateur bouts began,
was handing out the Ryder Cup to the professionals of the two
great golfing nations. And those charming ladies, former United
States golfing champions, the Misses Harriot and Margaret Curtis,
were preparing to launch the Curtis Cup play, beginning in 1932.

The first playing of the Walker Cup Match was in August 1922, at the National Links of America, Southampton, Long Island. The first playing of the Ryder Cup Match was in June 1927, at the Worcester Country Club. The U. S. amateurs and professionals won the inaugural bouts, and when the ladies went at each other at the Wentworth Golf Club, in England, our side won that one, too, though the great Joyce Wethered captained the British and defeated our Glenna Collett Vare in the singles.

A good deal of preface, what? Well, now I'm going to take a statistical swing at the present generation of golfing fans and golfing writers, with a bewildered speculation (on my part) as to how so good a guesser as Robert Louis Stevenson could have referred to what he termed "the wiser youngsters of today."

You see, the vast trend of golf news and golf comment, as these lines escape a stuttering typewriter, is all along the statistical line— the scoring record busted for this course and that, carefully barbered for the performance of the P.G.A. cast, around what was once known as the Winter Loop, and now extending from New Year's to Christmas Eve; the financial standing of the leaders; the average scoring for the last 100 rounds by the topnotcher, who is showing up poor Old Man Par with an average card of well below 70. That sort of tripe.

Years ago I wrote a magazine article on the mechanization of golf, with the advent of the steel shaft and the sand wedge, declaring between sobs that the grand old game in its top phases now was played more by artisans than by artists. "Strong-back Golf," I think was the title.

Briefly, here's the idea, or notion. The steel shaft, emerging in 1930 and continually improved by the deadly ingenuity of the Yankee manufacturer, eliminated the always variable factors of whip and torsion of the hickory shafts, which never could be precisely matched or duplicated, even in the same set. That's why the heart of the golfing artist of the old school cracked along with the shaft on his pet driver, or mashie, or midiron. The great golfers prior to 1930 spent years accumulating a reasonably matched set of clubs, where now anybody can acquire, for quite a price, of course, an outfit with absolutely no variation of whip or torsion, in any kind of weather.

And in place of what Mr. Bernard Darwin once called "the almost drowsy grace of Bobby Jones," the top performers of today simply take that club back in a short, compact swing, as nearly grooved as possible, and bang the ball with it—with a club for practically every range, where Chick Evans, scoring 286 at Minikahda to set that record while winning the 1916 U. S. Open, employed just seven clubs—the same number his caddie carried when he won the U. S. Amateur of 1920, at the Engineers Club.

Fourteen clubs, as of today—and the P.G.A. permitted 16 for a time, some of them with facets the U.S.G.A. ordered filed off before the U. S. Open of 1947. As for the sand wedge, Bobby Cruickshank, one of the great veterans, had always rated it an implement rather than a golf club, and estimates that it saves the expert golfer an average of five strokes per tournament; that is, for 72 holes.

With this in mind, let us examine the improvement in scoring as of the decade of 1931-40 over the good old Golden Age, sticking strictly to the Big Show, the U. S. Open, which always has been played on a fairly testing golf course and not on a stage dressed and groomed and set for a four-act scoring drama with a gasping gallery as audience. Those scores of better than 280, now slithering down toward 270 and under—average rounds of 66 and 67 and 68—they're not going in the book for the U. S. Open, as yet.

The best score in the U. S. Open of the Golden Age was 287, made in 1930 at Interlachen, by Bob Jones, which was a stroke above the mark set by Chick Evans in 1916. The average winning score in this decade, 1920-30, was 293 strokes. The best score, and still the record, in the 1930-40 period was 281 by Ralph Guldahl in 1937 at Oakland Hills. And the average winning score was 287½, which is precisely 5½ strokes per tournament better than in the good old wood-shaft days. And Bobby Cruickshank estimates the sand wedge as saving at least five strokes of that margin!

We will leave the "wiser youngsters of today," then, to exult over the rounds in the 60's, but not often in the Big Show, merely mentioning that back about 1920, George Duncan once knocked off a round in 56 on a Swiss layout—not a very large one, of course. And we will trundle along into an era in which, if figures really don't lie, liars did figure, at times—but not as statistically as of today.

Incidentally, they didn't need to do any prevaricating about a record score in the Canadian Open, the season before the Golden Age began. Douglas Edgar, the little English professional who came over to the Druid Hills Golf Club in Atlanta in the early Summer of 1919, went up to Hamilton, Ontario, homesick and displeased with American ideas of prohibition, and shot four rounds on a very excellent golf course as follows: 72-71-69-66—278. This naturally won the Canadian Open championship and stood up for a lot of years as the lowest score ever recorded in a national affair. It still remains the widest margin of victory—a margin of 16 strokes, with second place shared at 294 by Long Jim Barnes and a seventeen-year-old kid from Atlanta named Bobby Jones.

Having somewhat disposed of 1920, we now find ourselves in the following year with quite a delegation venturing over to Great Britain, where Bob Gardner, the old Yale man, the season before had escorted Cyril James Hastings Tolley to the 37th green before losing the final match in the British Amateur at Muirfield. Several British amateurs tried out in our tournament at the Engineers Club in 1920—Mr. Tolley, Roger Wethered, and Lord Charles Hope— and none of them qualified, which was sad and surprising.

We didn't do so well over the Royal Liverpool layout at Hoylake. Willie Hunter, the diminutive English amateur, won it, and Bobby Jones was batted down with a quaint brass putter, 6-5, in the hands of a genial gentleman, Allan Graham, and a sort of British-American pick-up team match presaged the inaugural Walker Cup bout that arrived the next year.

Then the British Open at Old St. Andrews, and the amazing victory of Jock Hutchison, the transplanted Scot, returning to his native heath after all those years and in the first round knocking in an ace at the 142-yard eighth hole, following it with a drive of 306 yards that trickled over the rim of the ninth hole, and missing another ace by three inches! Picking up four strokes on par at these two holes, Jock went on through some rather dreadful golf in the next two rounds, and against a par of 73 did a great 70 in the fourth round, to tie Roger Wethered, the tall English amateur, who lost a stroke—and eventually the championship—by stepping on his ball as he backed down from a dune after getting a line on the 16th green.

No blubbering about it either. No alibi.

"My feet are just too big," said Roger, with a grin. And Hutchison beat him in the play-off next day.

Bob Jones made his prize error in this British Open. After two rather dismal rounds, he ran into a string of boxcars or 6's in Round 3 and picked up his ball at the 11th green, thus retiring from the competition, though he played out that round and the fourth. That was the most regrettable act of his golfing life. And yet, five years later, the bitter memory of that juvenile mistake paved the way to a British Open championship and one of the great chapters of his career. Of which, later.

That 1921 Open was the curtain raiser of a calamitous decade in British golf, as the Golden Age swept across the blue Atlantic from the U. S. A. In those ten years only one British golfer won the British Open—Arthur Havers in 1923. Hutchison was born a Scot, and Long Jim Barnes was originally a Cornishman, but both were playing from the U. S. A. Barnes won at Prestwick in 1925. Walter Hagen won the classic fixture in 1922 and 1924, 1928 and 1929, and Bob Jones won it in 1926, 1927, and 1930, three times in four starts.

Stretching the string into the next decade, Tommy Armour, who started the game of life in Carnoustie, Scotland, and came to the U. S. A. as an amateur in 1920, turning professional a few years later, won the British Open in 1931. Gene Sarazen won it in 1932 and returned to win the U. S. Open at Fresh Meadow, the only competitor except Jones to win the British and U. S. Open the same season. And Densmore Shute, with a miraculously balanced par score of 73-73-73-73—292 at St. Andrews, tied with Craig Wood, another born American, and beat him in the play-off in 1933.

Quite a hangover, for the Golden Age!

Still sticking to 1921 and the Open championship, which, of course, is the Big Show, the brave lads came back to America, and Jim Barnes proceeded to spreadeagle a great field at the Columbia Country Club, Washington, D. C., by nine large strokes, with Walter Hagen and wee Freddie McLeod tied as runners-up, and Chick Evans nosing out his now established amateur rival, Bobby Jones, by a single stroke for fourth place. Mr. Jones had started his fourth round with two birdies and two pars and then a fine, fat 9 at the long fifth, where he went for the green with a brassie and batted two

out of bounds. At that period—and he never really got over it—
he had absorbed a large dose of the Walter Hagen idea of shooting
the works. First place or what the hell!

According to the records, it seems to have worked fairly well
for both of them.

Anyway, starting the following season, 1922, at Skokie, Mr. Jones
established a record in the United States Open which is almost as
unlikely to be matched as the so-called Grand Slam. In nine consecutive playings of the U. S. Open, he finished first or second
eight times. First, four times. Second, four times—twice after losing
in play-offs—so that he hit the leading score in six out of nine starts.

All this, starting at the age of twenty, plus five U. S. Amateur
championships in nine starts, three straight victories in the British
Open, and a fifty-fifty split in two British Amateurs—all this, mind
you, beginning in 1922 when Gene Sarazen, a twenty-one-year-old
professional, beat him out by one stroke for the U. S. Open, and Jess
Sweetser, a twenty-year-old Yale undergraduate, knocked him off
in the semifinal round of the U. S. Amateur and went on to beat
Chick Evans in the final.

No use trying to get it straight. From this point on, the story,
or saga, involving these Three Musketeers and their celebrated contemporaries in the Golden Age of golf is destined to be a garbled
continuation of the narrative beginning when the agitated Cavalier,
leaping upon his horse, galloped off madly in all directions.

For one phase, the build-up of the incredible Jones career involves
a stretch some of us older guys got to calling the Seven Lean Years,
a stretch of which the Four Million of golf, or most of them, are
extremely ignorant. The Four Million remember the Grand Slam.
They are likely to be somewhat shocked to learn that in the seven
years from 1916 to 1923, Bob Jones, his age climbing from fourteen
to twenty-one years, played in 11 major, or national, golf championships without winning one. Oh, yes, he won the Southern Amateur
a few times, and the first playing of the Georgia State Amateur;
and a lot of tourneys; but nothing in the Big Time.

Then, in the next stretch, the Eight Fat Years, from 1923 through
1930, he won 13 national championships in 21 starts, a score which,
absurdly enough, would rate him a better than even-money favorite
against the field—something nobody dares dream about, in golf.

Just as well ease out of it by suggesting, as a charming banality, that it could have happened only in the Golden Age of Sports.

And I'll let you all in on this much: it will never happen again.

Walter Hagen's record is nearest to that of Jones, rated, of course, on the United States and British Open championships, and the P.G.A. In a span of sixteen years, Sir Walter tucked away two U. S. Opens, four British Opens, and five P.G.A. titles, four of them in a row, for a total of 11 major league victories. And nine of these came in eight years, 1922-29, nearly the same period in which his amateur rival was going in the book.

There's a curious chapter in the Hagen-Jones rivalry, which serves to introduce an even "curiouser" one in the Hagen history.

In the early Spring of 1926, when that previously mentioned Florida boom was resounding, a lot of golf was being played all over that state, and a special 72-hole home-and-home match was arranged between Walter Hagen, professional at Pasadena, and Bob Jones, wintering at Sarasota.

The arrangement involved 36 holes at Sarasota one Sunday, and 36 holes a week later at Pasadena. Sir Walter, sleek headed, cold, smiling, playing the odd frequently—and close to the pin—finished the first half of that match 8 up! And on his home course the following Sabbath he kept the iron pressure on the desperate amateur and closed him out, 12-11, holing a 20-foot putt for a birdie 3 at the finishing green to end the match after Jones himself had canned a 30-footer for a birdie 3, in the effort to keep it going.

There was a lot of talk about a return bout, but the U.S.G.A. said no, emphatically, unless it was played for charity. From the gallery ticket sales Sir Walter picked up $7,000 from this affair, and when he gave Bob a little token of his appreciation in the form of a pair of platinum cuff links set with emeralds and diamonds, Bob said:

"Walter, you have now ruined me twice! This licking, of course, and I'll be busted the rest of my life trying to buy shirts to fit these links."

You may exercise the old imagination, if you weren't in circulation in those days, on what a kick the Four Million got out of that match. A lot of the opinion was to the effect that that would be about all for Bobby Jones in the Big Time—anyway in the open championships. Yet later that same season, 1926, Jones won the British Open at St. Anne's, with Hagen trailing by four strokes, and then he came home and won the U. S. Open at Scioto, the first "double" in golf history, with Hagen in seventh place, five strokes behind.

You couldn't go out on a limb, where Jones or Hagen was concerned, in those days. Anyway, you'd better not.

Take the Hagen-Compston episode, as the other half of the example.

In 1929, Sir Walter and his manager-genius, Bob Harlow, set out for Britain, where Sir Walter was seeking his fourth triumph in the British Open, at Muirfield. Mr. Harlow had arranged a special match at 72 holes for his champion with Archie Compston, a six-foot-four English professional, for a fee of £500, said to be the highest ever assigned to a professional golfer for one bout. Compston had trained for this match; Hagen was lately off the boat—where he had been living rather comfortably—and Compston gave him at Moor Park the most colossal drubbing on record in the top flight, 18-17.

And a fortnight later at Muirfield, Sir Walter won his fourth British Open—and Archie Compston finished third!

Touring exhibitions and special matches were sharing the spotlight at this time with the Winter Loop and the regular fixtures and educating the Four Million and their sisters and their cousins and their aunts in the traditions of golf and the difficult practice of standing still and holding their breath instead of leaping up and down and bellowing when the clutch was on, as at football and baseball.

Bob Harlow had Walter Hagen and Joe Kirkwood, the famous Australian trick shooter who came over here in the dawn of the Golden Age, on tour after tour, and in one of the Winter circuits, this pair won seven tournaments, Hagen four, and Kirkwood three, which was quite a feat in the days before the professionals began playing the road-show circuit, with a tourney a week. George Duncan and Abe Mitchell came over from Britain for a lot of touring; also Archie Compston and Arnaud Massey, the startling Frenchman who won the British Open at Hoylake soon after the turn of the century.

Arthur Havers was over also, in 1924, the year after he won the British Open, and it all contributed heartily to the grip of the game on the good old American public, though none of the visiting firemen in that era, or later, was able to capture the U. S. Open after the Ted

Ray conquest of 1920. The late Harold Hilton, famous English golfer, had won the U. S. Amateur away back in 1911, and Dorothy Campbell, playing from Britain, or anyway from Canada, won the U. S. Women's championship in 1909 and 1910—the only woman who ever won the British Ladies' and the U. S. Women's Amateur in the same season. And in 1924, as Mrs. Dorothy Campbell Hurd, and (I think) naturalized in this country, this same great competitor supplied a prime feature of the Golden Age by defeating in the final round of the National the tennis expert, Mary K. Browne, who had taken up golf just to show what she could do with that game— and had showed what she could do by defeating Glenna Collett in the semifinal round at the 19th green, after the great Glenna had won the qualifying medal.

And Glenna Collett, later Mrs. Edwin H. Vare, U. S. champion in 1922, went on to win five more U. S. titles and, as suggested earlier in this narrative, established a record for an amateur, masculine or feminine, in the U. S. book with six championships.

Where does all this escort us to? Somewhere along in the Golden Age, not long before that curious match of three-out-of-five bouts for the Mythical Championship of the World in 1928, between Johnny Farrell, who had beaten Bob Jones by a single stroke in the 36-hole play-off after a tie for the U. S. Open at Olympia Fields, and Sir Walter Hagen, who had won that British Open again, at the Royal St. George's Club, Sandwich, England. As I recall it, the mythical affair packed them in and went the limit. The wise guys said it was fixed, Bob Harlow says it wasn't, and his boss won three out of five, played at Detroit, New York, Philadelphia, Chicago, and St. Louis.

The combats between Hagen and Gene Sarazen went to an early peak in 1923 at Pelham Manor, where Gene was defending his 1922 P.G.A. championship, won at Oakmont. The brave lads were playing all 36-hole matches in those days, and it was Gene and Sir Walter in the final round. I'll never see a tougher match than this one, anyway not before checking in at Valhalla. And, as Damon Runyon used to say, a story goes with it.

The sixth hole at Pelham, 385 yards, was a rather freakish affair, a long, straight drive placing the ball at the foot of a steep hill, with a direction flag on top and the well-trapped green a steep little pitch beyond.

The boys were level at this juncture in the morning round, and they both drove well and pitched over the hill. I was walking near Gene and the "marker"; there was no umpire or referee. Gene's pitch had come to rest just off the green, on a sort of partition between two bunkers, over which players habitually marched on their way to the next tee. The grass had been worn away by this process.

Hagen's ball was on the green some 10 yards from the flag. An Autumn leaf had settled on Sarazen's ball, and as he inspected the position, he asked the marker if he could remove the leaf. The marker said sure, and Gene dropped the leaf in the bunker.

Then the marker said:

"Hold on there! That ball is in a path, and a path is a hazard!"

Hagen began sauntering over to see what was going on.

"Well, I've picked up something," said Gene. "What about it?"

The marker now was bewildered for fair.

"I dunno," he said, "but a path is a hazard, and. . . ."

"What'll I do?" cut in Gene, crisply.

Walter Hagen spoke up, in a thin, dry tenor.

"Aw, Gene," he said, "you ought to know the rules. Go ahead and play! There's no penalty."

Sarazen chipped loosely, lost the hole to a par 4, and didn't hit the fairway with his next three drives; but the match was square at the intermission. I had lunch with Gene, and he didn't talk any until we were finished and starting toward the first tee for the matinee round. Then he said:

"Were you at the sixth green this morning?"

I told him I was.

"Then you heard what Hagen pulled on me—showing me up before the gallery. I'll beat him for that if it's the last thing I do!"

Going out two under par, Sarazen was 3 up at the turn of the afternoon round, but the Haig, two under par for the second nine, was square at the home green, and the extra holes began with No. 1, a 494-yard par 5, on an upland green.

Sarazen was home with a drive and brassie. Hagen had outranged him by a couple of yards from the tee, but the ball was in a tight lie, an old divot scar. He addressed it with a brassie, switched to a spoon, shook his sleek black head, and drew the big iron. I have never seen a ball hit any harder. He was on that green with an iron bang of 240 yards, and the hole was halved with a birdie 4 each.

The second hole, 310 yards, was a sharp dogleg to the left, with a house and a tall cluster of trees in the out-of-bounds angle. Sir Walter hit a fine drive with a light tail-end pull past the angle, pin high and a wee pitch to the green over a shallow little pot-bunker. Sarazen went for the angle, a desperately bold and even reckless shot, and the ball was tagged by the top of one of the trees and dropped in tall rough, in line with the small green, but 40 yards short.

And then he blazed it out with a niblick, two feet from the flag!

For once the Haig flubbed one in the clutch, right into the little bunker. He nearly holed the recovery, and Sarazen canned his birdie 3, for the match and the championship.

Then the Haig won that P.G.A. tourney the next four years in a row. He was hard to keep down, that baby!

The Pelham affair, as mentioned, was in 1923, when Bob Jones finally broke loose from the Lean Years and won the U. S. Open at Inwood in a playoff with Bobby Cruikshank, who finished with a birdie 3 at the 425-yard home hole on which Jones had taken a gruesome 6. And that play-off! It was at 18 holes in those days, and they halved precisely three of them. On 15 greens one or the other picked up a stroke—or lost it, if you prefer. Bobby Cruikshank went on to the fringe of three other U. S. Opens, which he nearly won, but never again was he as close as when that 200-yard iron shot from hard turf in the rough was fired by Bob Jones across the lagoon at the green's front, six feet past the flag, on the last hole of that desperate play-off.

And then, while Bob Jones for eight successive years, to the end of his golfing days, was never without a U. S. championship, he was knocked off in the second round of the U. S. Amateur of 1923 at Flossmoor by Max Marston, who went on to beat Jess Sweetser, defender from 1922, with a stone-dead stymie on the 38th green of one of the toughest matches that ever went into the book.

The book! More and more it seemed always to have been in there before anything began.

As for the U. S. Amateur, Bob Jones finally won on his seventh start, at the Merion Cricket Club, after a putting lesson that Spring of 1924 by the late Walter J. Travis, at Augusta, Georgia. That same season, Cyril Walker eased him out of first place in the U. S. Open by three strokes, at Oakland Hills, with some amazingly consistent play. And Willie Macfarlane, another imported golfer of genius and charm, beat Bobby in the second playoff after a tie for the U. S. Open of 1925, at Worcester.

Later in that eventful year, Mr. Jones protégéed young Watts Gunn, his clubmate from the Atlanta Athletic Club, up to the U. S. Amateur at Oakmont, and Mr. Gunn, never having played in the Big Time before, proceeded to qualify and set a world record by winning 15 consecutive holes from Vincent Bradford in the first match, going from 3 down at the 11th to win, 12-10. He then beat Jess Sweetser, 10-9, and Dicky Jones, 5-3; and in the final bout, with his chaperon and clubmate, he had Bob Jones 1 down at the 12th hole of the morning round and was 2 under par at Oakmont before Mr. Jones assembled himself and began shooting 3's at him.

This eventually turned out successfully for Mr. Jones, in the only final-round battle between clubmates in U. S. Amateur history.

And now for 1926, and the conquest of Britain, and the triumphs of Sweetser and Jones in the British championships, and the Walker Cup team victory—the first complete Yankee cleanup, barring the Ladies' affair, and all administered in a mode that appeared to the somewhat complacent visiting delegation not to be really unpleasant to their hosts.

Jess Sweetser's conquest in the British Amateur at Muirfield was a triumph in more ways than one. Jess was on the verge of a dangerous illness. He didn't know how ill he was at Muirfield. He was complaining of a heavy cold, and he quit talking about it when some sprightly members of the United States Johnny Walker Cup team—the working press men—began inquiring what had happened to the Old Yale Spirit. Jess went on to win that championship, the first American-born victor in the British Amateur. And he won his match at singles in the Walker Cup engagement at St. Andrews and, with George Von Elm, won their foursomes bout.

Shortly after midnight, following that match at St. Andrews and the great dinner party at the Royal and Ancient Golf Club, Sweetser suffered a lung hemorrhage in my room at the hotel, where he joined me after my belated return from the dinner party and a valiant endeavor with several stubborn survivors to finish a couple of gallons of champagne which remained in the Walker Cup.

I spent my birthday that year sort of looking after Jess Sweetser and, with Bob Gardner, the Walker Cup team captain, and Bob

Jones, persuading a couple of hardheaded Scottish medical men that good old Jess really was able to take the train the next day for London, and the *Aquitania*, and home. They finally agreed and, as all the world ascertained a long time afterward, gallant Jess made the voyage in great shape, considering, and regained his health at Saranac and Asheville, and in two years was playing, and winning, in the Walker Cup Match again.

Now for the reflex action of that Jones error of 1921, five years before, when he picked up in the third round of the British Open at St. Andrews. The Jones boy may have been depressed at that time, but nothing to compare with his gloom after Andrew Jamieson had beaten him in the sixth round of the British Amateur at Muirfield. He wasn't driving well. He was spraying the big shots all over the place. But he had settled down in one round to defeat the defending champion, Robert Harris, with a card three strokes under par. And he went on to the quarter-finals, where Jamieson caught him three strokes over par and beat him, 4-3.

Bob rather solemnly told me later that if it hadn't been for the memory of that 1921 blunder, he'd certainly have chucked his tentative entry for the British Open and sailed for home on the *Aquitania*. But that 1921 mistake—something really had to be done about that. So he stayed on for the British Open.

And the first break he got was a driver.

Bob had tried out 11 drivers since landing in Britain, and none of them seemed to be working for him. When he got down to Sunningdale, where the Southern section was to qualify for the British Open, Jack White, veteran professional, then on duty there, had made up for him a driving club that resembled something from the workbench of the late Benvenuto Cellini, if that celebrated artificer had been addicted to golf.

The Jack White driver was the answer, or anyway a large part of it. Around the Sunningdale course, where the record at that time was 70, Bob Jones scored 66 in two practice rounds, and then, qualifying for the British Open, set a record which at this writing still endures: 66-68—134. This was just 10 strokes better than par on one of the finest inland courses in Britain, and seven strokes ahead of a great field.

"Incredible and indecent," chuckled the greatest of all golf writers,

Mr. Bernard Darwin, rating that 66 the finest competitive round ever
played in Britain. Well, there wasn't a 2 or a 5 in that round. There
were six 3's, and a dozen 4's. Twelve pars and six birdies. Out in 33,
back in 33. And (get this) 33 putts and 33 other shots!

One single mistake, in all that round, and it didn't cost anything. Bob's iron shot for the 175-yard 13th slid over the fast, flat
green into a pot-bunker, and he chipped out and holed the putt for
a par 3. That's the only time he was off the line.

Then he went up to Lytham and St. Anne's, and—never again on
the game as he played it at Sunningdale, he scored 72-72-73-74—291,
finished two strokes ahead of his fellow-competitor, Al Watrous, and
became the first amateur to win the British Open since Harold Hilton
in 1897, five years before Bob Jones was born.

And then what the newsprints blithely termed the "First World
Championship in Golf." Home again, the Macon meeting the Aquitania to take the golfing party off at Quarantine, the ticker-tape
parade up Broadway to the City Hall, and the reception by Mayor
Jimmy Walker—the Golden Age now glittering for fair! On to
Columbus, Ohio, and the Scioto Country Club; And six strokes back
of the field at half-time, and unable to eat breakfast before the last
two rounds. Four strokes back of Joe Turnesa, with seven holes left
to play, Bob Jones once more began batting down Old Man Par
and, with that birdie 4 at the 485-yard 72nd green, he went one single
stroke ahead of Turnesa.

For the first official World Championship ever racked up, in golf
. . . I remember how oddly subdued he was, after that last round.
He said something about it being a plain miracle, and that he was
glad of it, because he'd never have another chance to win both those
championships in the same year again.

But he did have the chance in 1930. And he won them again.
You can't tell what's in the book, in this game.

Later in 1926, George Von Elm got revenge for two previous beat-
ings in the U. S. Amateur, defeating Jones, 2-1, in the final round at
Baltusrol, where Jones had beaten his famous rivals, Chick Evans and
Francis Ouimet, in successive matches. And then, in 1927, after his
worst finish in the U. S. Open, 11th place at Oakmont, Bob suddenly
decided to have another shot at the British Open, again being played
at Auld St. Andrews. So he went over there, arriving less than a week

before the tournament, with his father and Stewart Maiden, his veteran preceptor, mentor, and model in golf. And again Mr. Darwin's charming play on words emerged in comment on his score for the British Open, 68-72-73-72—285, over the famous old par-73 course.

"This championship," wrote Mr. Darwin, "will always be remembered for the fact that Bobby performed the wholly indecent and profane feat of holing four rounds of the links in a score of three under an average of 4's."

Still a record, for the British Open at St. Andrews. When Sammy Snead won the championship nineteen years later, in 1946, his score was 290, which is two strokes better than par, and five strokes worse than Jones'. I can't help quoting Mr. Darwin again on that Jones finish in 1927, when, with a gallery of 20,000 massed about the great home green, Bob Jones holed the final putt to finish six strokes ahead of the field:

The scene that followed was wonderful. Not even when Francis Ouimet beat Vardon and Ray at Brookline was there such a riot of joy. Personally, I thought Bobby was going to be killed in the very hour of victory.

One moment stood he as the angels stand shaking hands with Andrew Kirkaldy, and the next he was not. For the crowd, unmindful of anything or anybody else, stormed up the slope and swallowed him. It was a real relief when, after what seemed whole minutes, Bobby reappeared, his putter held high over his head, borne aloft on admiring shoulders. It was a wonderful demonstration of personal popularity, but it was something more than that. It showed that the Scottish crowd, the most passionately patriotic crowd in the world, knows a great golfer when it sees one, and knew that Bobby was by so far the greatest there that it could not bear anyone else to win.

Well, Bobby left the little silver pitcher there, at the Royal and Ancient Golf Club ("of which I have the honor to be a member," he explained), requesting his fellow-members to take care of it during the year of his championship. You may guess if that registered with that Scottish gallery! And he came home and he won the U. S. Amateur at Minikahda, defeating Chick Evans one more time in the final round, so his stretch of United States championships was still intact after five years. And in 1928, he won the U. S. Amateur again and captained the Walker Cup team in the 11-1 victory at the Chicago Golf Club.

Jones kept getting involved in play-offs in the U. S. Open. He lost the 1928 affair to Johnny Farrell at Olympia Fields, and he holed a 12-foot putt at the last green at Winged Foot in 1929 to tie Al Espinosa—the most important shot he ever played—and won the play-off next day, which was extremely lucky for Mr. Jones, as he got licked in the first round of the U. S. Amateur later that year by Johnny Goodman at Pebble Beach.

But the string of national championships was still unbroken, extending to seven years, when 1930 arrived.

In the other brackets, Walter Hagen had run out his four straight wins in the P.G.A., Leo Diegel, the hard-luck guy, had won it in 1928 and 1929. And Tommy Armour, now the Silvering Scot, had added the P.G.A. crown of 1930 to his great victory in the U. S. Open of 1927. Glenna Collett had settled down to a straight run of three Women's championships in 1928, 1929, and 1930. In 1930, our side won the Walker Cup Match for the sixth straight time, and while Glenna was losing at Formby, England, to Diana Fishwick, in the British Ladies' affair, the curtain was rising with a stately leisure on the closing act of the Golden Age of golf, known popularly as the Grand Slam.

Of course, there's a lot of Jones in that closing scene. After the last trick at Merion, Francis Powers paraphrased Grantland Rice's most famous football line, adapting it to the 1930 situation in golf:

"Once again the Four Horsemen of the Apocalypse galloped away together, this time over the emerald fairways of Merion, and their names were Jones, Jones, Jones, Jones."

Yet there were so many, so many, in that stellar cast of the Golden Age! So many who played well their part: Macdonald Smith, the classic stylist, who pushed Bob Jones to the wire in the 1930 British Open at Hoylake, and again, two strokes behind him, was runner-up in the U. S. Open at Interlachen, picking up five strokes on the champion in that last round. There was Wild Bill Mehlhorn, slashing away at the top in 1924, 1926, and 1927; and Harry Cooper, tying Armour in 1927, and on the heels of the champ in three other major engagements.

There were Jesse Guilford, the Boston Siege Gun; Harrison Johnston, who beat the stubborn Dr. Willing in that curious 1929 U. S. Amateur at Pebble Beach; and, among the *femmes*, the sprightly Miriam Burns Horn, champion in 1927; Marion Hollins, a great promoter of feminine golf as well as champion in 1921; Edith Cummings, who beat Alexa Stirling in the final of the 1923 championship and Opal Hill of Kansas City, who took up golf at the age of thirty-five on the urgent advice of her physician and went on to win everything in the U.S.A. of any importance, excepting only the National.

They all, and scores of others in the glow of the spotlight, participated in the tremendous build-up of golf in the Twenties toward a peak unlikely to be equaled, for the game, and which most probably will remain forever unmatched as a climax of individual achievement.

Which brings us back to Old St. Andrews in the early Summer of 1930, following the winning of the Walker Cup Match at the Royal St. George's Golf Club, at Sandwich, 10 points to 2, with Bob Jones the captain of our side. Jones had sort of gone in training for this expedition by playing in two of the late Winter tournaments in his home state, finishing as runner-up in the Savannah Open, one stroke back of Horton Smith, the Tall Pine from Joplin, with a score of 279 to 278, figures which don't look so bilious even in these statistical days. Then, over at Augusta, playing two rounds at the long and very tough Augusta Country Club and two at Forest Hills, Bob Jones spreadeagled a great field of professionals in a mode reminiscent of Douglas Edgar in that Canadian Open.

This time, Horton Smith was runner-up to Jones, who topped the field by 13 strokes, with a score of 284.

It was while Bob was finishing his last round that Bobby Cruikshank, refreshing himself with a spot of tea on the lawn, handed me the following prediction:

"He's just too good," he said, referring to Bobby Jones. "He's going over to Britain, and he's going to win the British Amateur and the British Open, and then he's coming back over here and win the National Open and the National Amateur. They'll never stop him, this year."

Of course, I didn't let any of this escape in print at the time. And it still looks sort of incredible, now. But Bobby Cruikshank was right.

At St. Andrews, with a field of 270 competitors in the British Amateur, Bob had four tough bouts before he got into the final round. His first opponent was one Syd Roper, and all Syd, a hitherto unknown golfer, shot at him for the first 16 holes of a par-73 course was fifteen 4's and one 5. Syd started off on par precisely, 4-4-4-4, and was 3 down; Jones had 3-4-3-2, the eagle deuce resulting from the holing of a stiff pitch from the sand of a bunker on a hole of 427 yards. This start gave Jones a lead of 3 up, and he was just able to hang on to it.

Then he won an extra-hole match with the defending champion, Cyril Tolley, and two more tough ones, with Harrison Johnston, U. S. Amateur champion of 1929, and George Voigt, who had him 2 down with five holes to play.

And at last reaching the 36-hole stage, all the other battles being of the sudden-death variety, Bob went steadily away to win, 7-6, over Roger Wethered, after which a stalwart police escort convoyed him nearly a mile to the clubhouse from the 12th green through a gallery estimated at 25,000 adoring fans.

In the British Open at Hoylake, Bob Jones said afterward that there were at least five other competitors playing better golf than he was—Macdonald Smith, Leo Diegel, and Horton Smith, from the U. S. A., and Fred Robson and Archie Compston, British professionals. Messrs. Smith and Diegel, in fact, had him collared in the fourth and last round when he laced a spoon second 20 yards from the green of the seventh hole and used up five more strokes in a dreadful 7. Diegel was still tied with him when, an hour after Jones finished, Leo stood on the tee of the 532-yard 16th, with three more holes to play. But Diegel was bunkered on his drive and scored a 6, while Jones, also bunkered beside the green with his second, had blasted out four inches from the cup for a birdie 4. And that was the margin.

I will always believe it was while waiting for the jury to come in—Mac Smith and Leo Diegel—that Bob Jones decided he was playing his last season in competitive golf. I was getting the news from the front by the old grapevine and carrying it up to the secretary's room in the clubhouse, and I remember asking Bob, rather impolitely, when he was going to quit this darned foolishness. I reckon it was pretty rough on both of our sets of nerves.

"Pretty soon, I think—and hope," he replied. "There's no game worth these last three days!"

But he had two more engagements, and he knew that, for sure.

Well, if you think that Broadway parade of 1926 was something, you should have seen the New York greeting this time, the million homelings amplified along the thoroughfare by a trainload of Atlanta fans, quite a number of whom went on over to Minneapolis for the U. S. Open at Interlachen. And there, in case you are still skeptical about it all being in the book, I'll sort of boil down that championship to one shot in the second round, when Jones was completing two scores of 71-73—144 to be two strokes back of Horton Smith at the halfway mark.

The ninth, at Interlachen, is a dogleg to the right of 485 yards, with the second shot a big one across a pretty little lake, to a small and well-guarded green. Bob's drive was cut slightly, off to the right, the ball winding up in a tight and somewhat hanging lie. As usual, he decided to go for it anyway, and he laid into that spoon shot with all he had. And half-topped it.

The ball went away like a rifle bullet, certain not to carry the beastly little lake. And a ball in the water there would rate him playing 4 from the bank, with a probable 6, and a very possible 7, resulting.

They call it the "Lily Pad Shot" in Minneapolis to this day. But I didn't see it strike any lily pads.

The ball hit the water 20 yards from the farther bank, skipped like a flat stone once and again, and hopped out on a smooth, grassy slope, 30 yards short of the green.

Did you ever hear a composite gasp by 10,000 pair of deflated lungs? I did, then. And after it "the roar of the crowd."

Bob seemed to have regained his composure while walking around the lovely little lake. He stuck a wee pitch two feet from the flag and holed a birdie 4. That break saved him two strokes—at least. He won the championship by two strokes.

Who says it's not in the book, before ever a ball is hit?

Jones broke loose next morning with a score of 33-35—68 and seemed to have the Third Trick sewed up. Then he used 38 strokes on the first nine of the matinee round, and at the 13th green, Macdonald Smith, starting that round seven strokes in the rear, was only a single stroke down. But Jones canned a 40-foot putt for a birdie at the 402-yard finishing hole, and Mac Smith, after his gallant spurt, couldn't quite negotiate the eagle deuce needed there for a tie. He got his par 4, and was two strokes behind.

And the Third Trick was in the bag.

Last stop, Merion. That's the way the headlines were chanting it. And after winning the medal for the U. S. Amateur of 1930 with a score of 142, tying what was then the record, Bob Jones won his five matches, the closest margin being 5-4.

Looks easy, now. Yet that was the only championship tournament I can recall when the Jones boy couldn't sleep at night, when he was supposed to be sleeping. Bob himself seemed not to know what was the matter. . . . He was in the locker room during the intermission of his 36-hole bout with Fay Coleman. He was 2 up and was talking with Mickey Cochrane, celebrated catcher with the Philadelphia Athletics and quite a golfer himself. Mickey asked him how he was feeling.

"Fine," said Bob. "I never felt better. But I can't seem to get those shots going right. I don't know what's the matter."

Mickey Cochrane grinned and told him not to worry—any more than he could help. I walked away with Mickey, and when we got out of hearing the great catcher said:

"I know what's the matter. It's that fourth championship. He's got three in the bag and the strain is now bearing down. It's that way in baseball. When you're in a series and you simply have to win all four games, and you've won three of them, you'll go out there feeling all right, every way, and everything seems to go all wrong. The old strain is bearing down."

Anyway, Bob always managed to get going, and he beat Coleman that afternoon, 6-5, and in the semifinal round next day with Jess Sweetser, who had given him the worst drubbing of his major tournament career in the 1922 U. S. Amateur at Brookline, he won, 9-8. After the match Jess came over to Bob's locker while they were dressing.

"I tried like the devil to carry you to the 11th green," said Jess with a grin. "That would have made it 8-7, the same as at Brookline. And then I could have said 'Well, Bobby, we're all square, after eight years.' But I couldn't make it. You're 1 up!"

You hear some remarkable lines in locker rooms. Some of them sort of make your eyes sting.

And I'll never forget Bob's daddy, Big Bob Jones, getting a line from a fan trotting along far ahead of the vast gallery, pouring slowly down the long slope toward the green in the valley where Big Bob was waiting—worried as always. Big Bob wasn't following that final match, with Gene Homans. But he certainly cocked an ear when somebody on the hillside hailed the chap coming in from the front and asked him how they stood.

The trotting fan slowed to a walk.

"He's 8 up," he said. "It's in the bag."

Big Bob said nothing. His expression never changed a line. But I could hear him humming low under his breath. And if he had been singing the words, they would have been:

"There's a long, long trail awinding into the land of my dreams."

Sweet spot, Merion, for the curtain. Merion, where the Jones boy played in his first major championship, the U. S. Amateur of 1916, just half his lifetime before.

The curtain for the last scene which, as George Trevor said, "entrenched his record safely and forever, with the Impregnable Quadrilateral of Golf."

The curtain, too, for the Golden Age of golf, a game that will go on forever, but never again will lay hold upon the heart of sport with quite so firm a grasp.

TENNIS

by ALLISON DANZIG
Tennis Editor, The New York Times

When they call the roll of the immortals of lawn tennis, one name always goes to the head of the class. It's William T. Tilden, 2nd, and no arguments.

When it comes to ranking the women players, the debate becomes more lively but almost invariably it ends with Mlle Suzanne Lenglen, La Belle Suzanne, on top.

Tilden and Lenglen, the two most magic names tennis has given to the world since Major Walter Clopton Wingfield introduced the game under the Greek cognomen of *Sphairistike* in 1873, both came into the plenitude of their powers immediately following the First World War. The decade of the 1920's exactly spanned the career of Tilden as an amateur of international renown. For the first six years, the tall, gaunt egoist strutted across the courts as the unrivaled colossus, champion of the world, master of strokes and spin, strategist par excellence, a Nijinsky for zephyrous movement, and a showman whose love of the limelight and high regard for his own opinion made him a firebrand and an international incident.

Suzanne Lenglen, glamorous queen of transcendent grace, before whom Wimbledon, Paris, and the French Riviera bent the knee until she offended royalty, to cancel a presentation at the Court of St. James, held sway just as majestically and imperiously from 1919 to 1926. No other player might be mentioned in the same breath with her—not even the poker-faced American, Helen Wills, who in 1926 invaded Cannes, where La Belle Suzanne held court in a silken, perfumed bower, and was trounced for her brazen effrontery in a match that had them hanging from the trees and made the front pages of the American press.

If no other player of any consequence had come to the fore in the period of the 1920's, it still would take precedence over all others for giving the world the two most famous champions ever to hold a racket. Big Bill and Suzanne were as synonymous for the best in tennis as were Babe Ruth in baseball, Jack Dempsey in boxing, Bobby Jones in golf, Tommy Hitchcock in polo, Willie Hoppe in balk-line billiards, Red Grange in football, Paavo Nurmi in distance running. At their peak they could not only beat any rival from the world over; they could call the score.

But it so happened that in the decade in which Tilden and Mlle Lenglen held such absolute sway there were marshaled upon the cultured, priceless turf of Wimbledon and Forest Hills far more players of the first class than the world has ever known, before or since, in a comparable period. From every continent except South America they came to provide tennis of such superior brilliance as likely we shall not look upon again for many years to come.

From France there came the Four Musketeers—René Lacoste, Henri Cochet, Jean Borotra, and Jacques Brugnon—to topple Tilden from his Olympian perch and end the supremacy of the English-speaking nations in the international team championship for the Davis Cup. Except for America's Big Four—Tilden, William Johnston, Vincent Richards, and R. Norris Williams, 2nd—no other country has produced a quartet of contemporaries to compare with these world-renowned wearers of the Chanticleer.

It was little, pale-faced Cochet, with an artistry and magic touch that made him the greatest natural genius the game has known, who brought down the great Tilden in the quarter-finals of the national championship at Forest Hills in 1926. That day, which saw the end of Big Bill's six-year reign as the scourge of the courts, and also the rout of two other members of the Big Four by the French, was one of the most memorable in tennis history. It was the handwriting on the wall that pointed to France's elevation as the champion Davis Cup nation in 1927, and the end of the trail for those twin terrors of tennis, Big Bill Tilden and Little Bill Johnston.

It was Cochet, quiet, inarticulate in English, and cold almost to the point of sullenness, who humbled the aging Johnston in the deciding match of the cup series at the Germantown Cricket Club, Philadelphia. For once the aloofness and unfriendliness of the little French master melted. Throwing his racket thirty feet in the air, he ran forward with a cry of exultation to greet his beaten foe, and that started the wildest stampede ever seen on a tennis court.

From the packed stands poured hundreds of deliriously happy compatriots of the winning team, both men and women. Tears streamed down the faces of some as they embraced their conquering heroes and lifted them to their shoulders. And a few days later, a cavalcade of glittering Hispano-Suizas bore the Four Musketeers down New York's Fifth Avenue. With the huge, glistening Davis Cup mounted for all to see, they paraded in triumph to a crack French liner, where the trophy was received in full dress formality by the captain at the top of the gangplank as the entire crew stood at attention.

Sharing the lion's portion of the honors with Cochet was sharp-faced, sphinx-like Lacoste, the inscrutable "Crocodile," son of a multimillionaire manufacturer of motorcars. No one ever saw Lacoste so much as change expression on the court, much less give vent to his feelings in an emotional outburst. He was the machine, next to infallible in his control, with a defense that was adamant against every variety of spin and artifice and that amounted to offense in the depth and calculation of his return.

It was Lacoste who succeeded Tilden as champion of the United States in 1926; who defeated the colossus in the 1927 final, in one of the greatest matches ever played in this country, and who brought down both Big Bill and Little Bill at Germantown as France won the Davis Cup.

Borotra, the third member of the Four Musketeers, was one of the most glamorous figures ever to step on a tennis court. Gallic to his polished finger tips, he was the dashing, debonair boulevardier, captivating with his charm and bubbling friendliness in opera cape as he kissed milady's hand, and the toast of Wimbledon and Forest Hills in his blue beret as he stormed the net with a dynamic style that won him the sobriquet of the "Bounding Basque of Biarritz."

Not quite the player that was Cochet and Lacoste, tall, handsome Jean, who fairly exploded with vitality, even when he had beguiled his opponent into believing that he was the dying Gaul near the end of a killing contest, won his share of matches from Cochet. Lacoste was his poison. "Ah, René," he would say with a sad shake of the head, "he kills me weeth those lobs." Lacoste was a master of the lob, and when he got through with Borotra, the dynamic Basque, who incessantly rushed to the net to get in his sweeping, full-armed volleys, was a drooping, utterly weary figure.

Brugnon, the remaining Musketeer, was one of the great doubles players of tennis, with a return of service that was one of the classic strokes. A gentleman he was, with Old World charm and distinguished bearing, a man given to few words, and those always sensible and to the point. Poise and restraint characterized his playing, too, and he was one of the shrewdest and soundest performers the four-handed game has known.

The Four Musketeers, who made France tennis conscious with their exploits as not even the great Lenglen had made her, would have lent distinction to the Golden Age by themselves. But there were others of heroic stature whose talent ripened during this period.

From Spain there came Manuel Alonso, the Tiger of the Pyranees; from South Africa, Brian Ivan Cobb Norton; from Australia, James O. Anderson, Gerald Patterson, Norman Brookes, John B. Hawkes, and Pat O'Hara Wood; from Japan, Zenzo Shimizu and Ichiya Kumagae. There was Senorita Lili De Alvarez of Spain, Kathleen McKane Godfree, Eileen Bennett and Betty Nuthall of England, Kea Bouman of Holland, Fräulein Cilly Aussem and Fräulein Hilda Krahwinkel of Germany, and Miss Daphne Akhurst of Australia. And in America, too, there were, besides the Big Four, Helen Wills Moody, Molla Mallory, and Elizabeth Ryan. Helen Jacobs, Frank Shields, Wilmer Allison, John Doeg, and Sidney Wood were beginning to break into the picture, which also included Frank Hunter, Watson Washburn, and the Kinsey brothers, Howard and Robert.

Alonso was a dynamo of energy with a thirst to get to the enemy and tear him apart. He bristled with fight in every movement, though he was one of the fairest and friendliest men that ever played the game, a born sportsman. No one brought greater concentration to the court. He was so completely absorbed in the business of annihilating his opponent that he was oblivious of the crowd and the amusement he created with the fierce intensity of his attack.

In a tight match he was like one possessed. As he went through the agitated windup of his service, the flagellating movement of his racket was like the lashing tail of a tiger getting ready to spring for the kill with fang and claw. If the ballboy was slow in supplying him with ammunition, he cried out, "Come, boy, come!" with an impatient wave of the hand, and snatched the balls from him. There were times when he was so infuriated at missing a volley that he bit the throat of the racket.

Alonso never won the highest honors of the game, but he ranked next to Tilden after establishing his residence in the United States. He reached the final of the All-Comers at Wimbledon in 1921 and once at Newport he came within an inch of defeating Tilden.

Brian Ivan Cobb Norton came to the United States from South Africa about the time that Alonso arrived from Spain. "The Babe" they called him. He was a little man with fair skin and curly hair, a dangerous twinkle in his eyes, and his tongue in his cheek. He was an impish combination of a clown and an acrobat, with boundless energy and springs in his nimble feet, and he could have been a great champion had he been willing to pay the price. He liked a good time. He had Tilden tottering on the brink of defeat in the British championship challenge round in 1921 and he was the logical man to have succeeded Big Bill at the top in American tennis, for he was as quick as a cat, had all of the shots, and was a demon for attack. His great talent was wasted and his career ended prematurely.

Zenzo Shimizu was not a truly first-class player, but he had a great match with Tilden in the Davis Cup challenge round that rates among the classics. He was a tiny man, the soul of friendliness and politeness, with a big smile and a bow to the waist for everyone, and no one could possibly conceive of him as having any truck with Tojo.

Like Kumagae, Shimizu used the characteristic Japanese stroke, with the Western grip and an extreme rotation of the wrist to bring the face of the racket well over the ball and impart excessive top spin. It was amusing to see him, in his Sou'wester hat, and hardly as big as a minute, lower his head and put all of his strength into his forehand drive. It was more than amusing to see him do it against the great Tilden. It was positively incredible the way he stood up to the blasting force of the big American, who towered over him as a great Dane over a Pekingese.

They met in the challenge round at Forest Hills in 1921. Little Bill Johnston had dispatched Kumagae quickly in the opening singles, and the crowd of more than 12,000 looked for Tilden to make short shrift of Shimizu.

The world champion led at 5-3 in the first set, and then little Zenzo stood the gallery on its head. He took four games in a row. It was a joke. It couldn't be that Tilden was serious. Surely he was toying with his opponent and setting the stage for one of his dramatic comebacks after getting the fans worked up.

But it wasn't a joke. In the second set they stayed even to 4-all. The crowd was buzzing with excitement. It could scarcely believe what it saw. It saw little Shimizu knock back Tilden's fiercest drives with a control that refused to waver. It saw the American's cannonball service explode on the other's racket and almost bend him back, but the return was invariably good, and deep.

Why didn't Tilden go to the net? they asked. The great champion had lost his casual manner by now and was beginning to show concern. He did not like to volley. He preferred to stay back and beat his man into submission with his withering forehand and backhand drives or break down his control with mixing spin. Now he decided that he must go to close quarters. Shimizu met his volleying assault with a succession of passing shots, broke through his service, and won the set at 6-4. The crowd was stupified. Tilden was down, two sets to none.

In the third set, Tilden went into the lead by 4 games to 2 and the gallery began to breathe a little more easily. Then the tension mounted again. Making amazing recoveries and thwarting Tilden's most desperate efforts, Shimizu pulled even at 4-all. They just about gave up hope for the American when he lost his service again to fall behind at 4-5. The score went to 30-all in the 10th game. Tilden was within two points of defeat!

The crowd awaited one of the greatest upsets in history. It did not come about. Tilden, fighting with all his cunning and bringing every shot in his wide repertoire into play, saved the 10th game, pulled out the 11th from 15-40, and won the 12th for the set.

As the players left the court for the intermission, Tilden was haggard and dripping with perspiration. He seemed to be on the verge of exhaustion from the great physical effort he had had to make and from the sticky heat. Shimizu, too, looked spent, and he was beginning to get cramps in his legs. Which one would have the more in reserve when the battle was renewed?

After the rest period, they went at it again and played even to 2-all in the fourth set. Then the match turned into a rout. Shimizu was in bad shape with cramps. Play had to be interrupted while his legs were massaged. His resistance was ended, and Tilden rushed through to victory with the loss of only one more game, in the fifth set. The United States swept the series, 5-0, but few galleries have had a worse scare than the little Japanese gave them that day.

Long Jim Anderson was the best tennis player Australia produced after the First World War until the rise of Jack Crawford in the 1930's. He had a powerful forehand and a good backhand and he led Tilden by two sets to one in the 1922 challenge round and defeated Johnston in 1923. Gerald Patterson, who won at Wimbledon in 1919 and again in 1922, had an atrocious, corkscrew backhand, but he made up for it with his forehand and with one of the most powerful overheads of all time and a strong service. For a big man of heavy weight, he was strikingly graceful. Few players have had better footwork. The tremendous force of his overhead, was demonstrated when one of his smashes caught Borotra just below the temple in a Davis Cup doubles match at Forest Hills and knocked him unconscious into the bottom of the net.

Norman Brookes was well past his prime in the 1920's but he was still active and to be feared in doubles with the wizardry that made him champion of Wimbledon in 1914. It was that year that he played his memorable match at Forest Hills with Maurice (Red) McLoughlin, in which the first set went 17-15, the longest on record for singles in Davis Cup history.

Johnston and Williams, too, had won national fame before the war, but they were still going strong in the Golden Age. Williams, champion in 1914 and 1916, and one of the most blindingly brilliant players in history, with his daring half-volleys and risky position in the court, was one of the great doubles players in the 1920's, pairing with Tilden, Johnston, Vincent Richards, and Watson Washburn.

Johnston was one of the idols of tennis and one of the best of all time. He weighed only 125 pounds at the most and was small in stature, but he had the heart of a giant, one of the most dreaded top-spin forehands the game has known, and was a volleyer of the first class. It was Little Bill's misfortune that Tilden came along at the same time to rule the world; otherwise Johnston would have been the king of the courts. Little Bill got to the top five years before

Tilden, winning the championship in 1915. He triumphed again in 1919, defeating Big Bill in the final. He was still the second best in the world through 1925 and was runner-up in the championship each year from 1920 to 1925, with the exception of 1921.

In 1922, Johnston won the first two sets from Tilden in the final at the Germantown Cricket Club. The crowd in Tilden's home town, was cheering madly for the Californian. Each of them held two legs on the big challenge trophy, and Little Bill had his heart set on winning it to gain permanent possession. He lost the third set and then gained a 3-0 lead in the fourth. Victory was beckoning and seemed in store for him. But then Tilden cut loose and all but broke the heart of Johnston and the crowd as he hammered his little opponent into submission.

Mrs. Johnston rushed from the stands after the match was over to greet her husband and tell him what a wonderful fight he had made. Dripping wet from perspiration and worn down to the point of exhaustion, he brushed her and all others aside brusquely. He was utterly crushed by the ending of his high hopes of taking the cup.

Little Bill knew that he would never defeat Tilden again. He could beat every other player in the world. He could pound Anderson and Patterson of Australia into the ground in the Davis Cup matches, allowing them a mere total of 11 games in 6 sets that same year. He could defeat Vincent Richards and Frank Hunter at Wimbledon to win the championship in 1923. He could score 11 victories in 12 cup matches in singles between 1920 and 1926, but always he had to play second fiddle to Tilden.

Vincent Richards was the Boy Wonder of the courts, the Yonkers Prodigy. At the age of fifteen he won the national doubles championship with Tilden. He was a member of the Davis Cup doubles team at nineteen, displaced Johnston in the singles in 1924, to win both matches, and was a member of the winning doubles combination with Williams the next two years. From 1921 through 1925, he ranked second, third, or fourth in the country, and in 1926 he was the only member of the Big Four to survive the French uprising in the quarter-finals of the championship. Three times that year he defeated Tilden on clay and grass and he might have been ranked first. But at the close of the season he led a revolutionary movement that marked the beginning of professional exhibition tennis in the

United States and he was left out of the rankings, an injustice that brought down heavy criticism on the United States Lawn Tennis Association.

Richards was one of the great volleyers, probably the best of them all. His skill in the forecourt in executing half-volleys and lift volleys still had galleries marveling when he was in his forties. He had a fine temperament for the game, a sound knowledge of tactics, and wonderful concentration. No one fought harder on the court, and he had a poise and keen sense of humor that enabled him to remain relaxed no matter how great the pressure or how punishing the play. His sliced backhand was defensive, and his service did not compare with Tilden's in explosive content, but he was so much the master at the net and his return from the back of the court was so regular, deep, and calculated that he was a challenge for Tilden and Johnston in their prime.

Tilden's greatness is to be appreciated from the fact that he towered above all these world-famous players—Richards, Johnston, The Four Musketeers, Alonso, Norton, the Australians, and the Japanese. Until the French caught up with him in 1926, he was a prohibitive favorite against the field. The belief was that he could win by any score he chose in almost every match he played.

The tall, lean Philadelphian with the branching shoulders and the finest footwork the game has ever known, with the possible exception of Fred Perry's, was the master of every stroke but one. He was never quite sure of his overhead, which was surprising, considering that he had one of the finest services that ever exploded cannon balls.

Tilden was the exponent of the all-court game. No player in history has had a stronger attack from both sides. He could drive with stunning speed and unerring control from forehand and backhand. Along with this burning pace, he had a forehand chop and backhand slice that could break up his opponent's game. His knowledge and mastery of spin have probably never been equaled.

In his prime, Big Bill did not need to resort to changes of spin. His speed could knock over any man who faced him. But it pleased him at times to change his methods, for the sake of variety, and beat his man by ruining his control rather than with dazzling winners. His ability to analyze his opponent's game and exploit its weaknesses was unexcelled. He was a strategist of the highest order who knew every trick and when to play it.

Tilden was not the volleyer that was Richards, and he preferred to stay back and win with his ground strokes and service, but when he chose, he could go forward and perform with brilliance in the fore-court. In the 1927 championship final with Lacoste, he showed how fine a volleyer he could be. A weak knee, which troubled him at that time, was partly responsible for his going in so much. It was less of a strain for him to go to the net to end the rallies quickly than to keep racing across the baseline in the punishing rallies from deep court. Also, Lacoste's defense was so magnificent against drive, chop, and slice that Tilden found he had to go forward to get in a finishing blow.

A year or two after Cochet had displaced him as the leading player of the world, Big Bill maintained that the French artist of the racket was a greater player than he (Tilden) had ever been. No one else thought so. Expert opinion held that it was simply a case of the American passing his peak.

Tilden refused to admit that he had started to slip. With the vanity and the sensitiveness of a woman over her age, he insisted that he was as good as he ever was and that Cochet was beating him because he was playing a superior order of tennis. Considering that Tilden was still one of the great attractions in tennis when he had passed the age of fifty, and was in the headlines as one of the iron-men marvels of all time, it is understandable why it came so hard for him to accept the fact that he had passed his peak at the age of thirty-four.

Cochet may have had more natural ability and more of the touch of genius than Tilden, who slaved for years on the practice court to rise from obscurity, and did not win his first turf championship until he was twenty-seven. But, considering all the attributes and the years of supremacy, there can be no question that the American takes precedence over him, as well as "Little Do" Doherty, Brookes, Johnston, William Larned, Red McLoughlin, Ellsworth Vines, Donald Budge, Fred Perry, Bobby Riggs, Jack Kramer, and all the other giants of the past and present.

Tilden won the American turf court championship seven times, the seventh time in 1929, at the age of thirty-six. He has thirty-one national amateur titles to his credit. He won at Wimbledon three times, in 1920, 1921, and 1930. Had he chosen to go over, he could have won there many more times. From 1920, the year he and Johnston lifted the cup in New Zealand, until he was beaten by Lacoste in 1926, he won every Davis Cup singles match he played. After he left the amateur ranks, following the close of the 1930 season, he defeated the greatest players who became professionals, and he was still a worthy foe for them for one or two sets when he had reached the half-century mark.

Tilden was not only the greatest master of the racket of all time, he was also the greatest showman the game has known. He would rather have been an actor than a world champion and he spent a small fortune in the theater. He did not go over nearly as well on the professional stage as he did on the courts, where his temperamental scenes and flair for the dramatic made the headlines no less than did his victories. Because he was so overwhelmingly the favorite in every match and the crowd was for the underdog, he would sometimes play upon the heartstrings of the gallery by purposely getting himself in a hole until the fans were worked up to a high pitch of excitement. Then he would come on with an onslaught that blew his rival off the court and leave the crowd limp and marveling at his performance.

Throughout his career, Tilden was embroiled with the tennis powers who directed the amateur game. He was continually challenging their dicta, criticizing their policies, and finding fault with about everything they did until they were ready to sigh with relief when he went into the professional ranks.

His most famous controversy with them had to do with the Amateur Rule. Largely because he was making a substantial sum from writing about the game for a newspaper syndicate, the U.S.L.T.A. enacted the so-called player-writer provision of the rule, formulated by a group of well-known sportsmen in and out of tennis.

The rule restricted a player from writing current newspaper accounts of tournaments in which he was competing. He was permitted to write magazine articles and books and to send analytical reports to the papers of matches after the conclusion of the tournament, but he could not be a daily "reporter."

Tilden was among those who approved the report of the special committee, but it was not long after the rule was adopted that he was put on the carpet for failing to live up to it. Matters came to a head in 1928. He went overseas with the Davis Cup team and while playing at Wimbledon in the British championships filed daily articles on the matches for the press.

The solons of the U.S.L.T.A. met in executive session in New York and took punitive action. They suspended him from amateur competition. The suspension was announced as the American team was about to engage Italy in the Davis Cup interzone final. Tilden was acting as captain of the team, and so it lost its leader and star player for the matches, but the Americans still won easily from Italy.

The victory qualified them to meet France in the challenge round. When the French awakened to the fact that the suspension stood for this series also, that their ox was to be gored no less than Italy's, they let out bellows of rage. "*Mon Dieu!*" they screamed. "Thees you cannot do to us."

This was to be the first challenge round ever held on French soil. In honor of the occasion, they had built a beautiful new stadium in the Bois at Auteuil. For days the papers had been filled with accounts of the preparations for the matches and the coming of the great Tilden. It was to be one of the famous moments in the history of French sports, the most historic in tennis since the deputies of the *tiers état*, in 1789, took *Le Serment du jeu de paume*, or oath of the tennis court, in the court tennis court at Versailles, never to abandon their efforts until they had given a constitution to France.

Now they discovered that the leading actor in the big show, Mr. Tennis himself, was not to be permitted to take part. It was like putting on Hamlet without the Melancholy Dane. It was stupid, insane, a dastardly plot to ruin France's big moment of glory. A fig on amateur rules. Who cared about rules? Only crazy Americans could think of technical violations and money. The suspension was unthinkable. It must not stand.

Feeling along the boulevards ran so high that the American ambassador to France, Myron T. Herrick, found it necessary to intercede. He put through a telephone call to Philadelphia, to Joseph W. Wear, then the chairman of the Davis Cup Committee of the U. S. Lawn Tennis Association.

The Ambassador explained to Mr. Wear how strongly the French resented the disbarment of Tilden from the matches. For the sake of international good feeling, he asked that the lost leader be restored to good standing and allowed to participate in the challenge round.

Mr. Wear called a meeting of the high brass of the tennis association in New York. It was impossible to dismiss a request from so high a source. The solons prided themselves that their players were ambassadors of good will, that tennis was a boon to international good feeling in extending the hand of friendly competition across the seas. Now they were charged with creating an atmosphere of bitterness among the French toward Americans, of jeopardizing the friendly relations between the two nations. The decision was inevitable.

As much as it galled them, the solons ate their crow. They put Tilden back on the team, but with the understanding that when he returned home he was to be brought up on the charges of violating the rule.

When the French heard the news they tossed their hats into the air and shouted, "Vive, Teel-den!" Joyously, madly, they stormed the gates of Roland Garros Stadium at Auteuil to see their heroes defeat him and prove the supremacy of France over the world's best. They almost had a hemorrhage when the aging Tilden turned on Lacoste, who had conquered him in 1927 in the cup matches and the American championship final, and humbled him in the opening challenge round engagement. But that was the only match the Americans won from the French, France taking the other four; and the French drank of the ambrosia of victory from the Davis Cup.

Upon his return to the United States, Tilden faced charges, was found guilty of having violated the rule, and was suspended from amateur competition for the remainder of the year. But he had made the front pages of the press throughout the United States and in France, and his fame was greater than ever. The next year he was back in competition and won the championship, and in 1930, his last as an amateur, he triumphed at Wimbledon. At the end of the season, he followed Vincent Richards into the professional ranks, the first important defection from amateur tennis since 1926. For the next ten years he was to remain one of the top attractions in the professional realm, harvesting a fortune until, with the outbreak of war, he devoted his services to staging exhibitions for the armed forces and to raising funds for the Red Cross and other charities.

Only three players in history have won the American championship seven times. Tilden was one of them. The other two were Richard Sears, the first champion, and William Larned. Neither of them, by common consent, was in the same class with Tilden as a player.

As a personality, flaming, flamboyant, opinionated to the point of being intolerant of criticism, and a gallery player every moment he held the green-carpeted stage, Tilden was in a class by himself. Even when he had passed the age of fifty, his bearing and every gesture befitted the monarch whose spirit refused to knuckle to young upstarts with a racket or to the old gentleman with a scythe. He brought millions of dollars into the "gate" and, more than anyone else, he was responsible for the tremendous growth of tennis in the United States and the world over during the Golden Age.

Mlle Lenglen was the great player personality in women's tennis that Tilden was in the men's division. She was a prima donna with a figure that would have adorned the stage, though she was lacking in beauty, and she moved about the court with a flowing grace and ease of movement that was beyond compare. She was the queen, the supreme artiste, before whom the tennis world bowed—not only her opponents but high dignitaries who catered to her every demand and whim.

Not even Tilden was a more tempestuous figure than La Belle Suzanne, a flashing, vibrant personality, who carried herself with an hauteur that amounted almost to arrogance at times, stamped her foot, quarreled violently. In 1926, she kept the Queen of England and a big crowd waiting for over half an hour before she appeared for her match at Wimbledon. After a shrill dispute with the officials, she pleaded illness and withdrew from the tournament, where she had held absolute sway from 1919.

The British were outraged by what they regarded as a snub to Queen Mary, for which the French government felt obliged to apologize. Her presentation at the British court was canceled. That was the end of her amateur career. That year she joined the professional ranks.

Suzanne was no exponent of swat, as was her great American rival,

Helen Wills. Her whole game was scientific placement and control of the ball. She had almost unbelievable accuracy as she put the ball precisely where she willed and maneuvered her opponent until the opening was offered for the finishing thrust. She achieved this accuracy through hours of daily practice as a young girl, under the supervision of her father, who, the story is, would place a handkerchief on the court and keep her firing at it until she had achieved satisfactory marksmanship. The handkerchief was moved from one part of the court to another, and she hit ball after ball at the target until Père Lenglen was satisfied. Possibly the tax of those long hours of practice at so young an age undermined her health. She died at the age of thirty-nine, in 1938.

Mlle Lenglen's grace has never been equaled on the court. In white accordion-pleated skirt, sleeveless waist, and white shoes and stockings, with a scarlet bandeau around her dark tresses, she moved swiftly and easily about the court, her legs twinkling like a ballet dancer's and her long arm carrying the racket forward in sweeping strokes to meet the ball in dead center. When she chose she could drive with severity, both from her forehand and her more freely hit backhand, but her softer shots were highly effective because of her ability to conceal the direction of her strokes.

Suzanne rose to prominence directly after the First World War. At the age of fourteen she won the championship of Picardy, and in June 1914, she took the French hard-court crown at St. Cloud. Then came the war, and it was not until five years later that her fame began to spread and she became world renowned. She won the championship at Wimbledon in 1919 and every year thereafter through 1925, except for 1924. She also took the doubles cups those years with Elizabeth Ryan of California, who lived abroad and was famous in her own right, and she was French champion six times.

Mlle Lenglen never won the American crown. She played for it only once, in 1921, and suffered the most painful experience of her career on the court. She was drawn against Eleanor Goss, then the fifth ranking player of the United States, but Miss Goss defaulted. At that time the draw was made "blind," without seeding, and in the next round Suzanne came up against the American champion, Molla Bjurstedt Mallory, who had ruled the courts this side of the Atlantic since 1915, except for 1919, and was to win the title seven times in all.

Mrs. Mallory, who came to America from Norway, welcomed the chance to meet the great French player. There was no love lost between them. Suzanne, as the reigning queen of Wimbledon, had slighted her in the British tournament. This was Mrs. Mallory's chance to pay back a score. She was a fighter second to none, and she had a great pride. No one conceded her a chance of winning the match. That sent her out with blood in her eye.

Mlle Lenglen dismissed the match in her mind as unworthy of serious consideration. She would win by any score she chose. Her appearance upon the court at the West Side Tennis Club in Forest Hills, Long Island, was something out of the theater. In ermine wrap she made her entrance upon the stage, favoring her subjects with happy smiles while catering officials swarmed around and behind her and cameramen in droves recorded the scene. The great French player was in her element, the cynosure of all eyes, and with everyone dancing attendance upon her.

No one so much as took notice of her opponent. Grimly, Mrs. Mallory waited until the fuss over her rival had subsided. Then the court was cleared, the umpire and linesmen took their places, and the thousands in the stands leaned forward eagerly to see the celebrated Suzanne play rings around the American champion. What followed was one of the severest shocks Forest Hills has ever known.

Like a tigress, Mrs. Mallory went for the kill. She flew around the court as never before in her life. No ball, it seemed, could escape her racket, and she pummeled it back so hard and so deep from the forehand that it scored beyond redemption or extracted the error from her opponent. Always she played with that same grim expression, never relaxing, bending all her energies on annihilating her opponent.

Mlle Lenglen, so unconcerned and gay of spirits at the start, seemed amused at the fury and intensity of her opponent's play in the early stages. She gave the impression of a cat that was content to let its victim have its brief moment before pouncing. She looked toward the linesmen and smiled, and there was disdain in the shrug of her shoulders.

It wasn't long until her attitude of lofty indifference began to change. Mrs. Mallory was at her hammer and tongs without a letup. The American champion had one good shot. That was her forehand. She had only a defensive backhand and she never went to the net if she could avoid it. Her service merely put the ball in play and practically never scored or forced an error. It was simply on the might of her forehand and as much courage and determination as any woman ever brought to the court that she won the championship seven times. Those assets were now giving her the upper hand against the greatest woman player in history.

As Mlle Lenglen found the match going squarely against her, her confidence started to ooze. When she looked around now she was no longer smiling. She was plainly worried and unable to understand what was happening. She began to cough. The cough became heavier and more alarming as her opponent's lead increased. She put her hand to her heart and looked appealingly to the umpire.

Mrs. Mallory paid no attention to these distress signals. Such was her concentration that they may have escaped her. She hewed to the lines and hammered and hammered with the most destructive attack ever to come from her racket. The gallery did not know what to make of it. As Mrs. Mallory's lead piled up, the dead silence changed to electric excitement. History was in the making. The stands buzzed more and more noisily as Mlle Lenglen's cough became more violent. Some of the crowd were sympathetic and concerned for her health. Others exchanged knowing looks. To them the coughing was an act.

The first set went to Mrs. Mallory by the score of 6-2. There was no second set. After two points had been played in the next game, Mlle Lenglen, coughing heavily and weeping, defaulted. They administered to her, helped her on with her ermine wrap, and escorted her, on the verge of hysterics, off the court. Her conqueror, meanwhile, gathered up her rackets quickly and, with hardly a pause to accept the congratulations of those at the umpire's stand, strode triumphantly, still grimly, from the enclosure. Forest Hills never saw anything so dramatic, before or since.

Mlle Lenglen was charged with poor sportsmanship and of lacking the courage to take a licking, although there were many who defended her and thought she was treated unfairly. Some prophesied that her reign was at an end, that she would never be a champion again. It did not take longer than the following Summer for her to set them right. In her next meeting with Mrs. Mallory, at Wimbledon, she scored an overwhelming victory, and she was supreme in the British and French championships until she retired from amateur tennis.

Next to her one appearance at Forest Hills, Suzanne's most famous match was her meeting with Helen Wills at Cannes on the Riveria, in 1926. Although no title of any consequence was at stake, it created more of a sensation than any other women's match in history, with the exception of her debacle against Mrs. Mallory, and Mrs. Helen Wills Moody's default to Helen Jacobs in the 1933 championships.

The French girl was at the summit of her career, and Miss Wills was just reaching the plenitude of her powers. Except for her loss to Mrs. Mallory, Mlle Lenglen had not been beaten since 1917, and the preceding Summer, 1925, she had gone through the British championships by defeating five successive opponents in love sets. Miss Wills had ended Mrs. Mallory's reign as American champion in 1923 and successfully defended her crown in 1924 and 1925. Back in the United States there were many who predicted she would win at Cannes and establish her supremacy.

The California girl stood, and still stands, as the hardest hitter women's tennis has known. From both the forehand and the backhand she drove with a sustained speed and depth that broke down resistance. She was not a good volleyer and she had no inclination for the net, though she could hold her ground there, but such was the power of her ground strokes that there was seldom occasion for her to go forward.

Miss Wills offered a sharp contrast to Mlle Lenglen. She was placid and inscrutable on the court as her dynamic rival was animated and temperamental. "Little Miss Poker Face" they called the American, who was never known to change expression beneath the eyeshade she always wore. Suzanne said of herself, "I just throw dignity to the winds and think of nothing but the game." Helen was always dignified, proper, and a stickler for the strict etiquette of the court, so much so that her matches lacked color, and only the abnormal speed of her strokes saved them from monotony as she hammered her opponents into submission.

The fair-skinned Californian, with her classic features and never-failing poise, was a lovely picture of young womanhood. Nothing could excite her or make her unbend. There was something stately about the way she played tennis. It was a cold war that she waged without a trace of emotion. If she enjoyed any of her big matches, the closest scrutiny failed to reveal it. In triumph or disaster she treated both of those two imposters just the same, so far as you could tell from her countenance.

Helen did not have Suzanne's grace and quickness of movement around the court. Her game lacked the variety and subtlety of her rival's. Her whole strategy was to blow her opponent off the court. Her admirers were sure that her tremendous hitting power would put Mlle Lenglen under such pressure that the French champion's control would break down and Suzanne would be unable to dictate the pattern of the play as she had against others.

Cannes hadn't known such excitement in years as when the young American challenged the world champion on her favorite stamping ground. The seats were sold out long in advance. From all over France and from England came enthusiasts to see the women's tennis match of the century. Hundreds, unable to get in, perched themselves on the house tops and in the windows of neighboring buildings and in trees.

It was a noisy crowd that kept up a din of cheering for their idol. Suzanne was not in a happy frame of mind. There had been some domestic difficulty at home. The unruliness of the spectators got on her nerves. When she fell behind at 1-2 in the score and realized the dangerous challenge she faced, she turned angrily to the crowd. Like a queen giving orders to her subjects, she commanded them to be quiet, *fermez la bouche*, as the French say.

Suzanne won the match after a long, bitter fight in the second set, 6-3, 8-6. She never had a greater ovation than she received as she walked off the court. They called her the Jeanne d'Arc of tennis.

That was the only match in which she and Helen Wills ever met. A return meeting in the French championship was prevented when the Californian was stricken with appendicitis and had to give up tennis for the remainder of the year. Suzanne left the amateur ranks late in 1926, to take up a career as a professional player. Possibly, had they met a year later, particularly on the faster turf surface, where speed counts for more than on France's hard courts, the outcome would have been reversed.

With Mlle Lenglen out of the competition, Helen rose to world supremacy in 1927, winning the championship at Wimbledon and Forest Hills. In all, she was to win eight British titles—a record—and to equal the mark of Mrs. Mallory in taking the American seven times, and she was invincible in Wightman Cup team play against England.

It was Mlle Lenglen who launched professional tennis on a big scale. With Mary K. Browne, former American champion, Vincent Richards, Howard Kinsey, and others, she signed a contract with the American promoter, C. C. Pyle, to go on tour in the United States. Up to this time the professional in the United States had been purely an instructor, laboring in obscurity. Now he stepped forth upon the stage to reap handsome profits for his playing skill. It was some years before the movement got under full swing, but once Tilden joined up, late in 1930, the future of professional tennis was assured, and since then leading amateurs have followed the dollar sign to earn fortunes in exhibition play.

The Golden Twenties started the golden trail for both amateur and professional tennis. The concrete stadium at Forest Hills went up in 1923 rivaling Wimbledon as the mecca for the world's best, and housing crowds larger than had ever seen tennis in this country before. More than thirty nations came into the Davis Cup fold, and the Women's team match between England and the United States was inaugurated. Madison Square Garden in New York was filled to capacity, and receipts were as high as $50,000 for a single night's play as the successors of Lenglen, Richards, and Tilden hit the gold dust trail that they had blazed. Tennis had become bigtime, a major national sport and the most international of all competitions with the exception of the Olympic Games.

TRACK AND FIELD

by JESSE ABRAMSON
Track and Field Editor, New York Herald Tribune

Paavo Nurmi was the supreme figure produced by track and field athletics in the sports era that flowered after the First World War.

Peerless Paavo, the Ace of Abo, the Phantom Finn! He wrote his fame indelibly on the cinder paths of Europe and the board tracks of the United States, with a matchless combination of speed and stamina and the color of his glittering achievements that had no equal in his time or any time. The days of his distance-running dominance endured from the 1920 Olympics at Antwerp, the first postwar assembly of the world's foremost athletes, until the 1932 Olympics at Los Angeles, where, waiting in the wings for a final chance to demonstrate his greatness anew over the classic marathon route, he was declared ineligible for further amateur competition.

There was only one Nurmi. He shattered every record in the books from 1,500 meters to 10,000 meters, from one mile to six, up to one hour of running. Although he never considered himself a mile specialist, nor was he primarily a miler, he demolished the world mile record that had lasted for eight years and hung up a standard of 4 minutes 10.4 seconds that remained beyond reach for eight years more. His 5,000- and 10,000-meter records endured for eight and nine years. His record of 11 miles, 1,648 yards for one hour of running was not eclipsed for seventeen years.

In an era when the nine-minute two-mile, believed beyond human grasp, was regarded with the awe that subsequently embraced the four-minute mile, Nurmi became the first to cover the double mile in better than nine minutes. He attained this goal on the board track in the old Madison Square Garden in the peak accomplishment of his American tour; he did not duplicate the record outdoors until the twilight of his career.

In three Olympics, 1920 to 1928, he won six world championships, from 1,500 meters (under a mile) to 10,000 meters (more than six miles). At the height of his power, in 1924, when he was twenty-seven years old, he won three Olympic crowns in a span of 48 hours, plus a fourth, unofficial, title. He won two of his races, 1,500 and 5,000 meters, within an hour and a half, an incredible performance that stands alone in Olympic history. He shattered the Olympic records in both triumphs. Two days later he survived a cross-country test under insufferable conditions of heat that forced two-thirds of his opposition to give up under the baleful sun; he not only survived it but won it in his unsurpassed style, which combined wonderful co-ordination, relaxation, poise, grace, speed, and stamina. And the following day, when many of his challengers were either hospitalized or still gasping for breath from that harrowing test, the incomparable Finn went out and won another Olympic race, although it was a 3,000-meter team race not listed on the official Olympic agenda.

His five-month, 55-race tour of the United States in the Winter of 1925 gave tens of thousands of new fans a chance to see this nonpareil of track, and established him immemorably in the American saga of foot racing.

Track and field, more than any other game or sport, consists of so many different events embodying assorted skills that it is difficult to evaluate one record performance against another, although the track scientists have tried with graphs depicting and measuring ultimate human possibilities. What with sprinters, hurdlers, middle-distance and distance runners, jumpers, vaulters, throwers of assorted hardware, round, flat, and long, the track fan pays his money and takes his choice of singling out the specialist who transcends all in track and field.

But the fans were unanimous in their acclaim of Nurmi, although he appeared to shun the acclaim in his reactions away from the track. Taciturn, impassive, unsmiling in repose; vibrant, graceful, effortless in action, Paavo was as colorful in his racing—head erect, shoulders squared and rolling with his stride, arms held chest high—as he was colorless otherwise.

Unconquered and all-conquering from 1921 to 1926 in his native land—incubator of distance-running marvels—Nurmi stood head and shoulders above his distance-running contemporaries and above all track and field athletes. On the basis of his supremacy in his own realm of track, on his Olympic triumphs, his numerous records, he was accorded the accolade for his contributions in the Golden Twenties.

His influence on track was tremendous. His novel ideas on even pace revolutionized the tactics of distance racing. His records challenged the generation that followed him. He developed interest among track devotees and spectators as never before; he made the sport world track conscious and record conscious as no other individual before his time, although track had had such idols as Lonnie Myers, Bernie Wefers, Mel Sheppard, Arthur Duffey, Ted Meredith, Alf Shrubb, Jim Thorpe, and Hannes Kolehmainen.

The decade that produced Nurmi was not without many other titans, although none so enduring as Peerless Paavo, none who could sweep to victories such as his in three successive Olympics.

They were nonetheless mighty in their accomplishments, these contemporaries of Paavo's—Charley Paddock, the sprinter who became celebrated as the Fastest Human; Earl (Tommy) Thomson, whose world record of 14.4 seconds in the 120-yard high hurdles was unsurpassed for eleven years; Joie Ray, miler extraordinary in his consistency and longevity, and darling of the galleries—no match for Nurmi in man-to-man competition, yet he met the challenge of Paavo's presence in America by equaling his indoor record with a 4:12 mile; Sabin Carr, one of a long line of Yale vaulters and first to soar over the magic height of 14 feet, indoors and out; Harold Osborn, epitome of high-jumping class and all-around skill in the decathlon; Ned Gourdin and DeHart Hubbard, pioneers in establishing Negro pre-eminence in the broad jump; Clarence (Bud) Houser, little giant of the shotput and more particularly of the discus ring.

California, as a state, and the universities of California, Stanford, and Southern California, under the coaching direction of Walter Christie, Robert L. (Dink) Templeton, and Dean Cromwell, moved up in this decade following the First World War with an array of talent and a concentration of champions that astounded the rest of the country and the world, although it probably didn't surprise the Chambers of Commerce at all, considering that the Golden State had the weather to produce track champions and fruit in such wonderful abundance. The three universities and the athletic clubs of that state swept Amateur Athletic Union and intercollegiate team championships right through the decade and shared the headlines with the individuals that comprised the teams.

California had produced champions before, but never in such profusion as it did in the Twenties, with Paddock, Frank Wykoff, Charley Borah, Morris Kirksey in the sprints, Emerson (Bud) Spencer in the quarter, Jack Merchant in the hammer throw, Bud Houser, Glenn (Tiny) Hartranft, Biff Hoffman, Eric Krenz, and Harlow Rothert, shotputters and discus throwers de luxe; Leighton Dye, Kenneth Grumbles, and Robert Maxwell in the hurdles, Lee Barnes in the pole vault, and Robert King in the high jump, among many others of distinction.

In this era of Paddock and Ray and Carr and Osborn and Hubbard, Nurmi was the greatest.

Paavo Nurmi was born in Turku in the southwest of Finland on June 13, 1897. The world was at war when Paavo, as a youth of seventeen, became interested in running and joined his first athletic club. He had run cross-country as a boy, had participated in inter-apartment house races. His idol, and the idol of all Finnish boys, was Hannes Kolehmainen, father of Finnish distance runners, whose Olympic feats in 1912, when he won the 5,000- and 10,000-meter championships at Stockholm, and his subsequent exploits in America as a member of the Irish-American A.C., had made him the national hero.

Even as a boy, Nurmi had indicated his individuality and his purposefulness; he trained more than others, he developed his even pace by running behind trolley cars in lieu of electric rabbits. He had to go to work at the age of twelve when his father died. He knew hard work and did not shun it when he decided he would become a champion runner. He set himself a program that stressed speed, stamina, and condition and followed it with strict precision. It may not have been all fun, but it was what Paavo wanted. He grew up an unwontedly grave and taciturn fellow, whose reserve was never dented in the years when his name was a byword in the athletic world.

Nurmi developed his running ability gradually and consistently through the war years, but his best times did not indicate that he was headed for stardom. He made his most significant progress after he was inducted into the Army in 1919 when he was twenty-two.

Peace had come to the warring nations by then, and Paavo was allowed more time to train as a soldier than he had ever had as a civilian. He now had maturity; he also had the benefits of the sauna, the Finnish steam bath, for grooming his muscles after workouts.

The race that brought him to Finland's attention as a real comer took place in 1919 in the Army championships. Under a full military pack, including rifle, cartridge belt, and five kilos of sand, he ran 20 kilometers, and ran the whole distance. He won. It was an incredible performance. That year he ran 3,000 meters in 8:58.1, 5,000 meters in 15:31.5, 10,000 meters in 32:56.

By 1920 he was Finland's best. But he met misfortune in his Olympic debut at Antwerp. He could run fast and far, but his style was not flexible for a racing duel. In the 5,000 meters he was beaten by the home-stretch wallop of the fiery little Frenchman, Josef Guillemot. It may have been seasickness that knocked Nurmi off form. Later in the week, however, he annexed his first Olympic crown. He won the 10,000 meters, turning the tables on Guillemot. This time he was ready for the Frenchman's stretch bid. He also won the cross-country race.

Nurmi returned home and took stock of himself with calm self-appraisal. He decided that he had to develop his lap-by-lap speed beyond the limits of his opposition. He took to carrying a watch and clocking his laps. By 1921 he was ready to demolish world records. He cracked Alfred Shrubb's long-standing six-mile record by 18 seconds, sliced that much, too, from Jean Bouin's 10,000-meter mark, cutting it to 30 minutes 40.2 seconds. He ran a mile in 4:13.9, compared to the world standard of 4:12.6 which Norman Taber had put up with the help of four pacing quarter-milers in 1915. To improve his speed he ran half-miles. He tried for the Finnish 800-meter championship and was beaten a yard in 1:58.4. The defeat was memorable. He wasn't to lose another race until 1925, again in the 880.

In 1922, Nurmi attained another goal. He eclipsed Kolehmainen's 1912 world record of 14:36.6 for 5,000 meters, returning 14:35.3 in the same Stockholm stadium. He visited England and came away with British championships in the four-mile run and two-mile steeple-chase and hung up a 2,000-meter world record of 5:26.3.

The following year Nurmi achieved a mark that the Americans and English especially could appreciate. He shattered Taber's eight-year-old record with a 4:10.4 mile at Stockholm. Trailing Edvin Wide, Sweden's best, for one lap, Nurmi took command and went on to his record by steadily increasing his speed over the remaining three laps. His schedule had called for a 4:09.4 mile, but Wide's control of the pace in the first quarter wrecked his timetable. Nurmi had left nothing to chance. In training for this mile race he had marked out a quarter-mile track on a football field at Helsinki and trained himself to hit each quarter on schedule.

His 4:10.4 mile was sensational. A Finnish periodical devoted a full page to a picture of the stop-watch showing the record time. But Nurmi never thought much of the mile record he had made; although he had great speed, it was the steady speed of a distance runner, not the speed of a natural miler. Yet no one surpassed his mile mark until Jules Ladoumegue of France reduced it to 4:09.2 in 1931.

Four years of such topflight international competition had now prepared Nurmi for his epic year. He now knew to a split second what he could do at any given distance, and he knew what he had to do to put himself beyond competition. But in the Spring of 1924, getting ready for the Paris Olympics, he damaged a knee cap. He made slow progress. He intended to try a back-breaking assignment in the Olympics which no human had ever tried before. But Nurmi was a superhuman. He intended to win the 1,500 meters and 5,000 meters on the same afternoon. He gave himself a final tryout in Helsinki. Within a span of 45 minutes he raced to a world record of 3:52.6 at 1,500 meters, then raced 5,000 meters in 14 minutes 28.2 seconds, putting up a world mark that was to last eight years. He also ran a 10,000-meter trial in 29 minutes 58 seconds, time he never again was to equal.

Finland's athletic statesmen, however, doubted Nurmi's genius. They refused to let him enter the 10,000 meters track race at Paris.

The Paris Olympics saw Peerless Paavo at the zenith of his form. Within 90 minutes he won two distance races against the world's best. He won the 1,500 meters in 3:53.6, an Olympic record, coasting the last lap after running the opposition into the ground with his unrelenting pace. Then, pursued by Willie Ritola, a fellow Finn, American trained, he won the 5,000 meters in 14:31.2, for another Olympic record.

Two days later Nurmi demonstrated his superman ability in the 10,000-meter cross-country race. In sweltering heat that caused 24 of the 39 starters to faint, collapse, or quit the grind in exhaustion, Paavo strode majestically over fields, pavements, fences, and water jumps. Impervious to heat and fatigue alike, he won effortlessly. The next day, with many of his cross-country opponents still hospitalized from their exertions, Nurmi was ready for another race. It wasn't an official part of the Olympic program, but he won the 3,000-meter team race, leading his fellow Finns to victory.

An all-conquering will dedicated to a single aim was Nurmi. That year he pared the world 10,000-meter record to 30 minutes 6.1 seconds and smashed four of Shrubb's mileage records en route.

The United States saw this Fininsh marvel in 1925. Unlike other Europeans who came before and after him, Nurmi trained himself for the tour he was to undertake. He had never run on board tracks, but he mastered board running as he mastered everything in track. As Americans by the tens of thousands were to see him, Nurmi was a stolid, unsmiling, balding fellow, with a big, well-developed chest, long, muscular legs. In racing action he had a bounding stride, rolling his body to get the last extra inch to his steps, carrying his arms high.

With his even-paced style, Nurmi ran away from all American opposition from the mile up, shattering indoor records at standard and odd distances in almost every start. Record crowds greeted him everywhere. But even Nurmi had his limits. One night in the old Madison Square Garden, trying the first part of a double assignment, he overtaxed himself racing against Ritola.

Breaking one record after another en route, Nurmi developed a cramp and had to quit the race. It became celebrated as the "veal potpie incident" in the saga of Nurmi. He was supposed to have eaten that dish. More likely, however, Nurmi exhausted himself with his killing pace and succumbed to its effects. That wasn't charged up as a Nurmi defeat. His only setback occurred in the Yankee Stadium at the end of his tour when he elected to run a half-mile against a half-mile champion, and Alan Helffrich outsped him easily. Nobody, not even a Nurmi, could be supreme at all distances.

From here on, Nurmi went downhill, although not all of a sudden. In 1926 he set a world record of 8:20.4 for 3,000 meters but was beaten in world-record time in a 1,500-meter race by Otto Peltzer of

Germany, and in another world-record two-mile race by Wide. In 1927 he set a world record for 2,000 meters. By 1928 he was coming back to the field.

In the Olympics at Amsterdam, an "old man" of thirty-one with aging muscles, he was beaten by fellow Finns in the steeplechase and 5,000 meters, but proved he was capable of winning an evenly fought race when he outdueled Ritola in the 10,000 meters, beating him in the homestretch. Later, at Berlin, he blasted a nineteen-year-old world record held by Jean Bouin by running 19,210 meters in one hour. He made a brief return visit to the United States in 1929, but the supreme Nurmi was no more. He lost his first mile race to Ray Conger in 4:17.2, and shortly returned home.

In 1931, in the fading twilight of his career, Nurmi finally achieved a long-sought goal that had eluded him in his prime. Although he had become the first to better nine minutes for two miles by racing the distance in 8:58.2 indoors in 1925, he did not achieve comparable time outdoors until six years later when he posted a world record of 8:59.5 in successful defense of his prestige against two new Finnish challengers, Lauri Lehtinen and Lauri Virtanen.

The records that existed when Nurmi arrived on the scene, and the records he left are compared in the following table:

Distance	Nurmi's Records	Former Records
1,500 meters	3:52.6 (1924)	3:54.7, Zander, 1917
2,000 meters	5:26.3 (1922)	5:30.4, Zander, 1918
3,000 meters	8:20.4 (1926)	8:33.1, Zander, 1918
5,000 meters	14:28.2 (1924)	14:36.6, Kolehmainen, 1912
10,000 meters	30:06.2 (1924)	30:23.2, Ritola, 1924
20,000 meters	1:04:38.4 (1930)	1:06:29, V. Sipila, 1925
One mile	4:10.4 (1923)	4:12.6, Norman Taber, 1915
Two miles	8:59.5 (1931)	9:09.6, Alfred Shrubb, 1904
Three miles	14:11.2 (1923)	14:17.6, Shrubb, 1903
Four miles	19:15.6 (1924)	19:23.4, Shrubb, 1904
Five miles	24:06.2 (1924)	24:33.4, Shrubb, 1904
Six miles	29:36.6 (1931)	29:59.4, Shrubb, 1904
One hour	19,210 meters (1928)	19,021.90 meters, Jean Bouin, 1913

Athletic greatness in any era is measured by the records of the contestant, the men he beats, the championships he wins, and the length of time he remains on top. Charley Paddock qualifies on these points as the No. 1 sprinter of the decade that followed the First World War. Paddock, by the nature of his specialty, was much more restricted in record-breaking feats than a distance runner like Nurmi; there was also much less scope for bettering the speed of homo sapiens. From the turn of the century, man, at best, had improved only a yard or so per hundred yards.

In a decade that produced such sprinters as Loren Murchison, Morris Kirksey, Jackson Scholz, Charley Borah, Chester Bowman and Roland Locke, with Frank Wykoff, George Simpson, Eddie Tolan, and Ralph Metcalfe coming on as the Twenties gave way to the Thirties, Paddock left his imprint on the track world.

From 1919, when he emerged into the spotlight as a surprise winner in the Inter-Allied Games of that year, until 1928, when he made his third straight Olympic team as a fading star, Charley Paddock was the World's Fastest Human in public acclaim, even though he was beaten now and again in national and international competition.

But Paddock had the flamboyant personality to keep himself in the limelight, winning or losing, so that his name remained synonymous with sprinting class, whether he was setting world records with the help of an alleged sympathetic and co-operative starter whose rhythm he knew perfectly, or making a round-the-world sprinting tour with his great contemporary, Murchison, or exposing a possibly nonexistent conspiracy among Americans, including himself, to wear out Harold Abrahams in the 1924 Olympic 100-meter final, or capitalizing on his athletic fame so that he was often in hot water with the Amateur Athletic Union, or forcing George W. Wightman to resign from the Olympic Committee in protest when he was included on the 1928 team, or running to a nonstandard 175-yard record through a fall of bricks, as the Franklin Field stadium wall collapsed in his path, or writing a book called *The Fastest Human*.

One way or another there was always excitement around Paddock, and the magic of his name remained up to his retirement following the 1928 Olympics.

Considering his fame, it is surprising to recall that Paddock won only one Olympic championship, the 100 meters. That was at Antwerp in 1920. He was the national 100-yard champion in 1921 and 1924, the national 220-yard champion in 1920, 1921, and 1924.

His international career as a first-class sprinter had its inception in the Inter-Allied Games in Paris in 1919. He went into those games with no national reputation, for he was only an eighteen-year-old at that time, although a second lieutenant of artillery. He was a rather plump youth, he had a peculiar waddle in his walk, and a high-pitched voice that sometimes broke into a falsetto, particularly when he laughed, which was often.

Whatever impression anyone gained from that combination as to his sprinting ability was considerably altered when he shot out of his holes.

He had a high-knee action and a tremendous bouncing stride, amazing leg drive combined with a feather-footed touch so that he hardly seemed to light on the track as he flew over it. The ordinary lunge and shrug finishes used by all the top sprinters were not good enough for Charley. He developed the jump finish, for which countless high-school coaches thereafter damned him. It was termed a "grandstand play," and he himself said there was some truth in the assertion that it was a "freak finish by a freak performer." He admitted that the jump finish—he actually took off 10 to 14 feet from the tape, which he broke with both feet off the ground, both arms flung up and outward—was useful only to a sprinter like himself with an exaggeratedly high, bouncing stride.

With it, Paddock equaled the world 100-yard record of 9 3/5 seconds four times in 1921, when he was a student at Southern California, equaled the mark again in 1924, set a world record of 20 4/5 seconds for 220 yards in 1921, shattering Bernie Wefers' twenty-five-year-old figures, and matched his own standard again in 1924. Paddock might have shaded these figures by a tenth second, but tenth-second timing was not officially recognized in his day. In 1926, in his eleventh year of competition, counting his school running, he was unofficially credited with 9.5 for 100 yards in defeating a California successor, Charley Borah.

In the two years, 1921 and 1924, when Paddock achieved his most glittering record feats, he also took over the world 100-meter record of 10 2/5 seconds, and his 220-yard speed also earned him credit for the 200-meter record with the same time. He put up a 300-yard record of 30 1/5 seconds, and a 300-meter record of 33.2 seconds in 1921. He never tried any distances beyond that.

Following the custom of his day, Paddock also went in for whole-sale records at intermediate distances and earned a basketful of "bastard" marks at 90, 110, 125, 130, 150, 175, and 200 yards, some of which still remain in the books as "noteworthy performances." The distances weren't often run except by record hunters. In one of these races, at 175 yards, in the Penn Relays, the crush of people craning their necks for a look at Fast-Time Charley caused a brick wall to crumble, and Paddock sped right through falling bricks to get his record.

In the 1920 Olympics, Paddock came through triumphantly in the 100 meters, as expected, but was beaten in the 200 meters by Allen Woodring, the balding Syracuse flier who had made the team as a substitute and ran in borrowed shoes. In 1924, Paddock was beaten by the Englishman, Harold Abrahams, in the 100 meters, and nailed by Jackson Scholz, fellow American, in the last stride of the 200 meters, when Paddock made the fatal error of turning his head. By 1928, Charley still retained enough speed to make the Olympic team in the 200 meters.

Paddock had a brief fling at indood sprinting in the old Madison Square Garden, but he wasn't the hair-trigger starter required for success in the short 60- and 70-yard board-floor tests. The man who was a marvel in these indoor sprints was Murchison, Paddock's side-kick on a trip around the world. They were contemporary, and their sprint careers lasted about equal length. Murchison indoors was unbeatable. Even in a race as hazardous to consistent form as 60 yards, Murchison ran up a winning streak of more than 40 sprints. Murch, small, blond, and compact, was so fast and so sure footed on boards, on the straightaway, or around a turn, that he could afford the luxury once, in Madison Square Garden, in an international relay, of picking up a baton dropped by Huber Houben of Germany, re-turning it to him, giving him a head start and beating him by 20 yards in 220.

Murchison shattered indoor records from 60 yards to 220, won the national outdoor 100 in 1920 and 1923, the 220 in 1918 and 1923, and was a hard-luck favorite who fell ill on the eve of the 1924 Olympics.

(Paddock and Murchison were closely linked as sprinters. Paddock was killed in an Alaska air crash on July 21, 1943, while serving as an officer in the Marines, while Murchison, struck down by illness, became a wheel-chair invalid.)

Another glittering figure of the Twenties was Joie Ray, the miler out of Kankakee, Illinois, who carried the Illinois A.C. colors to fame on boards and cinders for a period of thirteen years, starting in 1915. For durability and consistency there was none greater than Chesty Joie, a small, blond, cocksure champion with winged feet, whose cockiness was matched by his achievements.

It was Joie's fate never to win an Olympic championship, and his destiny in his last years as a miler to pursue Nurmi in his American indoor races of 1925 but never to beat him.

But these setbacks could not detract from the many years of glory that fell to Chesty Joie. In American competition, up until Nurmi's advent, he was in a class by himself in the classic mile. He won the national mile championship eight times, seven years in succession from 1917 to 1923, in times ranging from 4:14 2/5 to 4:20 in the days when a 4:20 mile was out of reach of everyone except the very top class. He won 16 national titles in all, from a half-mile to 10,000 meters (6¼ miles), dominated the indoor miles and kindred distances in cup competition with a stranglehold grip. Racing then wasn't a matter of all-out pace from gun to tape; it involved strategy and man-to-man duels of brain as well as heart and legs. And in these races Ray was supreme.

Records were simply a by-product of the competition then; the public and the runners were not as record-crazy as they later became when Nurmi made stopwatches a must for every track fan. Ray held the indoor mile record of 4:14.6 when Nurmi arrived and began whittling it down. He whittled it down to 4:12. That was a challenge to Joie. On the night that Nurmi quit the 5,000-meter race in the old Garden, Ray was scheduled to race him subsequently in the mile. When Nurmi was forced to withdraw from the mile, Ray went out and equaled his indoor record of 4:12—ten years after he had won his first national title.

In 1928, in his last fling in racing, Ray moved up to the marathon distance, which no topflight miler had ever essayed successfully. Ray made the Olympic team in the classic distance grind, and he made a brilliant bid for the Olympic championship at Amsterdam, only to fail on blistered feet in the closing miles.

Mention of Nurmi and Ray always must bring up the name of Willie Ritola, a compatriot of Paavo's, who was identified throughout his racing career as an American although he carried Finland's flag in the 1924 and 1928 Olympics. Arch rival of Ray's in many an indoor brush at 3,000 meters and two miles, Ritola was unfortunate in that he came along in the same age as Nurmi. Only Ritola could give Nurmi a run in the 5,000- to 10,000-meter range at Paris in 1924. Ritola won the Olympic 10,000 meters that year, defeated Nurmi in the Olympic 5,000 meters in 1928. In between those years, Ritola carried off 15 American championships from two to six miles, and, as the chief rival of Nurmi in the celebrated 1925 indoor tour, he set a three-mile record of 13 minutes 56.2 seconds that even Nurmi couldn't dislodge and viewed with admiration.

The history of track and field records proves that by and large the performances in any era are bettered in virtually all events. But the years following the First World War did not produce any record-breaking titans in the quarter and half. The shadows of Ted Meredith's mighty feats hovered over the efforts of his successors. His world 440-yard record of 47 2/5 seconds, set in the intercollegiates of 1916, remained unassailable and almost unapproached through the Twenties. Quarter-milers like Joe Tierney of Holy Cross, Bud Spencer of Stanford, and Rut Walter of Northwestern were acclaimed for getting within respectable distance of Ted's seemingly imperishable mark.

Ray Barbuti of Syracuse received renown in the 1928 Olympics by winning the 400 meters and saving the United States from a complete shutout in the individual flat races, although Barbuti was a virulent competitor rather than a speedboy. Meredith's world record of 1 minute 52 1/5 seconds in the half-mile, also set in 1916, was not eclipsed for ten years, and no American half-miler surpassed it until the end of the Twenties.

The Olympic year of 1920 also produced a marvelous hurdler in Earl Thomson, Canadian-born but American-trained, who, as a Dartmouth student, put up a world record of 14.4 seconds in the 120-yard high hurdles, a figure that endured for eleven years.

The runner who can dominate the mile, main event of indoor

track in public appeal, has always captured track's headlines, and in the years that followed Nurmi and Ray, from 1926 to 1928, it was Lloyd Hahn, short-striding, choppy power runner from the plains of Nebraska—converted from a sprinter to a first-class miler by Jack Ryder of the Boston A.A.—who was well-nigh unbeatable at that distance, and also in the half-mile and 1,000 yards. There was one exciting occasion in 1927 when he set the pace all the way and outlasted Wide of Sweden in a 4:12.2 mile, a fifth of a second back of Nurmi's and Ray's standard, and another thrilling occasion a year later when he shattered all records, indoors and out, by stepping off the 880 on the I.C. 4-A banked board track in 1 minute 51.4 seconds.

Hahn was great when he could set the pace and control it all the way, and he had almost unending success through three years in the United States. But it did not prepare him temperamentally for the sort of racing he was to encounter in the 1928 Olympics at Amsterdam, and his shocking failure there marked him as just another indoor mile wonder who couldn't make good outdoors in the Olympics.

All through these years there was another who entranced the track public with his consistent success. Whenever a marathon, particularly the famed Boston A. A. Marathon from Hopkinton to Exeter Street, was run, you would be sure to find Clarence DeMar in it, and most often the winner. The old man of the marathon had been an Olympic team member as long ago as 1912, and had first won the Boston grind in 1911. He was old, was Clarence, as runners go, in his fourth decade, when he shuffled home ahead of the field in 1922, '23, '24, '27, '28, '30 in the big Boston test. DeMar and the marathon were linked inseparably in the Twenties.

In the field events, the broad jumpers, high jumpers, and pole vaulters achieved the greatest progress through the Twenties and produced some mighty figures in the sport. Ned Gourdin of Harvard, one of the early Negro pioneers in an event that has become almost a monopoly for his race, became the first to leap beyond 25 feet in the long jump. He went three inches beyond that distance in the Harvard-Yale vs. Oxford-Cambridge meet in 1921. A year later DeHart Hubbard of Michigan arrived as champion and took possession of the event, winning the national title six straight years, and the 1924 Olympic title, and putting the world record at 25 feet 10⅞ inches.

Harold Osborn was the high jumper of the era. The blond Illinois ace, comparatively small, with springs in his legs and passion for leaping over a crossbar, put up a world record of 6 feet 8¼ inches in 1924, and made the lofty height of 6 feet 6 inches virtually par for him in any competition. He was the best in a superb group of jumpers that included Dick Landon of Yale and the New York A.C., Leroy Brown of Dartmouth and the New York A.C., Johnny Murphy of Notre Dame, D. V. Alberts of the Chicago A.A., and Bob King of Stanford.

The pole vaulters had been content with a 13-foot ceiling in their specialty until Charley Hoff of Norway showed the way toward the 14-foot mark. But that magic height was cleared for the first time in 1927 by Sabin Carr of Yale.

The United States has always been supreme in track and field, which, considering its population and the scope of its organized athletic program in schools, colleges, and clubs, was as it should be. And yet, in the Twenties, as demonstrated in its record in the Olympic Games of 1920, 1924, and 1928, the United States was less overpowering than in any other decade in the fifty years of modern Olympic history. It was a sign of the times that the greatest track figure of the Twenties should be not an American but a Finn—the Peerless Paavo of Abo.

POLO

by Tom O'Reilly
Columnist, the Morning Telegraph, New York

There is no point in being modest about this matter. If you claim
familiarity with the modern game of polo and missed seeing a performance by the late Thomas Hitchcock, Jr., you can camp on the
Meadow Brook Club's famed International Field the rest of your
life and still remain a stranger to the game.

Hitchcock had to be seen to be believed. You could compare his
mallet to Shakespeare's pen, Michelangelo's brush, or Mae West's
buoyancy and still sound inadequate. At times it seemed like a magic
wand that made the other swift, graceful centaurs who peopled
America's velvety polo fairylands just disappear into thin air. Hitchcock undoubtedly inspired the green-eyed English libel that "Polo
is a Persian invention, a British sport, and an American profession."

Moreover, the timing of Hitchcock's arrival on the polo stage was
as unfair as that observation, because never were there so many truly
great mallet stars performing at the same time as in the Golden Era
following the First World War. There were afternoons when Devereux Milburn, Winston Guest, Malcolm Stevenson, Watson Webb,
Louis Stoddard, Earl W. Hopping, Pat Roark, and Lewis Lacey, and
the brothers Miles from Argentina (*Si, Señor*, with a brogue, yet!)
gave peerless Tommy a rough time of it.

But those were the exceptional occasions when Hitchcock proved
he was human. Usually he outclassed everyone. He was ranked at
10 goals (the absolute top) for eighteen years. He was polo history's
lone performer of whom it could be said "He was worth 10 goals no
matter what position he played." Thus the story of American polo's
greatest days must be dominated largely by the saga of Ten-Goal
Tommy.

Nobody except his mother could say of Tommy Hitchcock "I knew

243

him when. . . ." When he was fourteen, the gracious "Lady of Aiken" taught him polo with a group of other Long Island youngsters, who called themselves the Meadow Larks. Had not World War I intervened, Tommy, who was born at the turn of the century, might have experienced the customary slow climb from low-goal competition to high-speed polo, but I doubt it. Most great athletes, such as Bobby Jones, or Babe Ruth, seem to leap from total obscurity to fame with few tiresome stops, and Hitchcock was great, indeed. From the time he first appeared in a United States National Open championship, in 1919, until his death in 1944 in an Army airplane crash in England, Tommy Hitchcock, Jr. was the first choice of everyone naming a United States international polo team. He was the world's best.

Hitchcock's World War I experiences have been retold often enough to become trite if they were not, like most of his fighting exploits, magnificent. At sixteen he left St. Paul's School to fly with France's Lafayette Escadrille. He served with distinction as a pilot until his bouncing kite was shot down, at 1,000 meters, over the German lines. He spent four months in German hospitals and many more in prison camps. While being transferred, between camps, he leaped through the window of a train crossing a river near the town of Ulm, and escaped. Walking only at night, guided by a compass, and fed with food saved from his rations, he covered one hundred miles to the Swiss border, near Berne, in eight days. He became a man early.

It has been said that genius is difficult to live with, and on the day of a polo match Tommy was intense to the point of fanaticism. A broad-shouldered, six-foot, light-heavyweight, with powerful arms, light blue eyes, a shy smile, and straight, unruly brown hair that tumbled down over his forehead, Tommy could be the soul of affability off the field, or even before a match. Yet on dismounting, after the final whistle of a game, he was such a bundle of taut nerves that he seemed to give off sparks. Unlike his colleagues, he rarely changed clothes at the club. Quickly he would bundle into a polo coat, climb into a car, and go home. He played at such a pitch that it took time for him to get unwound. Usually he appeared miserable while posing with his mates for pictures around the cup after winning a tournament final. He was impatient to get away.

This gave some people the mistaken impression that Hitchcock was a cold person. Actually he was the fieriest of all devotees in a notoriously wild game, marked for its extremes. In high-goal polo there is no such thing as a so-so match. The contest is either terrific or terrible.

Even in defeat Hitchcock was always terrific. I saw him outmounted and occasionally outhit, but never outplayed. Physically, his attributes included the customary flawless riding ability, powerful, accurate hitting, and superb condition. During the off-season he rose early on each working day to box three fast rounds with a trainer before breakfasting and departing for Wall Street. He chose boxing as a conditioner because, he said, "I think it brings a fellow to the point of exhaustion quicker than any other exercise." He had to wear large gloves in these workouts because he was a powerful puncher.

Mentally, his gifts were a natural fearlessness plus absolute concentration and a lightning-like ability to anticipate, and act instantaneously on the next move of friend or foe. There were days when high-powered opposition seemed about to shake his team to pieces until Hitchcock, riding at No. 3, would become a mounted dervish whose slam-bang tactics, catlike quickness, tremendous hitting, and omniscient direction appeared to pull his mates together by sheer power of will. He was a performer who gave all he had—which was plenty—and left an audience limp.

In 1921, coming of age, he rode as No. 2 on the United States international team that invaded England and brought home the Westchester Cup. His mates were Louis E. Stoddard, Sr., No. 1; J. Watson Webb, No. 3, and Devereux Milburn, back. The alternates were Earl W. Hopping and C. C. Rumsey. They had a rather easy time of it, defeating the British in two straight matches, 11-4 and 10-6. The greatest polo player in British history, Captain Leslie Cheape, had been killed by the Turks during the war, and the English side included Lieutenant Colonel H. A. Tomkinson, Major F. W. Barrett, Lord Wodehouse, and Major Vivian N. Lockett. Young Hitchcock was playing with long heads, and they taught him much. They also ranked him at 10 goals.

Poloists the world over admit that there never was a greater strategist in this curious game—which combines the speed of horse racing with the physical contact of hockey, the deft touch of golf, and the tricky team play of basketball—than Devereux Milburn. Much of the credit for Hitchcock's polished performances in international competition must go to Milburn, one of the great backs of all time, who was always around to help with shrewd advice.

Indeed, it was largely Milburn who devised the revolutionary American strategy of forsaking the short, snappy passing game, then in vogue, for a type of team play that depended on powerful drives, with the ball soaring down the field and horses racing in pursuit. Hitchcock was the perfect man around whom such an attack could be built, and from that 1921 series until his death he remained the first choice for any of our international teams, even though a complete new school of exceptionally talented players came to the fore.

Tommy's international reputation was only one year old when it became apparent that, despite all the traditional fuss surrounding our matches with the British, the most serious threat to America's claims of polo supremacy would come from Argentina. In 1922, a quartet of Argentines, led by Jack Nelson, set out for London and a season of tournament play. They included, in addition to Nelson, the Miles brothers, Juan and David, and Lewis Lacey, a Canadian who lived his life and played his polo at the Buenos Aires Club. Although this team had been playing together for two years, it arrived in London unheralded. It then proceeded to win the Hurlingham Champion Cup, the Whitney Cup at Ranelagh, and the Roehampton Open Cup.

This success brought an invitation to play in the United States Open championship, which was promptly accepted. In the final match of our national tournament, the Argentines walloped a Meadow Brook team, made up of Skiddy von Stade, Hitchcock, E. C. Bacon, and Milburn, 14 to 7. The ranchers from below the equator were so hot that a special series was arranged between them and our 1921 international team.

In these matches, J. C. Cooley played at No. 1 in place of Louis Stoddard, Sr., and, while the United States won in straight games, the margin of its triumphs—7-4 and 5-4—indicated that players from Argentina never were going to be any pushover on a polo field. It was also obvious that South America's mallet-trained thoroughbreds were something special, because after the final match they were put up at public auction and returned handsome prices, leading up to the later sale of Jupiter, a blazed-faced Argentine pony, for which Stephen Sanford paid a cool $22,000.

Hitchcock played with the Meadow Brook team which won our National Open championship in 1923 and included Raymond Belmont, Bobby Strawbridge, Jr., and Devereux Milburn. The big international event of that year, however, was a series, arranged by General John J. Pershing and Lord Cavan, between the British and United States Armies.

The British Army had many officers with fancy handicap ratings, and the quartet of Lieutenant Colonel T. P. Melvil, Majors E. G. Atkinson, F. B. Hurndall, and Vivian N. Lockett was expected to overwhelm our less publicized military performers on International Field, Westbury, Long Island. As it turned out, the Yanks, captained by Major Louie A. Beard, and including Majors A. H. Wilson and J. K. Kerr and Lieutenant Colonel Lewis Brown, Jr., gave their opposite numbers from Blighty a handy polo lesson. The U. S. won the opener, 10-7, dropped the second game, 12-10, and then poured it on in the final, to win 10-3.

In the great idiot year of 1924, when Wall Street was washed in the lunar rays of a paper moon and every ash man dreamed of leaping "from Poland to polo in one generation," the mallet pastime honestly reflected the national nuttiness. The British arrived to play for the Westchester Cup, and when the Prince of Wales announced plans to attend the matches the U. S. Polo Association calmly scaled the 40,000 seats at Meadow Brook's International Field to a $100 top, causing such a box-office rush that Broadway speculators would not waste their valuable time finding you a pair for less than a mere mortgage on your apartment house.

The Empire had plucked the transplanted Canadian, Lewis Lacey, from Buenos Aires and planned building a team around his talents. This so frightened the United States that the association nearly wore itself out getting ready for the fray. Fully 18 players were invited to take part in trial matches to select the American quartet. When finally Webb, Malcolm Stevenson, Hitchcock, and Milburn rode out on the field, they had their choice of ponies from a pool provided by Stoddard, Harry Payne Whitney, Sanford, J. S. Phipps, R. Penn Smith, Robert H. Hassler, G. M. Hecksher, Rodman Wanamaker, 2nd, George G. Moore, W. Averell Harriman, Herbert Pulitzer, Walter Camp, Jr. and H. C. Phipps.

Lord Wimborne was the chief British backer, and there was plenty of internal disagreement when the Hurlingham Committee sent over, as teammates of Lacey, the same Army quartet which Major Louie Beard's cavalrymen had walloped, with Major Geoffrey H. Phipps-Hornby thrown in as lagniappe. Apparently, Lord Wimborne's monocle couldn't see as far as India, where Captain C. T. I. (Pat) Roark was bouncing maharajas over the sideboards and, to make matters worse, Lacey tore a shoulder ligament in practice and played through the series with one arm in a sling.

It was a short series. We won, 16-5 and 14-5, with the highly capable Bobby Strawbridge, Jr. replacing Stevenson after his seventh-period fall in the opener. Socially, it was a great series. From a competitive viewpoint, it ranked below two other events which received far less attention.

The first of these was the 1924 Olympic championship in Paris, which we entered in a rather offhand manner. Hitchcock played No. 1 on a curious United States team, which included Frederick Roe, Rodman Wanamaker, 2nd, and Elmer Boeseke. In the final round we were licked, 6-5, by (guess who?) four Argentines, named Arturo Kenny, Jack Nelson, Captain Enrique Padilla, and Juan B. Miles. Nelson scored the winning goal in the final seconds. Hitchcock sustained one of many crashing falls which, later, caused a physician to forbid him to play unless wearing a specially constructed pith helmet in place of the ordinary polo cap.

The second big surprise, if you discount the amazing omission of Roark in England's international lineup, came in our National Open championship. People looking over the entries came across a team called the Wanderers, that included Lacey, Hitchcock, Elmer Boeseke, Jr., and Louis Stoddard, Sr. Immediately they concluded that the Wanderers' triumph would be a mere formality.

To the amazement of these sophisticates, a quartet from California's famed Midwick Club—E. G. Miller, Eric Pedley, Arthur Perkins, and Carleton F. Burke—beat the Wanderers, 6-5, and won the title. Reviewing the year's work, it must have been obvious to all Long Islanders that the most dangerous threats to their supremacy lay not so much in England as in South America and our own West.

In 1925, when a veteran team, including Averell Harriman, Webb, Stevenson, and J. C. Cowdin, won the National Open by defeating Hitchcock and Co., Major Louie Beard took another Army outfit to

England for a return meeting with the British soldiers, before the King and Queen at Hurlingham. This time his mates were Major A. H. Wilson, Captain C. H. Gerhardt, and Captain P. P. Rodes. Just to prove our 1923 victory had been no fluke, the Yanks walloped a British quartet, made up of Captains R. L. McCreery and J. P. Dening, Lieutenant W. S. McCreery, and Major D. C. Boles, in straight games, 8-4, 6-4.

There was much talk of this Army rivalry being built into a big thing, and a Major George S. Patton, whose club won the Hawaiian Island championship a year later, issued a solemn comment on training for military men. It included, among other things, the following: "There are constant and real physical hazards in polo and, talk as we will of the necessity for cool judgment in combat, it is none the less a fact that no man can stay cool in battle unless he is habituated to the exhilarating sense of physical peril. No sport, save possibly steeplechasing and football, is so good a school in this respect. . . . The War Department, then, in encouraging polo is doing a very economical thing . . . rendering more efficient a body of men on whom, should war recur, the honor of our country will depend."

How could "Horsey Georgie" possibly have known that he was to lead the Army in another kind of international contest—in which there would be plenty of occasion for "real physical hazards."

The big event of 1926 was the appearance in our National Open championship of a team from Argentina. It was a red-hot outfit, that included Jack Nelson, C. N. Land, Lacey, and Manuel Andrada, the great gaucho performer. They got by Hitchcock and Co. all right, but in the final, Laddie Sanford's Hurricanes threw Pedley, Pat Roark, and Bobby Strawbridge, Jr. at them. The Hurricanes won, 7-6, in one of the toughest championship finals in Open history.

The British tried again to retrieve the Westchester Cup in 1927, but this time they approached from a new tack. The Hurlingham committee turned the whole matter of a challenge over to its Army-in-India Association. A full-fledged and beautifully turbaned Royal Indian—the Maharaja of Ratlam—turned up as the team's chief backer. Other maharajas, and patriotic Englishmen at home and in Australia, had loaned the team prize ponies. The players were Captain C. E. Pert, Major A. H. Williams, Captain C. T. I. Roark, and Major E. G. Atkinson.

Three of the grand old-timers on our side were making their final appearance in Westchester Cup competition. They were Webb, Stevenson, and Milburn. Hitchcock completed the quartet, of course. It was the same old story. America won, 13-3 and 8-5, as the old boys departed in a blaze of glory. After this series, the Army-in-India finished second in our National Open, losing, 11-7, to the newly formed Sands Point Club of Harriman, Hitchcock, Cowdin, and Stoddard.

Undoubtedly, 1928 was an important turning point in American polo's Golden Age, because it marked the first serious challenge from Argentina for a series of matches to decide the championship of the Americas and the arrival on the international scene of younger players who would carry most of this country's competitive burden. When the Argentines arrived on Long Island with a lineup that included Arturo Kenny, Jack Miles, Jack Nelson, and Lacey, the lone full-time North American veteran left to face them was the twenty-eight-year-old Hitchcock.

Tommy felt somewhat nervous about this and insisted that Malcolm Stevenson ride with him at No. 3. Trial matches to find a No. 1 and a back were not much help because no matter what lineup Hitchcock arrived at, Pat Roark and Webb would come out with a club that beat them. Averell Harriman was eventually selected to ride at No. 1, with Winston Guest at back.

It should be said here that whether the ponies were bred in Argentina, England, India, or our own West, nobody ever had a faster string of polo mounts than those bred and trained for Harriman by Jimmy Crawford in New York's own Genesee Valley. Harriman went into polo with the same efficiency he showed as a businessman, making certain that in the essential matter of getting first crack at the ball nobody was going to outrace him. It was this attention to detail that had made him a fine varsity oarsman at Yale, although not a heavy fellow, and also a first-class polo player.

The United States was lucky to win the first game, 7-6, on a soggy field. The Argentine, Miles, gave Hitchcock one of the toughest afternoons of his playing career. Argentina won the second game, 10-7, even though Lacey, in a collision with Hitchcock, suffered a fall that pinned him under his pony and was mighty dangerous.

It became evident that the Argentines had figured out how to bottle up Tommy at No. 2, and a change was mandatory. For the final game, which we won, 13-7, Hitchcock moved back to No. 3, with "Little Earle" Hopping, one of the ruggedest young players of his time, at No. 2. It became obvious that in the future Hopping and Guest would be in the forefront of international competition. Harriman could have made it too, but the poor fellow got all mixed up with business and Russia.

Another significant note was the appearance of two kids named Stewart Iglehart and Ebbie Gerry, who rode with Hitchcock and Harriman to win the Monty Waterbury tournament that season, while a young Englishman named Gerald Balding rode with a tough old cowboy named Rube Williams on the Old Oaks team that won our Junior Championship.

The year 1929 found many people who had been toying with the idea of buying a polo string deciding to compromise with a box of apples. Laddie Sanford's Hurricanes again won the National Open, with Webb replacing Pedley, who had returned to the West Coast. The Junior title was won by four young fellows named Ebbie Gerry, Stewart Iglehart, Jimmie Mills, and Cocie Rathborne. Some years later I asked a famous poloist which asset of a mallet star disappears first when he starts to slip—his eye, riding, or hitting? Probably thinking of 1929, he replied, promptly, "His bankroll." Could be.

The British, in 1930, sent over the best international polo team they had assembled in years. It included Gerald Balding, Lacey, Roark, and Humphrey Guinness, all exceptional performers. But the British were just a bit too late. By this time Hitchcock had gathered around him Pedley, at No. 1, Earle Hopping, No. 2, and Guest, back. That was one of the greatest teams ever to ride for the United States. They beat the British, 10-5 and 14-9. Sanford's Hurricanes again won the National Open, this time with Pedley back in his old spot, replacing Webb.

That was the year—1930—a kid named Mike Phipps broke into the Yale lineup, and people began to talk about a big Western cowboy named Cecil Smith, from Texas. At that time, too, little Pete Bostwick, the steeplechase star, was starting to dabble in polo, and they came no gamer. Husky Manuel Andrada commented, after Pete, weighing a fat 110 pounds, had maneuvered his horse in such a way as to ride the 200-pound, black-jowled gaucho off the ball, "Leedle man, beeg bump!"

Following the Golden Age, Phipps was to join with Iglehart,

Winston Guest, and Raymond Guest in forming the famous Templeton team. The Greentree four was to be organized by John Hay (Jock) Whitney, with Hitchcock, Pete Bostwick, and Gerald Balding the solid men. The West was to challenge Long Island for recognition in the polo picture with the start of the intersectional series at Chicago's Onwentsia Club, where the Westerners gave the Easterners the shock of their lives by walloping Hitchcock's crowd in two of three games.

Phipps and the Guest brothers, Winston and Raymond, rode with Tommy, with "Little Earle" Hopping as spare. Playing for the West were Aidan Roark, brother of Pat; Elmer Boeseke, veteran Midwick star; Cecil Smith and Rube Williams, the two famous cowboy horse dealers from Texas; and Eric Pedley, hustled on from California for the third game.

Another crack team, Old Westbury, was to be formed by Cornelius Vanderbilt (Sonny) Whitney, and included Phipps, Smith, and Iglehart. In 1939, the United States was to find itself in the unprecedented position of having four 10-goal players—Hitchcock, Phipps, Smith, and Iglehart—as World War II ended international competition and brought down the final curtain for the great Tommy.

It was brilliant competition in the Thirties, with many fine players bouncing that apple around, and the future of polo is bright, in the capable hands of experienced veterans like Pete Bostwick, Phipps, Iglehart, Smith, and Bobby Strawbridge. But it will be a long time before we see the like of the Golden Twenties, and longer still until another Hitchcock turns up.

BILLIARDS

by JOE KING
Of the New York World-Telegram

The Golden Age of billiards is generally confined to the years from 1920 through 1930, but for Willie Hoppe there was no time clock. The peerless billiardist was world champion of the scientific game of 18.1 balk line in 1906, and he carried on to win the world title for the first time at the more spectacular and popular game of three-cushion billiards in 1936. When the great stars of the Golden Age soared into the firmament, they found Hoppe already there, and when their fabulous era faded into history, Hoppe shone on. The Boy Wonder is a champion for the ages.

Willie, of course, was part of the Golden Age. He stood against an entirely new galaxy of challengers in the Twenties. Back in gaslight he had fought Vignaux, Slosson, Sutton, Cline, Old Jake Schaefer. At the Grand Hotel in Paris, in Grand Central Palace, New York, in Chicago's Orchestra Hall, in the New York Theater Concert Hall, and in the Garden on Madison Square.

In the dazzling incandescence of the Ruth-Jones-Tilden-Dempsey period he stood against Young Jake Schaefer, touched with the genius of Old Jake; against the cocky, uncanny shotmaker from California, Welker Cochran; against the dogged, analytical German, Eric Hagenlacher; against Edouard Horemans, the Belgian with the magic, but nerve-wracked, cue.

And Hoppe sailed serenely on, into the neon age, the generation of Jake Schaefer, 3rd. As he lasts so well, we will ask him to wait still another moment, while we tell of a master of the green-clad table who was more peculiarly associated with the Golden Age, who rocketed up with it, and who fizzled out at its end as the Great White Way etched untimely lines in his baby face.

He was Ralph Greenleaf, the invincible champion of the old game of pool, formally called pocket billiards, which was the shabby, other-side-of-the tracks cousin of courtly balk line. Greenleaf lifted pool up to the staccato tempo of the hurried, flamboyant Twenties. The game never commanded such prominence before or since. He carried the role of champion with an air and wore a tuxedo as if that were his style. He was slender, with good shoulders, wide blue eyes in a bland, juvenile face, hair slicked down tight and parted in the exact middle. He was saucy, arrogant, petulant, childlike, a typical spoiled darling of the times. But he was colorful and theatrical at the pool table, his absolute control of the cue ball was no less than mystifying, and his flair for daring combination play wrecked the tedious safety game of the old champions.

For a comparison, Hoppe was a true athlete, appreciative and thrifty of his physical gifts and resources. Greenleaf remained the reckless boy from Monmouth, Illinois, who had whipped champions when he was a tot, and he did not conserve his talent.

The old gentlemen from the New York Racquet Club came downtown to see and admire Hoppe. Greenleaf, in his finely tailored tuxedo, an innovation in the sport, was welcome for exhibitions in the exclusive clubs, but he could also walk in his flip way among gangsters, who idolized him. He would play in a sordid parlor on the Cicero side of Chicago, or in Brownsville, Brooklyn, in its infamous speakeasy days, and the shady denizens would carry him in triumph on their shoulders to the Cadillac waiting unharmed outside the door.

Hoppe was respected as a great, enduring man by all classes. Greenleaf epitomized the glitter and glamor of those flashy, lawless times, and he was the envy of the frustrated in all walks of life as well as those who did pack a rod. Back in the shadows of the gallery at his matches were the big shots of Broadway, munching their cigars, and perhaps casting back in mind to the boyhood parlor in the basement —the stale smell of gin and smoke, the cigarette dangling from lip, the hustling after a sucker, the cold appraisal of girls who would and who wouldn't, the utter disgrace of making an honest dollar.

But Greenleaf was the overpowering champion, the Babe Ruth of his sport, while Hoppe was not. Young Jake brought the home-run punch to the refined game of balk line. Hoppe would tell you that. Schaefer won the classic tournament of the Golden Age, in Chicago in March 1925, from the most brilliant field of the period—Hoppe, Cochran, Hagenlacher, Horemans, and the Japanese, Suzuki. Young Jake humbled Hoppe by 400-173 and set a new grand average record of 57 5/32. This beat his own mark of 51, which he set when he first relieved Hoppe of the title in 1921.

Willie commented on this tournament: "My game has not fallen off so much as the game of the other players has improved. When you get two players, one averaging 57, and another 45 (Horemans), in a tournament in which competition is so keen, then it is no disgrace to be beaten. My grand average of 26 was good enough ten years ago to win any balk-line tournament, but the pace has been increased, especially by Schaefer."

The elder Schaefer forced the change from straight rail to the balk line, and the younger Schaefer, in the intense rivalry of the Golden Age, was the chief cause of the many experiments with balk line which, however, failed to save the game after its glorious resurrection in the early Twenties.

But at pool, there was no conflict for Greenleaf. He was the grand slam, the forward pass, the cannon-ball serve, the home-run incarnate, on the green baize of his game. In the world's championship of 1924, a cautious old champion, Bennie Allen, fought a strong defensive game through the 13th inning, with Greenleaf ahead by a shade, 42-38. Ralph stepped up for the 14th inning and ran 83 and out. The gentlemanly Jerome Keogh, in the national tournament of 1924, was putting together a good, sound, old-fashioned game with a lead of 16 to minus 1 for three innings. Keogh sat down for the fourth inning and, before he got up, Greenleaf ran 101 unfinished, and the match was over.

Then, in December of 1929, at Detroit, in the world's title tournament, lightning struck. Greenleaf scratched in the first inning against Frank Taberski, and in the second inning he ran 126 for victory by 125-0. Here, obviously, was a man better than his game. A championship run of 126, and a two-inning match were undreamed-of records. They were fanciful to such a steady-going old master of safety play as bespectacled, pedantic Taberski, and staggering, galling blows, too, for of all the old-timers, he bristled highest at sight of this fresh young kid who mocked the conservative, obstructionist game which had held true since the time of Alfredo DeOro.

But grim, phlegmatic Taberski alone stood up to Greenleaf and the home-run cue, in matches marked by acrimony, where the roll of the balls was secondary to the crackling clash of personalities, which flashed brighter for the spectators than the floodlights over the placid, green playing field. Taberski did not have the ineffable touch and the imagination of the breezy kid, but he had the stanch spirit to fight on, when other challengers "dogged it," as they say in pool, and crept lamely back to the mourner's bench, that first row behind the referee where Greenleaf's rival prayed for his defeat.

Greenleaf first won the world title in 1919 in Philadelphia when he was twenty. He took every tournament thereafter—although he lost twice in challenge and league play, the latter time when he was ill—until grizzled old Taberski whipped him in 1928 in Chicago, in the most dramatic evening in the history of pool.

Taberski had claimed a default because Greenleaf violated a minor rule not concerned with the playing of the game. This lapse was charged to the referee. Taberski refused to play for three days, and when he agreed, the officials, fearful that the wall of animosity between the two would fall again on all, decreed that the play-off, should there be a tie, must follow immediately. That was Taberski's job, to make a play-off. And he did. He won the final match of the tournament, 125-97, and it was the Home Run Kid who wilted for the first time in the play-off, and went down tamely in the early morning hours by 125-41.

The atomic explosion of the 126 unfinished came the following year, but in 1930 the string seemed ended for Greenleaf, who had more entanglements than pool, when Erwin Rudolph, a steady-going, eminently respectable journeyman pool player, defeated him, 125-120, in the final game of the tournament in New York. Baby Face fooled them all. With a last grand exposition of his virtuosity, he won 20 straight matches, to go unbeaten through the tournaments of 1931 and 1932. But thereafter he fell down to the level of the rest and, while he won again, he had passed on with the Golden Age as one of the minor stars but one of genuine quality and spirit, one of blue-white brilliance.

While Hoppe shone serenely on. Although he was "all through" when the Golden Age began—and "all through" again when it ended, as we shall see.

The master billiardist of all time was upset by dynamic Young Jake, at 18.2, in 1921, and the old New York *Telegram*, in an editorial, attempted to foresee the future: "At thirty-four, Hoppe is ex-champion. That he will rewin the palm in contests with Schaefer is to be questioned. There is a new era dawning." There was. The second era of Hoppe was about to dawn in rosy light, and there was to be a resplendent third era of Hoppe, too.

But no one would be so brash as to predict that early in 1922, when Hoppe, the perfectionist, actually miscued at a vital point and failed to regain the title in a challenge match, which Schaefer won by the narrow margin of 1500-1468.

Hoppe, that Summer, seemed none too sure: "I have not touched a cue since that miscue in Chicago, and I don't intend to for some time to come. I don't think there is anything wrong with my shoulder, aside from the strain of twenty years of continuous playing."

Almost twenty years, then, from the time he took the Young Masters' World Championship, at 18.1, in Paris in 1904, and the whole of the Golden Age was just ten short years.

Hoppe did come back, we know. But let us see his problem back there in 1922. He had to match a player who counted billiards faster than any man who lived, including Hoppe. Schaefer proved that with his 51 grand average in the tournament of 1921.

Now billiards is a unique game in sports. Nowhere is the atmosphere so tense and the tightness of the players so clear to see, because there is no action to relieve the pressure except the slow pacing of the billiardist about the table, the hush while he strokes, the anticipation while the balls perform his bidding. The opponent in the corner of the ring is immobilized. He is helpless. He cannot pitch to the homer hitter, he cannot try to intercept the forward pass, he has no chance to return the cannon-ball serve, he does not get stroke and stroke alike with the grand-slam golfer. He just sits, and his nerves, as well as those of his rival, are stretched tautly across the table, and the graceful roll of the balls, so impersonal, tells better than in any sport, as nerve after nerve is impinged, whether this fellow has failed to face the issue or the other fellow has made a superlative shot when it mattered most.

Hoppe could whip almost everybody while he sat in the corner.

He alone was never helpless when he sat out. His personality, his reputation, his remorseless play, his integrity and gameness created a shimmering fear which danced across the nerves of his opponent on the table. Hoppe's nerves were never there.

His rivals tried to beat Hoppe, just as the golfers tried to beat Jones. But Hoppe and Jones never had any antagonist except the game itself. Hoppe with his cool concentration and finesse with three inanimate objects on a small green table; Jones with his relentless chase of Mr. Par over the greensward.

But nerves would not do against Schaefer. He had the nerves of a scrod. Hagen and Sarazen, in their classic match at Pelham in the P.G.A. championship of 1923, approximated the frigidity of a Hoppe-Schaefer duel. There had to be a technical difference, an advantage in technique, for Hoppe to hog-tie the trained, powerful sinews of young Schaefer, bursting with energy which the old man of thirty-six could not match. There was, and this is it. Schaefer could make the most difficult shot and go on to a smashing run, but when he missed that balking shot, he often left the balls open for a run by his opponent. Hoppe, with his cynical regard of those three small telltales on the table, never gave them a chance. He would essay a shot which would stop Schaefer, but his vision went further, and when he missed, the balls would roll into an impossible "leave." There was no shot to be made off them.

That is why Hoppe could come back in November of 1922, at the Hotel Pennsylvania, New York, just a few months after he had laid down his cue, to defeat Schaefer in the final match of the 18.2 tournament, 500-283.

In 1924, Hoppe made his greatest contribution to the saga of the Golden Age. He defeated Schaefer in a challenge match in Chicago, 1500-1196. He took on Horemans in New York and beat him, 1500-958, scoring 500 to 16 in one block. He went on to Boston to smash down Cochran, 1500-1189.

After that, Willie became intrigued with three-cushion. Balk line was not a moneymaker any more, and Hoppe was used to $20,000 to $25,000 a year. He went into training for the more popular game, which had its stronghold in Chicago. By training, we mean just that. Willie always took care of himself, kept in condition. He worked out at baseball in the Summer many a year, hitting and chasing flies. He walked interminable miles in the Winter. He played golf for years but had to give it up when he became too valuable and his arm was insured and the guarantor company objected to the risk. He was abstemious, and he was wary of late hours, while Greenleaf, for a short flashback, was the most convivial and genuinely hospitable champion of the Golden Age in his limited sphere, excepting only untutored, roughhouse Ruth, who embraced the world.

Hoppe had unfortunate experiences at three-cushion. Bob Cannefax, the champion at that game, cut the cloth in 1926 and was suspended a year for this misdemeanor, which was intended to force Hoppe—a classicist, who played the balls rather than the cloth— to concede a new fast fabric to the three-cushion man who could not roll his fast-action game on an old cloth slowed down after long play. In more mysterious circumstances, the cloth was cut again during Hoppe's match with Gus Copulos, the Greek, who ran 17 for a record.

Hoppe, the old gentleman of billiards, with his impeccable sportsmanship and his delicacy of manners, could not abide such tactics and yearned again for the balk line, but his heart was not in the old game. Even though he staked the 18.1 title against Schaefer in 1926 and lost it for the first time since he took it from Ora Morningstar in 1914. In the match, Schaefer set a record grand average of 34 72/104, but Hoppe showed he, too, had learned about the home run and the grand slam and Greenleaf, by running a new high record of 200.

Again, in 1927, Hoppe stepped back into balk line to defeat Hagenlacher in the grand ballroom of the Hotel Pennsylvania, to resume his old-accustomed dominance of 18.2, by 1500 to 1387. The old fans will remember that title match as one of the closest and tensest they ever saw. The lead changed hands four times in the final block, and after a hushed audience saw Hoppe run off the final 41 billiards, cheers broke out.

But as the effulgence of the Golden Age dimmed in luster, Hoppe again faded out. Mainly through injustice. The National Billiard Association, not a sports body but a creature of the Brunswick-Balke Collender Company, which had a virtual monopoly of bowling and billiard equipment, decreed Hoppe could not play in the balk-line tournament of 1928 if he went through with his plans for the three-cushion tournament.

The late Jack Doyle, the most respected man in the game on Broadway, led an uprising. "We feel a great injustice has been done to Willie Hoppe," he stated in behalf of New York's room owners. "He is the greatest figure in billiards. What difference does it make if he wins a dozen titles? There should never be a restriction on talent."

But the N.B.A. had its way, only because of its financial hold on the players, through tournament prize money and through salaries granted to champions and their foremost challengers. By 1930, Hoppe had revolted against the N.B.A., and this action broke the N.B.A. for a time. But all was confusion, and Willie apparently had disappeared also in the destruction of this commercial "sports" body.

But you can't keep a Hoppe down. In 1937 he regained the 18.1 title, which he first won in 1906, from Schaefer. In 1940 he ran off 20 games in succession to squelch all opposition at three-cushion. Schaefer and Cochran were among the defeated, and Hagenlacher, Horemans, and Suzuki long since had been forgotten. As Hoppe sailed serenely on, a great champion of the Golden Age, and a champion also for the ages.

SWIMMING

by L. DE B. HANDLEY
Noted swimming authority, former Olympic coach

Two names inevitably flash to mind when memory drifts back to the swimming achievements of the Twenties—John Weissmuller and Gertrude Ederle. Old-timers may argue pro and con their being the greatest swimmers of the period, but none will dispute that one feat of each stood out boldly above all others—Johnny's world record of 0:51 seconds for 100 yards free style, and Trude's conquest of the treacherous English Channel.

Weissmuller's mark is memorable as the most enduring in natatorial history. He set it in 1927 and for sixteen years it defied all attacks—truly amazing longevity in a sport as fast stepping as swimming. When Alan Ford finally shaded it to 0:50.6, then to 0:49.7 in 1944, moreover, many wondered how much these better times were due to the building of more modern and speedier pools.

Trude earned lasting fame in swimming the Channel in 1926. Not only was she the first woman to achieve the grueling exploit, but she effected the crossing through very rough water in 14 hours 30 minutes, smashing the then existing men's record for the course, 16 hours 23 minutes, made by Sebastian Tiraboschi of Argentina, and creating a mark for women not beaten to date. New York City authorities thought so highly of the feat that upon Trude's return they gave her an official reception and arranged for a Broadway parade, during which she received one of the most enthusiastic popular ovations ever accorded a city guest.

Both noted aces enjoyed brilliant careers aside from the quoted feats. Weissmuller, popular Tarzan of the silver screen, won his first national outdoor championship at 220 yards free style in 1921; he garnered the Olympic 100- and 400-meter titles in 1924, the 100-meter again in 1928; he shattered world free-style records from 100 to 880 yards, and the back stroke mark for 150 yards, and he was invincible in the sprints until his retirement in 1929.

Some believe that Weissmuller, despite his 880-yard record, never fully exploited his capabilities at courses beyond 440 yards because of the unwillingness of his coach, Bill Bachrach, to pit his two top aces against one another. At the peak of Johnny's career, Sweden's great free-styler, Arne Borg, came to this country and joined the former's club, the Illinois A. C. of Chicago. Borg was at his best from 800 meters, upward, as made clear by his 1500-meter record of 19:07.4, untouched in eleven years, so Bachrach decided he should specialize in the longer events, Weissmuller in the shorter. Whatever the in-fluence of the decision, Johnny unquestionably possessed endurance aplenty, for he won several important distance races.

Tall, rangy, and broad chested, Weissmuller was gifted with ex-traordinary buoyancy. He swam so high in the water that his back showed above surface almost to the waist. A happy-go-lucky, fun-loving youth, he early displayed a flair for showmanship. He and Stubby Kruger, Hawaiian dorsal champion, concocted a comedy skit, which they performed at swimming meets and which went over with a bang. Literally, indeed, it stopped proceedings at the 1924 Olympics. The applause of the crowd was so insistent, the cries of "encore" so compelling, that they had to repeat the act twice while officials fumed at the disruption of the schedule. The stunt was barred after that.

Johnny withdrew all too soon from the amateur ranks. Years later, time trials indicated he had retained his phenomenal speed.

Trude Ederle, a shy and retiring lassie, leaped into the spotlight in 1922, at the age of fourteen, by scoring a startling upset victory in the international three-mile swim for the J. P. Day Cup, in New York Bay, for which had been brought over Europe's foremost naiad, Hilda James of England. Trude was rated a rank outsider, never hav-ing competed in a race longer than 220 yards, yet she convincingly defeated more than 50 opponents. Very soon afterward, she began to crack free-style records (all records herein referred to are world marks, unless otherwise stated) and before she was through she had broken standards from 100 to 800 meters. She earned the national 220- and 440-yard crowns that Summer.

It was my privilege to coach Trude from novicehood, and I

attribute her success very largely to the good offices of her older sister and fellow-star, Margaret. Trude was a fine competitor, but she lacked confidence in herself and easily became discouraged. With rare wisdom, Margaret, whom she worshipped, coaxed and encouraged, scolded and bullied, as circumstances prompted, always getting results.

An instance in point: When Trude was within a mile of completing her record-breaking swim from the Battery to Sandy Hook, the tide turned against her and she began to lag. Margaret rose to the occasion, shouting from the piloting motorboat: "Get going, lazy bones, you're loafing." "Loafing, am I?" shouted back the indignant Trude. "For that I'll make it if it kills me." And she did.

Like Weissmuller, Trude forsook the amateur field before attaining the limit of her possibilities, attracted by the lure of the Channel swim.

But the story of the Twenties is not told by the performances of a couple of topnotchers. The decade was memorable because it brought to full fruition more than fifteen years of keen study devoted by Americans to the development of the crawl stroke, thereby launching a period of astounding international improvement; because it saw the Women's Swimming Association of New York, a little club formed in 1917 by a handful of business girls, mushroom into the world's greatest organization of its kind, produce an amazing sequence of record breakers, and play a leading role in furthering the universal progress; because it marked a stretch of unprecedented and not since equaled success for our swimmers and divers, highlighted by triumphs at three consecutive Olympic tests.

To clarify the notable strides made in natatorial methods, it will be necessary to touch on the evolution of the crawl and explain that its increasing efficiency was brought about by a gradual quickening and narrowing of the leg drive, which consists of a series of alternating scissoring kicks, termed "beats" in swimming parlance.

Dick Cavill of Australia, who first used the crawl in competition at the turn of the century, made just one change from the preceding racing stroke, the trudgen, retaining the same arm action, but replacing the single, wide scissor kick by two narrower beats to each cycle of the two arms.

Swimmers of the New York A. C., trying in 1903 to imitate

Cavill's leg action from hazy press descriptions, unwittingly acquired a four-beat drive, giving birth to the American crawl, and subsequently technicians decided to widen the first kick, producing a thrash composed of one "major" and three "minor" beats.

Early in 1917, however, some of us at the N.Y.A.C. conceived the idea that greater propulsion and less resistance might be attained by again narrowing the first kick and balancing the action with a second major beat of the same scope. Trials disclosed that the number of beats had to be raised to six to establish perfect rhythm, and here we ran into an unforeseen obstacle.

None would give a practical test to the conceived innovation. Our star clubmates deemed the experiment entirely too risky, and letters sent to some thirty of the country's leading coaches and contestants revealed that everyone, without exception, believed the six-beat would prove far too fast and tiring ever to be used effectively for more than 100 yards or so.

Then two champions of the W.S.A., Claire Galligan and Charlotte Boyle, unexpectedly came to the rescue. At the request of the late Charlotte Epstein, founder of the club and outstanding pioneer in the promotion of swimming for women, I had undertaken to serve as volunteer coach of the W.S.A. teams, for the club could not afford a professional mentor. When I explained the theory of the six beat to the two stars, they eagerly consented to give it a whirl.

The rest is history. In the Spring of 1918, the enterprising pair displayed the new stroke in taking first and third in the national 500-yard championship, and that Summer they broke American records with it at 880 yards and one mile, conclusively proving its availability and value.

Men still hesitated, however, fearing the swift thrash might be beyond their less supple muscles, and foreigners had no chance to learn it, so not until the 1920 Olympics at Antwerp did the stroke gain general recognition. There some W.S.A. girls used it in racing and gave requested demonstrations. Before long, it became the accepted standard the world over. A couple of years later, another W.S.A. ace, Ethel McGary, national long-distance champion for seven years, introduced in turn the eight and ten-beat drives, and the former has had many successful exponents, including Trude Ederle; the latter just a few.

The overwhelming leadership maintained by Americans through the decade speaks eloquently in Olympic results. At Antwerp in 1920, they won six of nine events for men, four of five for women; at Paris in 1924, seven of nine for men, six of seven for women; at Amsterdam in 1928, five of eight for men, five of seven for women. A grand total of 18 victories in 26 world tests for men, 15 in 19 for women.

It deserves mention in passing that the W.S.A. not only was the largest contributor to the three Olympic women's teams but reigned supreme at home in the Twenties, winning 132 of 193 national senior championships contested, or more than twice as many as won by all rival clubs combined.

The most concrete gauge of the universal progress spearheaded by Americans is afforded by the wholesale slaughter of records, so here is an outline of the ten-year cuts made in the times for the current Olympic or approximate events: Men—100 meters free style, 1:01.4 to 0:57.4; 400 meters, 5:14.4 to 4:50.3; one mile, 23:34.5 to 21:06.8; 100 meters back stroke, 1:15.6 to 1:08.2; 200 meters breast stroke, 2:56.6 to 2:45.0. Women—100 yards free style, 1:06.0 to 1:00.9; 400 meters, 6:30.2 to 5:39.2; 100 meters back stroke, 1:36.7 to 1:21.0; 200 meters breast stroke, 3:38.2 to 3:11.2.

Lack of space precludes mention of the host of our swimmers who earned titles or shattered records, so it may be well to confine the roster, with a few exceptions, to those who established world leadership through individual Olympic victories. They include, chronologically, Norman Ross, Duke Kahanamoku, Warren Kealoha, Clarence Pinkston, Ethelda Bleibtrey, Aileen Riggin, John Weissmuller, Robert Skelton, Albert White, Ethel Lackie, Martha Norelius, Sybil Bauer, Caroline Smith, Elizabeth Becker Pinkston, George Kojac, Peter Des Jardins, Albina Osipowich, and Helen Meany. Of these, five were double winners at the same Games, Ross, Weissmuller, White, Des Jardins and Miss Bleibtrey; four scored at successive Games, Kealoha, Weissmuller, Miss Norelius, and Mrs. Pinkston.

Kahanamoku and Ross, whose Olympic victories of 1920 virtually drew the curtain on brilliant careers, were among our most colorful aquatic personalities. A native of Honolulu, the smiling Duke was credited with placing Hawaii on the map, for before anyone on the mainland knew of his existence, he caused a world-wide sensation by shattering the record for 100 yards. Some questioned the feat, but Duke confuted the skeptics in 1912, when he first won our national title, then proceeded to Stockholm, where he captured the Olympic 100-meter classic. In all, he bettered the standard for 100 yards four times, for 100 meters, three, and he won the sprint at the Olympics eight years apart.

Pleasant in manner and a fine sportsman, Duke became a universal favorite. He was gifted with an excellent baritone voice, too, and he played the guitar skillfully, so he was in great demand as an entertainer at aquatic gatherings, ever ready to oblige. The sport suffered a great loss when he retired.

Ross hailed from the Pacific Coast but eventually landed in the Illinois A.C. fold. A remarkable all-around athlete, he once carried off at a single meet 11 first, and some second and third, prizes in a wide variety of track, field, swimming, and canoeing events. He fought in the First World War and swept the free-style tests at the Inter-Allied swimming championships, then won the Olympic 400- and 1500-meter titles in 1920. He lowered records from 200 meters to 880 yards, ripping the time for 400 meters from 5:21.6 to 5:14.4, and concluded his successes by winning the 1921 national indoor 220-yard championship.

Kojac, a strapping New York six footer, deserves rating as one of the greats of the era. He is remembered chiefly because of his amazing iconoclastic back-stroke work, including the slicing of records for 150 yards from 1:42.0 to 1:37.4, and for 400 meters from 5:59.2 to 5:43.3, but he excelled as a free styler also. Indeed, he battled the flying Weissmuller to a virtual dead heat when the latter, in 1928, hung up the American long-course mark of 0:57.8 for 100 meters, which stood until 1946. Some eyewitnesses thought Kojac won.

There is no way of computing relative ability in fancy diving, for scores depend on the far-ranging standards of judges, but it may be said of our Olympic men winners—Pinkston, Kuehn, Des Jardins, and White—that they materially furthered progress by perfecting general technique and introducing more difficult dives than ever before used in competition.

Of the feminine history makers, the Misses Bleibtrey, Riggin, Norelius, and Meany were products of the Women's S.A., and so were Agnes Geraghty, Helen Wainwright, and Eleanor Holm, Olympic finalists, who cannot be passed unnoticed, as the first two were leaders at home for a number of years, while Miss Holm, already a national champion, soon was to become the world's greatest dorsal swimmer, the Olympic winner of 1932.

Ethelda Bleibtrey had the distinction of carrying our naiads to victory at the Hellenic Games in Antwerp, for she won the two individual free-style events on the card and was largely instrumental in the capture of the relay. A sickly lassie when she joined the W.S.A. in 1918, Thelda swiftly grew healthy under a strict training regime. Within a year, she had developed into a fine specimen of athletic girlhood, able to garner the national 220- and 880-yard titles. Eventually she bettered free-style records from 100 to 440 yards, and the back-stroke mark for 150 yards. So great became her fame that several foreign countries invited her to visit them. But she passed out of the picture in 1923.

Aileen Riggin was one of the most popular and beloved undines of all time and among the outstanding all-around stylists. She was a "natural" in watermanship, my most valuable subject in experimental work. In one instance, when I was testing the theory that the legs set the rhythm for the arms in crawl swimming, she blithely ran up the leg drive from two to twelve beats, maintaining perfect co-ordination of arm and leg action throughout. Let anyone try it.

Scarcely fourteen when she won the Olympic springboard diving in 1920, hard pressed by Helen Wainwright, who was only a few months older, Aileen and the latter presently rose to the heights as swimmers also, earning many national titles and cracking a number of records. At one national gala, Helen scored enough points to win team honors for the W.S.A. single handed. Beautiful, dignified women nowadays, these two were mischevious little imps as children, often in hot water because of their playful pranks.

At the Antwerp Games a formal dance was held for the fair Olympians, and the youngsters naturally were left at home. But no sooner had their teammates departed than Aileen and Helen "borrowed" glamorous evening gowns from their rooms and crashed the party. A severe later scolding didn't prevent their having a wonderful time. The two still were gathering laurels when they decided to give up their amateur status and accompany Trude Ederle, fresh from her Channel swim, on a country-wide tour in an aquatic act.

It has been said of Martha Norelius that her crawl stroke was faultless. Experts at the Paris Olympics pronounced her swimming the poetry of motion. A coach inevitably is critical, but I never tired of watching Martha in action. Besides winning the 400-meter free-style events at the Games of 1924 and 1928, she annexed national titles from 100 yards to three miles and played havoc with records. Suffice that she blasted the figures for 400 meters from 5:53.2 to 5:39.3, and for one mile from 25:40.0 to 25:13.4. Unfortunately, false charges of a slight breach of rules, preferred by a misinformed A.A.U. official, caused the irate ace to abandon the sport before the mistake could be rectified and before she had nearly attained the limit of her superb speed.

Sybil Bauer, who wore the colors of the Illinois A.C., had the unusual experience of competing for several years in free-style swimming without getting anywhere, then shifting to the back stroke and immediately leaping to glorious success. She queened it over the field from 1921 to 1926, won Olympic honors at Paris, and monopolized dorsal records after reaching the top. It speaks for her class that she ripped the time for the classic 100 meters from 1:35.0 to 1:26.6.

Ethel Lackie, another Illinois A.C. star, held the spotlight for only three years, but she took full advantage, winning national and Olympic free-style sprint laurels in 1924, retaining the home titles in 1925-26, and dropping the standards for 100 yards to 1:00.9, and for 100 meters to 1:10.0.

Helen Meany, on the other hand, maintained her place among the elite throughout the decade. She qualified for all three of our Olympic teams, won the springboard diving at the Games in Amsterdam, and captured ten springboard and four platform national titles in all. As a youngster, she made her mark in swimming, also, and helped clubmates to shatter the record for the 400-yard free-style relay.

Elizabeth Becker Pinkston, a member of the Philadelphia Turners, was the heroine of an Olympic romance. At Paris in 1924, where she won the springboard diving, she became acquainted with Clarence Pinkston, who had taken the men's platform diving in 1920, and mutual attraction soon resulted in wedding bells, so that comely Betty traveled to the 1928 Games as a young matron, there to lift the platform-diving crown.

Agnes Geraghty was the only American girl ever to break the Olympic 200-meter breast-stroke record. She did it in the heats at Paris, but a slight mishap prevented her repeating in the final, and she was beaten. At home, however, she won 10 national titles and smashed standards aplenty.

It is worthy of note, in concluding, that no major change in swimming technique has taken place since the introduction of the ten-beat crawl, with the one exception of the development of the butterfly breast stroke, and that with the passing of the Twenties, American natatorial supremacy began to wane. Our mermaids were again able to triumph at the 1932 Olympics, but our male swimmers suffered a pretty bad drubbing at the hands of the vastly improved Japanese. They did somewhat better at Berlin in 1936, but by then the Danish and Dutch girls had progressed immeasurably and reaped among them the lion's share of the women's laurels. All of this affords overwhelming evidence that the decade of the Twenties definitely marked the Golden Age for American swimming.

BASKETBALL

by TOM MEANY
Sports Columnist, New York Star

During the third decade of this twentieth century, basketball was principally distinguished as a game in which the home team rarely lost. This was notably so during the early Twenties, when a team had to be at least 10 points the better outfit to win on the road. During the latter years, you had to be only about five points the better team to have an even chance of winning away from home.

There was no mystery, such as the absence of home cooking, about why visiting teams won so rarely. The general tendency was to blame it on the referees, who officiated for the same teams at home, game after game. This was something of a libel on the officials, if not a downright slander. The bald truth of the matter was that there was no such uniform interpretation of the rules as was to come later. What was a legal play on one court was little short of first-degree assault and mayhem on another court 50 or 100 miles away.

The net result was that few teams cared to stray from their home floors. Only in college conferences, such as the Eastern Intercollegiate League, the Big Ten, etc., were home-and-home schedules maintained with any degree of regularity. Intersectional games were about as rare as total eclipses of the sun. It was a great sensation when, at the conclusion of the 1919-20 season, New York University, led by Howard Cann, journeyed all the way to Atlanta, Georgia, to win a National A.A.U. basketball tournament and become the first truly national champion the college game had ever known.

College basketball was not a major sport in the Golden Age, save for isolated instances such as that of N.Y.U. related above. The Eastern Intercollegiate League was prospering well enough, but only the University of Pennsylvania, spurred on by the deeds of the Mc-

Nichols brothers, was filling its huge Palestra in Philadelphia. The capacity of such of the field houses in the Middle West as were already built never was taxed.

In the newspapers of the Twenties, basketball received only a little more space on the sports pages than the doings of the college rifle teams. The truth was that college basketball didn't share in the Golden Age because it was experiencing growing pains. It was moving fast by the end of the Twenties and was to blossom forth with ever-growing strides from December, 1934, when the University of Notre Dame played N.Y.U. in Madison Square Garden in the first of the many intersectional games which have played there to packed houses since.

Professional basketball, which in those days attracted more customers than college basketball, was in a wild state of disorganization. Players sold their talents for what they would bring on the open market. A player in the East would be with Troy, New York, one night and with Scranton, Pennsylvania, the next. The same shifting of talents was noticeable in western Pennsylvania and the Middle West, where the pro game also had the ascendancy over the college.

Skilled pro players could command anywhere from $40 to $125 an appearance. And they would play as many as 100 or more games a season, with as many as 10 or a dozen different clubs, which meant that team play, as it is now understood, simply didn't exist in professional basketball at the beginning of the Golden Age. And many college players, if they were good enough, competed on the preliminary teams appearing on the same card with the professionals. They were euphemistically called "semi-pros," although "semi-amateurs" would do just as well.

The first man to bring order out of this chaos was the late Jim Furey. He put a stop to wildcat basketball, in the East, at least, by assembling the Original Celtics, under his managership, to play Sunday nights at the Seventy-first Regiment Armory in New York City and to play with no other team. He guaranteed them a straight salary, so that they could concentrate their skill with the one team.

There were other Original Celtic teams preceding the Furey group, just as there have been others since, but this was the first time the Celtics, in the true sense of the term "team," were organized. Furey's team was coached by Johnny Witte, and this first group, which began

playing at the Seventy-first in the Winter of 1922-23, consisted of
Johnny Beckman, Pete Barry, Ernie Reich, Dutch Dehnert, Horse
Haggerty, and Joe Trippe.

It is doubtful if any team ever dominated its sport as the Celtics
did basketball. There have been examples of individual dominance,
such as Willie Hoppe in billiards, Bobby Jones in golf, etc., but never
a superiority so apparent on a group basis. This well may have been
because the Celtics were the first team, in the true sense of the term
in basketball; because, for the first time, five men played together,
night after night, from the start of the season until its finish.

This cohesion of the Celtics gave them a chance to work up
plays among themselves, the opportunity to evaluate the personal
skills and idiosyncrasies of one another. They could sense, for
instance, when Johnny Beckman was going to cut for the basket as
quickly as Johnny could himself.

Another gift which the Celtics had was that of speed, individual
speed and team speed. They were faster by far than any of the teams
they played, for basketball had not yet become the swift game it is
today. Basketball during the period just prior to the emergence of
the Shamrock five was a game in which shooting skill was everything,
with the ability to take a physical pounding the second qualification.
By their speed, the Celtics gained more shots at the basket than the
other team, a fact which enabled them to score more frequently
against quintets composed of better individual shots, and the speed
of the Celtics enabled them to avoid a great deal of the punishment
which was the lot of the plodding players of that era.

In all of the Celtics, both the original five players Furey had
assembled for his first season at the Seventy-first, and Nat Holman,
Joe Lapchick, and those who were added later, the bump of curiosity
was well developed. Basketball was a still expanding sport in those
days, and many of the maneuvers which are now standard operating procedure hadn't even been thought of until the Celtics began
experimenting.

Because the skill of the Celtics enabled them to win a great percentage of their games by decisive margins, it also gave them the opportunity to experiment without endangering the result. They could
afford to try out their theories under actual game conditions. Not all
the plays which the Celtics gave to basketball were developed acci-

dentally, as the pivot play was. Many were the result of dressing-room discussions, which were later put into practice during the game.

Just as the Celtics were the first team to play as a unit, so were they the first to develop a spirit of pride in their organization. It meant something to be a member of the Original Celtics, just as, in the early days of baseball, it meant something to be a member of the Baltimore Orioles. The Celtics, too, were pioneers.

The success of Furey with the Celtics stimulated other organizations in metropolitan New York, of which one of the best was the New York Whirlwinds, with Holman, Barney Sedran, Harry Riconda, Chris Leonard, and Dave Friedman. Holman and Leonard went from the Whirlwinds to the Celtics, and two other noted players who later wore the Shamrock were Lapchick and Davey Banks.

League basketball among the professionals was as loose as everything else about the game in that period, although the Eastern League and the Metropolitan League had at least the rudiments of organization. The Celtics, however, had no part of either circuit. They were good enough to stand on their own. It wasn't until the mid-Twenties that anybody was persuasive enough to sell them a bill of goods. And the salesman was none other than George Preston Marshall, the somewhat peculiar genius who now owns the Washington Redskins in the National Football League.

If professional basketball had to be put upon a big time basis, it couldn't have asked for a better promoter than Marshall. His own team was the Washington Palace Five (named after his laundry in the nation's capital), and he had clubs operating in the league in Brooklyn, Philadelphia, Rochester, Fort Wayne, Chicago, and other spots.

For two years the Celtics remained aloof from Marshall's loop, of which the late Joe Carr was the president. Carr, who later headed the National Football League, forbade any of the American League clubs to play exhibitions against the Celtics. It was then the Celtics came into Carr's loop, and for two years they dominated it to such an extent that they finally were disbanded and parceled among the other teams of the league. Cleveland got the cream of the crop, Holman, Lapchick, and Barry, and won the pennant.

The Celtics did a great deal to spread the gospel of basketball in the Twenties. They played exhibitions all over the country, engaging in as many as 125 to 150 games a season and maintaining a winning average of over .900 per cent! It was the Celtics who cracked open the South for basketball, playing against college teams such as Georgia Tech, Alabama, Mercer, and Rice Institute. They had one schedule rule—to play every night and twice on Sunday, if possible.

It was the Celtics, through Dutch Dehnert, who put the pivot, or bucket, play into basketball. They were winning a game by a rather handsome margin and decided, as they so often did, to put on a show for the fans. Dehnert stood on the foul line, his back to the basket, and the other members of the team passed the ball in to him and he passed it right back. Finding the player guarding him had committed the unpardonable sin of turning his head, Dutch pivoted, and dropped the ball into the basket himself. Thus was the pivot play born.

One of the great contributions to basketball in the Twenties was the decision of Marshall to have the American League play intercollegiate rules and eliminate the two-hand dribble. This opened the game to promising college players, and the range of the American League, from Washington to New York to Chicago, was the first wedge toward a universal, instead of a parochial, interpretation of the rules.

It was the American League that gave entry to the best college player of the decade, Vic Hanson of Syracuse. The pros of the Twenties are fairly well in agreement that Hanson was the top collegian to try his skill with them, as they are likewise almost in unanimity that the best professional of the Golden Age was Johnny Beckman.

While the Celtics were the top team, after Furey had stabilized them, Marshall's American League numbered several good clubs, including his own Washington Palace Five, the Chicago Bears of George Halas, the Cleveland Rosenblums, and Fort Wayne. It should be noted, however, that all of these teams were generously sprinkled with Eastern pros of the old wildcat days.

In the colleges, during the Twenties, no one team had a monopoly. Penn dominated the Eastern League at the edge of the decade, but then the title began to pass around, precisely as was the case in the

Big Ten. City College of New York, N.Y.U., and St. John's of Brooklyn, powers to be in the East later on, were just stirring from their cocoons as the Golden Age drew to a close. For college basketball, indeed, the Golden Age was just around the corner.

ICE HOCKEY

by George C. Carens
Sports Columnist, Boston Traveler

Glance back into your sports almanacs and you will find that the Seattle Metropolitans won the Stanley Cup in the early Spring of 1917. This trophy represents to ice hockey what the World Series represents to baseball, the Davis Cup to tennis, the Olympic Games to the world's runners, jumpers, and weigh-throwing specialists. Thus, as long ago as World War I did top honors in hockey cross the Canadian border into the state of Washington in the Pacific Northwest and leave the frozen fastnesses of our friendly neighbors to the north.

Why, then, did nearly half of America's Golden Era of Sport— the turbulent, terrific Twenties of which we write—come and go before ice hockey was established in the U.S.A.'s biggest urban communities? Simply because no Canadians had succeeded in selling the game South of the border and there was no certainty that this foreign sport would command the support needed to warrant such a risk.

Americans never could understand the appeal of cricket. Hockey seemed suited for American schoolboys and collegians in the northernmost states of the Union, but there was a lack of indoor playing surfaces with large enough seating capacities to justify an invasion of Canadian athletes to show their skill on steel runners.

True enough, New York had an indoor ice surface at the turn of the century—the old St. Nicholas rink. Harvard and Yale had launched their hockey rivalry on that surface in 1900. This forerunner of the huge modern covered rinks was doomed as a hockey center when its ice-making machinery wore out and could not be replaced because war orders had priority. So the St. Nicholas rink was rebuilt to house boxing shows, and nearly a decade was to pass before the magnificent new Madison Square Garden was erected to provide a place in which hockey might prosper.

Canada had so much outdoor ice, so many skaters, and so much enthusiasm for hockey that the game needed none of the refinements of this modern age to maintain its popularity in its native habitat. The Dominion teemed with puck chasers who laughed at frost-bitten toes and were happy to test their skill before groups of home-town zealots, or even in privacy. So disinterested were most Canadians in the commercial possibilities of their national sport that three franchises in the National Hockey League virtually went begging for purchasers when the Golden Era of Sport was ushered in during the early 1920's.

These unwanted bits of paper were being hawked by one Thomas Duggan, a world traveler, who had already done his part to affect the course of sports history in the New World by bringing to North America the innermost details of the pari-mutuel system of betting from Old France.

It was bruited about that Duggan had picked up one of these franchises in a Quebec pawnshop. Another traced back to Hamilton, Ontario, where it certified that the one-time affluent Tigers of that city would hark to the beck and call of its possessor. The third seemed to trace back to Montreal. A fly in the ointment was that there were financial liens on each of the documents.

In Boston, about that time, a Yankee from Vermont, who became a chain-store tycoon before his death in 1947, had caught the hockey "bug" by sponsoring amateur clubs. This man was Charles F. Adams, whose ardor for the game was so great that he would insure itinerant stick handlers that they would not go hungry if they would show up regularly for league encounters. The Shoe Trades Athletic Association, the Westminsters, and similar fly-by-night teams were winning acclaim on the sports pages, and the public response to their efforts impressed C. F. deeply.

Boston capital erected the Arena in 1910, but it was destroyed by fire in 1918. A couple of years after it was rebuilt in 1921, the aforementioned Duggan discovered that Boston's amateur "angel" was a prospective customer for one of the National League franchises. The asking price was $15,000, and, for all his enthusiasm, Adams preferred to share the risk. He sought a fifty-fifty arrangement with the

Arena management, but the seeming lack of a clear claim to the title was a hindrance.

Convinced that hockey interest would grow, Adams went along on his own and produced the first entry from the States in the N.H.L. —the Bruins of 1924-25.

This was a daring move, since the club must be manned by Canadians and there was a decided lack of eagerness on the part of executives above the border to yield their rights to established stars. Nor did they relent when a native of Montreal, the widely known and highly respected Arthur H. Ross, was assigned the dual role of manager and coach. Although the Stanley Cup competition was about 30 years old when the Bruins were about to be launched, the bigwigs in Canada possessed neither the vision nor the courage to co-operate with this experiment of seeking a new source of league income.

Starting with a victory, 1-0, over the Montreal Canadiens, on December 1, 1924, the Bruins' opening campaign proved one of disillusionment, for only five more victories were recorded in a 30-game schedule. Nevertheless, a second club was brought across the border for the 1925-26 season, when the Hamilton Tigers' franchise was moved to New York and operated by a team called the Americans, under private, rather than rink, ownership. Again the Bruins fell far short of championship stature, although the 17-15-4 record lifted them from the cellar and landed them fourth in the seven-club league.

Encouraged by the trend, owner Adams decided to raid the source of supply and opened negotiations with the Patrick brothers to buy the Western Canadian Hockey League—lock, stock, and barrel.

Clearly such a plethora of talent was more than the Boston team could absorb, so the League governors permitted a dispersal sale that would enable C. F. to regain a goodly portion of the $300,000 he invested. Eddie Shore, Frank Frederickson, Harry Oliver, Perk Galbraith, and Frank Boucher were among the stars retained by Art Ross, but the newly formed New York Rangers were ultimately permitted to buy Boucher's contract for $15,000 and he joined the Cook brothers in the new Garden, where this gifted offensive combination proceeded to rewrite the history of hockey.

For the Rangers won the Stanley Cup in the second year of their existence—1927-28—thereby beating the Bruins to supreme honors in the game, but only by the margin of one season.

Rugged body contact provided a spectator appeal from the moment the sport was introduced along the American Atlantic seaboard. Danger was apparent at all times, and in the Stanley Cup series of April 1928, the Rangers lost their goalie, Lorne Chabot, when his left eye was severely gashed by a high-velocity shot from the stick of Nelson Stewart of the Montreal Maroons. Knocked unconscious, Chabot was soon on his way to the Royal Victoria Hospital, leaving Manager Lester Patrick in a serious dilemma. He asked permission to use Ottawa's Alex Connell, who was present as a spectator, but the request was refused, and in this emergency, despite his forty-four years, the silver-haired New York pilot took over the assignment himself—and the Rangers won the game, 2-1.

This pulsating performance was not repeated, since a minor league goalie was called up for the remaining games, but Patrick's courage was one of the incidents that endeared him and his Rangers to the American public, who cheered loudly as the Rangers went on to take the odd game in five—and the Old Mug.

A year later, when the Bruins beat the Montreal Canadiens for the same trophy, Tiny Thompson scored three shutouts in five games, while single tallies by Cooney Weiland in the first two games put the Bruins into a commanding lead. Dr. Bill Carson capitalized the Bruins' advantage by scoring the winning tally for the pay-off—a denouement thereafter known as "the $25,000 goal."

In its current solid state, the impression may exist that all has been one sweet song for the National Hockey League since C. F. Adams took his plunge. Actually, the N.H.L. barely escaped competition from a proposed American Hockey League in the Summer of 1925, a year before the big Adams purchase in western Canada and while the new Madison Square Garden was being built. Colonel John Hammond had seen his first hockey game in the Boston Arena in 1923—a college game—in company with George V. Brown, boss of the Hub rink. That visit, plus the entry of the Bruins into the N.H.L., gave Brown the idea of forming a rival circuit. He proposed a Toronto-born hockey executive from Pittsburgh to head the new league, and a meeting was called in New York.

Chicago, Cleveland, St. Paul, Minneapolis, Pittsburgh, and Boston were in agreement, so the A.H.L. was a virtual certainty if Hammond would go along with a New York club. The proposed league's prospective mogul arrived for the meeting with Colonel Hammond very much the worse for wear, causing the New Yorker to leave in disgust. . . . On slender threads do vital agreements—sporting or otherwise—sometimes hang!

Monopolistic aspects of major league hockey may have retarded the expansion of the game, but there is general agreement over the quality of play and evenness of competition since the game was introduced in the U.S.A. When castles were toppling during the Great Depression, hockey was picking up new customers, perhaps because the rough-and-tumble play provided an escape mechanism for harassed Americans.

The era of seven-man hockey ended before the Bruins skated onto the ice at the close of 1924, but Americans have seen hockey's evolution from the skillful, scientific, close-checking methods to the helter-skelter game of the hour, resulting chiefly from constant concessions to the demand for more and still more speed, brought about by forward passing in all zones. The present-day rules make oldsters contemplate what stratospheric totals would have been achieved by the Rangers' line of Boucher and the Cook brothers, or the Bruins' Dynamite Trio of 1929-30, which scored 43 goals by Cooney Weiland, 41 by Dit Clapper, and 18 by Dutch Gainor in the 44 regular-season games, and an overall total of 193 points, including play-offs.

Some look back on Cyclone Taylor, Newsy Lalonde, Howie Morenz, Auriel Joliat, Frank Nighbor, and others as real giants of the game, but in this writer's book the greatest of all will always be Eddie Shore. I say this with a single reservation: It is to be regretted that Hobey Baker, magnificent performer on ice and on the gridiron for Princeton, could not have had the opportunity—and the desire —to match his skill with Canada's greatest hockey players.

Hobey's sweeping strides on skates, his roving type of play, so admirably fortified by jet-propelled action, his puissance and pleasing personality all combined to make him the idol of American sports fans. Destiny decreed that he should plummet to his death as an Army flier just before the first Armistice Day, November 11, 1918.

Suffice to say he had the same style that Shore later brought from his native Edmonton to become the greatest of all Bruins.

It would be trite to call Shore the stormiest petrel of sport, for there have been others. I sat in press boxes during all except the first five of Ty Cobb's twenty-four years of combat—and I use the word advisedly—on major league diamonds. His fiery spirit may have been equaled, but never outmatched. I watched Red Grange's wraithlike jaunts on the gridiron and sat in on the 1928 Davis Cup developments in Paris when an American ambassador appealed directly to Washington that Bill Tilden's disqualification be lifted in the cause of world peace. . . . But above and beyond all other memories will stand Eddie Shore's courage in the clutch, regardless of the odds.

In conclusion, while hockey was the last of the sports to win U.S.A. acclaim in the Golden Era of the Twenties, the game nevertheless produced thrills that still hold a place in the consciousness of our sports fans nearly a quarter of a century later. Whether the ebb and flow of economic conditions or the desire of the hockey supporters will one day force the rule makers to return to a more scientific game is a moot question, but it must still be said that hockey has only just begun to scratch the surface of its possibilities in the good old U.S.A.

YACHTING

by William H. Taylor
Associate Editor of Yachting; Pulitzer Prize Winner

The most significant development in yachting between 1920 and 1930 was the enormous increase in small amateur-sailed craft and the relative decline of big, professionally-manned yachts in the 100-feet-and-over category, a trend which eventually completely changed the complexion of the sport. But to the general nonsailing public, "yachting" was still the spectacle of huge luxury yachts and of great sloops and schooners sailing for famous trophies.

The America's Cup, blue ribbon of international yacht racing since 1851 for the largest active racing classes here and abroad, was raced for twice during the period, in 1920 and again in 1930. To the public's mind the outstanding figure in the whole sport was that of the Irish chain-store baron, Sir Thomas Lipton.

Actually, Sir Thomas (God rest his cheery soul) knew little more about yachting than that it cost a great deal of money but was well worth the price in the publicity he gained and the friends he made, both personally and for Lipton's tea. In the yachting cap and broad smile he habitually wore, he was photographed hundreds of times at the steering wheels of his various Shamrocks, but he never steered one in a race. For that matter he never sailed in any of the America's Cup races, which he used to watch somewhat uncomprehendingly from his steam yacht, Erin. Nevertheless, he was the personification of yachting to the landlubber public, and to this day yachtsmen all over the country race annually for the various Lipton trophies that he and his agents scattered with a lavish hand.

The Cup race of 1920, Sir Thomas' fourth, was a revival of the one scheduled for 1914, Lipton's Shamrock IV and the two American defense candidates having spent the intervening war years on the beach. Resolute, the Herreshoff sloop, sailed by that grand old man

of American yachting, Charles Francis Adams, assisted by the late
Bob Emmons, was selected after a series of trial races over the Gard-
ner-designed *Vanitie*, which had an equally able afterguard and crew
headed by George Nichols and C. Sherman Hoyt. After nearly thirty
years, old-timers still argue about which was the faster boat. Either
probably would have been fast enough.

An enormous fleet, including dozens of big excursion steamers,
loaded to the guards with spectators, followed the five races held off
Sandy Hook—the last Cup series sailed in those waters, abandoned
for subsequent Cup races because of traffic and pollution. In the
first race, *Resolute*, far in the lead, broke down because of rigging
failure—a chronic faults of hers—and *Shamrock* won. In the second,
Sir William Burton, Lipton's amateur racing skipper, capitalized on a
series of breaks to win; but *Resolute* took the next three races by
convincing margins, and the America's Cup went back to Tiffany's
vaults, in which gloomy surroundings much of its life has been spent.

Sir Thomas went back to Britain and made his customary report
—that he couldn't win "because of something the Americans put in
the water over there." Some dutiful stooge always asked, "And what
was that, Sir Thomas?" which provided the opening for his pet tag
line, "The American boat."

In 1929, Sir Thomas issued his last challenge for the Cup that had
helped make him famous, and vice versa. To meet him, the New
York Yacht Club organized four syndicates of wealthy members
who were sufficiently undismayed by the "temporary financial upset"
of that Autumn to build a quartet of sloops, each of which, before
the season's campaign was ended, had cost her backers a half-million
dollars, or better, to build, equip, and operate. They were designed
by four leading naval architects of the period, W. Starling Burgess,
Clinton H. Crane, Frank C. Paine, and L. Francis Herreshoff.

Charles Francis Adams, then Secretary of the Navy, and George
Nichols again appeared as skippers at the helms of *Yankee* and
Weetamoe, respectively. Landon K. Thorne and Paul Hammond
sailed *Whirlwind*, which was a failure in the trials. And Harold S.
Vanderbilt, in command of the Burgess-designed *Enterprise*, emerged
as the greatest big-yacht racing skipper of his time. With a keen, cold,
brilliant mind, an infinite capacity for study and experimentation, a
genius for organizing, and a high degree of skill and experience in the

actual sailing, he built up what had at first appeared an outside-chance contender into the logical choice as the Cup defender in the course of the 1930 trials.

When *Enterprise* met *Shamrock* V off Newport, before a spectator fleet fully equal to those of the old Sandy Hook days, she won four straight races. There was never a serious doubt, after the opening stages of the first race, that she would. Neither *Shamrock* V nor her all-professional crew, headed by Captain Ted Heard, were a match for *Enterprise* and those who handled her.

Poor old Sir Thomas went back to Britain to die. He was in his dotage in 1930, only rarely flashing a glimpse of the personality and wit that had made him a popular idol. Indeed, there was some speculation as to whether the 1929 challenge was born of his own flickering urge to "lift the auld mug" or of his business associates' appreciation of his still-potent publicity value.

The rebirth and growth of ocean racing was one of the most significant and lasting features of the 1920's in yachting. Previously there had been a few trans-Atlantic races in very large yachts, whose owners generally bet big stakes and then stayed home while professional crews sailed the races.

Around 1906, a few adventurous yachtsmen had started racing to Bermuda, from the East Coast, and to Honolulu, from the West Coast, but few were interested, and long before World War I they had died out. Yachting remained almost wholly a shoal-water pastime. About 1920, however, a new type of yacht gained popularity, an able, seagoing type, mostly schooner rigged, developed by such able designers as John G. Alden, William H. Hand, Charles D. Mower, and William J. Roue from the famous Gloucester fishing-vessel types. In them, amateurs began making longer cruises in deep water, and in 1923 both the Bermuda and Honolulu races were revived.

The Bermuda race drew 22 starters in 1923, 15 in 1924, 16 in 1926, 24 in 1928, and 42 in 1930. They battled all kinds of weather, from Summer gales and Gulf Stream squalls to fog and calms. They established ocean and long-distance racing as one of the leading phases of the sport, and out of these races came the evolution of the modern fast, able, comfortable cruising-racing yacht, probably the finest type of craft the sport has even seen. Out of them, too, came a breed of hard-driving, sea-wise, able sailors, for these boats, all under

75 feet long, were commanded and navigated by amateurs, and many carried no professional hands at all.

Among the Bermuda race prize winners in the 1920-30 era were John G. Alden, three times winner of the race and equally able as a sailor and as a designer of ocean racers; Robert N. Bavier, one of the best seamen and helmsmen of a generation; George B. Drake, W. Finlay Downs, Russell Grinnell, Raymond Ferris, who won a Bermuda race in his little schooner *Malay* with a crew of green kids picked up in a last-minute pierhead jump at New London, and Olin Stephens, whose *Dorade*, though she placed only second in the 1930 race, was the forerunner of a whole new type of ocean racing yachts. No less famous on the West Coast, as winners of the Honolulu races, were A. R. Peddar, Don Lee, Clem Stose, and Morgan Adams.

Trans-Atlantic racing, dead since 1904, came back in 1928 with the race from New York to Santander for trophies given by the King and Queen of Spain. Five big schooners, mostly of a type going out of fashion in the Twenties, raced for King Alphonso's cup, and William B. Bell's *Elena*, with a professional skipper, John Barr, was the winner. But there were four much smaller, amateur-sailed schooners racing for the Queen's cup, and two of them, Paul Hammond's *Nina*, the winner, and Jack Curtis' *Pinta*, beat the big yachts, boat for boat, although *Nina*, for instance, was only 50 feet on the waterline, against *Elena's* 96 feet. The race marked the end of trans-Atlantic racing in big yachts and the beginning of a series of such races in yachts less than 75 feet in length, amateur manned.

The six-meter class, sloops under 40 feet long, built to the international rule of measurement, was introduced in this country in 1922 and provided some fine international competition for the Seawanhaka Cup, British-American Cup, Scandinavian Gold Cup, and other famous trophies. By 1930, American Sixes had raced, here and abroad, against yachts flying the flags of Great Britain, Cuba, Sweden, Finland, Norway, Denmark, Holland, and Italy. Such outstanding skippers as C. Sherman Hoyt, Clinton H. Crane, Henry L. Maxwell, C. F. Havemeyer, Jr., Herman F. Whiton, Cornelius Shields, and Briggs S. Cunningham were prominent in the class during the Twenties.

The events outlined above were highlights of a decade in which, as previously noted, the number of yachts and of amateur sailors multiplied several fold, while the average tonnage of both sailing and power craft shrank in inverse proportion to their numbers. There were, of course, a good many large yachts built during the period— a few big schooners well over 100 feet long and, in the opulent later Twenties, several classes of racing sloops from 60 to 80 feet in length, like the 10- and 12-meter sloops, the Class M sloops.

There was also a new crop of big, diesel-powered luxury yachts, replacing the steam yachts of an earlier era, some of their owners spending a million dollars or more in a race to see who could build the biggest and most lavishly equipped craft. Many of them ended up, minus their gold-plated doorknobs, as patrol and escort vessels in the naval service in World War II.

Such vessels, however, meant far less to the sport than the thousands of small cruising and racing boats built during the same era for owners most of whom, prior to 1920, had had no part in the sport. Such boats, for instance, as the 23-foot sloops of the Star class, selling in those days for well under $1,000. That class grew from a total of 101 boats, in 1920, owned principally in the Long Island Sound area, to 793 registered boats in 1930, distributed all over the world and holding annual world championships. It was typical of the popular development in yachting through the 1920's.

ROWING

by ROBERT F. KELLEY
Former Rowing Editor, The New York Times

Rolling right along with the Tildens, the Hitchcocks, the Ruths, the Dempseys of the Terrific Twenties, rowing moved over the waterways of the world, with America producing some of the greatest crews in its history. In that introductory sentence is as significant a description of rowing as can be fashioned. Where every other sport produced its individual stars to mark this remarkable period, rowing produced crews.

The sport, one of the oldest we have, is also one of the most anonymous. As the late, great Bill McGeehan expressed it, "There can be only one logical reason for rowing in an eight-oared crew, and that would be to escape from your enemies."

But the sport that contributed, in the Yale-Harvard regatta, the oldest intercollegiate athletic event in the country reached during those Twenties a flowering that matched the blaze of color that splashed through the garden of sports. That was in its demonstration to the rest of the rowing world of the fact that American oarsmen had come of age, that they could more than hold their own with every other country's sweepswingers.

This came with the opening of that fabulous decade when the United States, for the first time, joined in Olympic rowing and won the 1920 test at Antwerp, to the amazement of all and the considerable consternation of the famous Leander crew of England, which had dominated international competition to this point.

The United States Naval Academy, under the guidance of the thin, typical Cape Codder, Richard A. (Old Dick) Glendon, who had started as a locker-room boy around the old Boston Athletic Association boathouse in Boston, and came on to a lasting place among the great teachers of the sport, won that 1920 race.

They were to be followed, during those Twenties, over the Olympic trail by Yale, in 1924, and California, in 1928, each contributing its bit to the march of rowing during the period. All three won lasting pages in the record books.

There was interest, but considerable doubt of success, when the United States Olympic Committee announced there would be a rowing representation from this country for the 1920 Games. A national regatta was arranged for Worcester in Massachusetts, and the Naval Academy crew decided to pass up that year's Poughkeepsie race and concentrate on the National, the winners of which were to represent this country at the Olympics.

Syracuse won at Poughkeepsie and then remained in training to come to the national regatta. But Navy won over the Orange, as well as another Navy crew and the Duluth Boat Club, covering the 2,000-meter Olympic distance in 6:20, a record for the Worcester course, which had been in use for a good many years. Two days later, the Annapolis eight embarked for Belgium, with rowing machines rigged on the deck, arriving off the Antwerp waterfront, which had so lately seen the ravages of World War I, on August 6.

The equipment had to be shipped up through canals and locks for 20 miles to the Royal Natique Boathouse, which was royal because it was also the club of Albert, King of the Belgians. The boat-house itself was pretty badly wrecked by warfare, and the shells had to be protected from weather by tarpaulin. The men stayed at an inn a mile distant, and Old Dick Glendon, after a few abortive attempts at coaching from a bicycle, managed to find an old launch to work from.

Except for American newspapermen assigned to the job, nobody paid much attention to the Navy eight. Leander, which had furnished the winners of the 1908 and 1912 Olympics, boasted one of the best crews of its ancient history and was universally favored to add a third Olympic triumph to its list. In addition to the English and Americans, French, Norwegian, Dutch, Swiss, Belgian, and Czechoslovakian eights were entered.

The preliminaries warned of what might happen in the final, for the American crew came through well, but so, also, did Leander, and the latter remained very much the favorite before the start of the final. Nor had this English crew been overestimated. It was easily one of the best in England's modern history.

Navy led for a brief while at the start. Then the Britons came back and moved to the front. The Americans refused to be shaken off. Rowing a shade lower than the 40 strokes a minute which the leaders were setting, Navy clung to their flanks.

But if the Midshipmen wouldn't be shaken off, neither could they seem to bring the others back to them. The finish loomed nearer and nearer, and finally, with less than 300 yards to go and Leander still leading by a good half length, it seemed all over but for the polite British cheering.

Here the little Baltimorean, S. R. Clark, a good coxswain, lifted his megaphone to the skies. One highly dramatic account filed to America that night had it that he had begun to sing the Star-Spangled Banner. In later years, Clark denied this, saying he didn't even then know the words. Whatever it was he yelled through the megaphone strapped to his shin, the crew responded.

Clyde King of Iowa, one of the great stroke oars in American history, raised his beat. The men behind him caught it, and Leander had nothing left to answer with. Foot by foot, Navy came up on England and then went away, to win by three-quarters of a length.

In 1912, Leander had set a mark of 6 minutes 10 seconds for the 2,000 meters. These two great eights of 1920 clipped five full seconds from the record in what was the tautest eight-oared fight the Olympics were to see until the Los Angeles Games.

Yale's 1924 victory at Paris served to demonstrate that a good crew could prevail at any distance, for the Elis first won the Olympic trials at 2,000 meters, beating a Navy Officers eight that included many of that famous 1920 boatload, and then, a week later, rowed four miles to triumph over Harvard before sailing for Paris. When they took their first Olympic heat in 5:51 1/5, it became apparent that only an accident could prevent their victory. They went on to win in a four-crew final from Toronto, Italy, and the Thames Rowing Club of London.

This Yale boat, like most good crews, had a better than average stroke oar in Al Lindley, but also, like most fine crews, it had real power in the waist of the shell in H. T. (Ox) Kingsbury, afterward to row in an Oxford varsity as a Rhodes scholar, and Ben Spock.

When another Olympics came around, in 1928, there was still another phase of rowing, with the emergence of the West to the dominating role it was to play for a good many years as California and Washington moved to the top of the pile. This 1928 winner was California, with a very excellent pair in the stern sheets, Peter Donlon at stroke and Don Blessing in the coxswain's seat.

Those Olympic triumphs stand out boldly in the period, but there were other great crews and great races—many of them. There was Navy's black-haired Tom Eddy, a story-book stroke, and Washington's first Poughkeepsie victors, the 1923 crew, captained by Don Grant from his coxswain's seat, and stroked by Dow Walling, with one of the strongest oars ever to have raced at No. 5 in Fred Spuhn, afterward to be remembered for his coaching at Yale and Princeton.

But probably the greatest group to race in those years came, strangely enough, from the sidewalks of New York. This was Columbia's boatload, which remained pretty much intact during the years of 1926, 1927, 1928, and 1929. In those four years, this crew was defeated at Poughkeepsie only once, and then by the California eight of 1928 that was to go on to the Olympic championship.

The Columbians won as freshmen and two out of three times as varsity. Sam Walker, Alastair MacBain, George French, Gordon Piercy, William Lightbowne, Thomas Kerrigan, Horace Davenport, Eric Lambart, Arthur Douglas, Bill Blesse, V. F. Murphy, and Bill Sanford rowed with them at various times, and Bob Berman coxed them throughout their career. Of that group of oarsmen, Davenport, Lambart, and MacBain were probably the best.

Columbia, until 1925, had been going through a slump that, in 1920, brought a serious discussion on the advisability of abandoning the sport. Then Young Dick Glendon, son of the man who had given Navy its 1920 Olympic champions, came up to coach, and there followed these remarkable years.

All these Columbia eights were good ones, even the one which was destined to finish second to California, at Poughkeepsie, in 1928, after the toughest sort of a four-mile battle. The 1929 crew was probably the best, and it triumphed not only over eight other crews but over the river itself, in one of the most dramatic varsity races Poughkeepsie has seen in modern years.

This regatta of 1929 was the one in which four crews sank in the

turbulent waters of a Hudson River that had been stirred up by a
shift in tide against the wind, following delays through the afternoon
that saw the varsities finally going away from their stake boats in
the semidarkness of early night.

Never before in the history of the event had there been such a
setting as that provided for this race. In the full flush of the sports
uproar, the biggest crowd in the town's history descended on Poughkeepsie during the day. It was estimated by police forces at more
than 100,000. They clung to vantage points all along the sides, and
on the bridges and rode the observation train and a fleet of chartered
excursion steamers and yachts in the river.

Captain Davenport's Columbia eight had come through the season
to this point undefeated. It was among the crews that arrived at the
starting line early and then had to wait for the big field to get to the
stake boats. California, Cornell, Washington, Syracuse, M. I. T.,
Pennsylvania, Navy, and Wisconsin made the rest of the field.

When they were finally all backed to their stake boats, the light
of day had almost gone behind the towering cliffs of the Palisades,
and they presented an unforgettable picture, 81 men moving into
position for what was expected to be one of the great races of history.

The tide had shifted so that it was against the oarsmen, and there
was further delay as they sought to stay straight. Two false starts
were called back, and finally, on third trial, Navy's boatload led the
pack away from the start. At the end of the first mile, Navy was
still holding a slim lead, with a surprising Washington crew, which
had not been highly regarded before the start, moving into second,
ahead of Columbia. California, which had rigged its shell too low
for this water, was already dropping out of it.

At the two-mile mark, M.I.T. began to settle at the stern and
finally had to stop rowing, the crowd realizing then for the first
time what the crews were up against. Out in the worst water, Columbia was sticking with Navy and Washington, the others dropping
away. At the end of the third mile, the California, Cornell, and
Syracuse shells swamped, leaving their oarsmen to flounder in the
water and be picked up by their coaching launches.

For the second mile, and a good part of the third, it seemed this
Columbia crew was not going to be able to do it. Navy and Washington were sticking to their work and, well into the third mile, had

a lead of almost a length. But Columbia, behind the long- cool-headed stroking of the Scotsman, MacBain, refused to become flustered and finally began to overtake the others.

At the two and a half mile point, they had Navy, and at the third mile they had Washington. Through the closing mile, they assumed command and then had to fight to stay alive in the waters. They finished, rowing superbly and putting the crowning final touches to a career that has never been equaled, before or since, in the long annals of college rowing.

SIX-DAY BICYCLE RACING

by FRED HAWTHORNE
Of the New York Herald Tribune

They were a fabulous lot in the Golden Age of cycling, whether it was for pleasure or racing for the great American dollar (worth just one hundred copper cents, no more, no less).

Frank L. Kramer, Pat Powers, Ike Dorgan, Harry Pollok, Harry Mendel, Hype Igoe, Tad Dorgan, John M. Chapman, Bill Wellman, William (Bunk) Macbeth, W. O. (Sheriff) McGeehan, Duke Ballard, and Wild Bill (Umpawaug Hill) Doig were among those identified either with the running of the six-day race in the old Madison Square Garden, or the present structure, or covering it for the newspapers. Many of these have long since seen their last "jam" and listened to the last frenzied roar of the crowd. Perhaps the six-day grind will never return to the Garden, but all those who knew the game, all those who rode in the race, all those who recorded it for posterity, will never forget its thrills and its wild drama, its absurdities and its clowning. And for the majority there never was, nor will there ever be again, a sports event to equal it.

There are names that will never die when old cycle-racing fans meet and start reminiscing. Starting with the rugged days when the race was a one-man-against-the-field proposition, in the old Garden at Madison Avenue between Twenty-sixth and Twenty-seventh streets, the name of Dutch Waller still remains fixed in the minds of those "who saw him when." Dutch, the gaunt, grizzled, sinister man a-wheel, was never seen on the track without a long black cheroot clinched between his teeth. No matter how fierce the pace, Old Dutch never relinquished his grip on his cheroot and many a time he carried it to victory, in the rugged days when it was every man for himself. In that hardy era a rider could pedal continuously for twenty-four hours at a stretch or sleep for twelve, were he so minded, and Dutch Waller was never one to dodge a challenge from a race rival.

Charley Miller was another one-man team who did all right for himself in his chosen profession, as did Charlie Ashurst, Teddy Hale, the big, bearded Englishman, and a host of others who were not so prominent.

In later years, because of harrowing tales, printed in the "yellow" press, picturing the riders as gaunt ghosts a-wheel who were kept in the race only through the use of drugs, and other such stories, the city fathers made it a misdemeanor for any cyclist to be on the track more than twelve hours out of the twenty-four.

Then came the team races and the "Berlin" point system, with the racers required to compete three times every twenty-four hours in a series of official one-mile sprints for points. These sprints and the mileage covered during the dashes were part and parcel of the whole race. If two or more teams were tied for the lead in distance covered at the finish of the race, the team with the highest point total would be declared the winner.

This change in the race rules had the effect of speeding up the grind, while detracting from the total mileage covered. The old record, established in the old Garden some thirty years ago, stood at well over 2,700 miles and has never been equaled or surpassed, due to the change in the rules. But that was more than counterbalanced by the greater thrills furnished in the official one-mile sprints.

Some of the greatest riders in the history of cycle racing were developed during the Golden Twenties. Outstanding were men like Alf Goullet, former Australian; Reggie McNamara, another Australian, known as the "Iron Man" because of his amazing durability to withstand innumerable crashes on the banked board tracks; Willie and Arthur Spencer, Bobby Walthour, Jr.; Oscar Egg of Switzerland; Franco Georgetti, Maurice Brocco, and Gaetano Belloni of Italy; Pete Van Kempen of Holland; William (Torchy) Peden of Canada; Alphonse Goosens and Marcel Buysse of Belgium, and many others, including Walter Rutt and Bob Stoll of Germany.

The hardiest athletes in any sport and of any era were the six-day riders. This has been attested time and again by the track physicians who do the "repair" work on injured riders. Falls that would either kill an ordinary man or put him in a hospital for several weeks are merely incidental in the life of a six-day racer.

Apparently hopelessly mangled and with broken bones and cracked heads, these athletes of the flying wheel return to the track within an hour or two and often go on to win the race.

McNamara is a notable example of this durability. It has been said of the Iron Man that, in his long career on the track, every bone in his body was broken, some of them three or four times, and his skull fractured. Yet McNamara was active in the game until he was in his late forties. Reggie was never known to have been helped to his feet or carried off the track because of crashes. Invariably, on regaining consciousness after some particularly hard fall, Reggie would get up on his own two feet, brushing aside his trainers and handlers, shoulder his way around the flat of the Garden track, call for a new wheel, and continue in the "jam" in which he had been thrown.

And as for losing weight as the result of six days and six nights of riding, the six-day man actually gains several pounds. It may be due to the fact that the average rider eats solid meals as often as six or eight times every twenty-four hours, and by solid I mean all of that —two-inch steaks, whole roast chickens, quarts of milk, raw eggs, and bunches of celery and in-between snacks while on the track. No landlady running a boarding house would keep a six-day rider under her roof and expect to remain solvent after seeing him eat his first meal.

In the Golden Days of Sport, in addition to the advertised prize money of $50,000, the six-day riders used to reap a harvest every night of the race by winning "primes." These were special sprints requested by spectators with more dollars than sense.

Many a night the announcement would go over a loud-speaker in this fashion: "Mister McGoofie offers $500 to the winner of a one-mile sprint," or "The gent's clothing firm of Ginsburg, Levy, O'Houlihan, and Ginsburg offers a two-pants suit and a hand-tailored overcoat to the winner of a one-lap sprint," and the race for an extra pair of pants would be on.

Refrigerators, washing machines, lamps, long flannel underwear, dog biscuit, hair restorer, a year's subscription to a fashion magazine, or a set of aluminum kitchen ware with a ton of coal—all these were grist for the riders.

In the more esthetic days of the six-day bike race, ladies dripping with ermine, white fox, and sable, squirred by immaculate males in tails, would drop in at the Garden after midnight and dress the picture up and add a bit of chichi to the proceedings. Such celebrities of the stage and screen as Peggy Hopkins Joyce, Clair Luce, Jimmie Durante, and Leon Errol were six-day sitters-in.

Perhaps the most violent addict of them all was the bandy-wobbly-legged Errol. During a December race in the old Garden, Errol was playing in a show in Philadelphia and, to see the race, he had a time schedule that he maintained all week. He had a taxi waiting for him every night and, immediately after his last curtain, Errol would grab his regular clothes, leap into the cab, and make a beeline for the Broad Street Station, dressing on the way.

Boarding a midnight train for New York, he would usually arrive at the Garden around 2 A.M. and shove his way to the press box, where he would convulse the newspaper lads, and the crowd as well, by doing some of his trick routines impromptu. It was a rugged routine, but Errol made the round trip every twenty-four hours.

Jack White, night-club entertainer, also would spend hours in the press coop, doing his trick falls all over the place and offering, if not delivering, munificent prizes for "jams."

And so they've taken the six-day race away from the Garden. Shades of John Chapman and Pat Powers. Shades of the Golden Age of Sport. Shades of the stolen lap and the big "jam." But perhaps the old-timers are holding six-day races in cycling's Valhalla. "There he goes! He's out for a lap!"